International Studies in Human Rights

Also in this series:
Ramcharan, B.G. (ed.): International Law and Fact-finding in the Field of Human Rights. 1982. ISBN 90-247-3042-2.

The Martinus Nijhoff series "International Studies in Human Rights" is designed to shed light on current legal and political aspects of process and organization in the field of human rights.

HUMANITARIAN GOOD OFFICES IN INTERNATIONAL LAW

The Good Offices of the United Nations Secretary-General in the Field of Human Rights

by

Dr. B.G. Ramcharan
Ll.B. (Hons) (Lon.), Ll.M. (Lon.), Ph.D. (Lon.);
Barrister-at-Law (Lincoln's Inn.);
Diploma of the Hague Academy of International Law;
Diploma in Air and Space Law;
Diploma in International Affairs;
Visiting Professor of International Law and Organizations
at the University of Ottawa.

The 1981 Reid Lectures delivered at Acadia University, Wolfville, Nova Scotia, Canada.

1983
MARTINUS NIJHOFF PUBLISHERS
THE HAGUE / BOSTON / LONDON

Distributors:

for the United States and Canada

Kluwer Boston Inc.
190 Old Derby Street
Hingham, MA 02043
USA

for all other countries

Kluwer Academic Publishers Group
Distribution Center
P.O. Box 322
3300 AH Dordrecht
The Netherlands

Library of Congress Cataloging in Publication Data

Ramcharan, B. G.
Humanitarian good offices in international law.

(International studies in human rights) (The 1981 Reid lectures delivered at Acadia University, Wolfville, Nova Scotia, Canada)
Bibliography: p.
Includes index.
1. Civil rights (International law)
2. United Nations. Secretary-General. I. Title.
II. Series. III. Series: Reid lectures ; 1981.
K3240.4.R35 1983 341.4'81 82-24564
ISBN 90-247-2805-3

PRINTED IN THE NETHERLANDS

CONTENTS

FOREWORD

While there is increasing reference to and reliance upon, the practice of good offices in connection with humanitarian issues in international relations, little scholarly work has so far been done to review and analyze the law and practice of humanitarian good offices. It is the great merit of this pioneering work by Professor B.G. Ramcharan that it presents a comprehensive insight into the practical dimensions and potentialities of the good-offices function in humanitarian matters, in particular in connection with the role of the United Nations Secretary-General. Human rights organs of the United Nations and other international organizations have developed legal and political devices to deal with pressing and important humanitarian concerns but there is an increasing awareness that legal and formalized procedures do not always provide an adequate and expeditious response to these concerns. The study by Professor Ramcharan can be seen as a convincing argument in favour of putting greater reliance upon less formal and complementary approaches to humanitarian and human rights issues. In this respect the office of the Secretary-General of the United Nations carries many potentialities which need to be further developed. Imagination, humanitarian commitment and political will on the part of the Secretary-General are indispensable preconditions for constructive developments in this direction. At the same time the United Nations is seized with important proposals to establish a High Commissioner for Human Rights and a Special Representative for Humanitarian Affairs whose functions would also have a strong good-offices component. In my view these proposals are not meant to weaken the role of the Secretary-General or of any other humanitarian or human rights organs but rather to strengthen the capacity of the international community to deal effectively with pressing humanitarian concerns.

A number of important conclusions emerge from this book which may be of considerable interest to all those who as policy makers or scholars are involved in humanitarian concerns:

First, the legal competence for the exercise of humanitarian good offices by the United Nations Secretary-General finds increasing acceptance in international law and praceice.

Second, the methods for the exercise of humanitarian good offices which have been developed are rich and varied and can be applied or adapted as the case or situation may require.

Third, a crucial issue regarding the exercise of humanitarian good offices is one of will and judgement.

Fourth, much attention should be given to the question whether the exercise of humanitarian good offices can be better organized through the designation of one or more focal points within the structure of the United Nations and whether good offices can be rendered in a less *ad hoc* manner.

Fifth, pending decisions to establish such offices as those of a United Nations High Commissioner for Human Rights and/or of a Special Representative for Humanitarian Affairs, greater use should be made of existing competences and potentialities of the United Nations Secretary-General to render humanitarian good offices.

For helping to re-inforce these conclusions, Professor B.G. Ramcharan must be congratulated for what is, on any account, an important contribution to the study of the actual and potential role of humanitarian good offices in international law and practice.

Theo C. Van Boven
Former Director,
United Nations Division of Human Rights

ABBREVIATIONS

AJIL	American Journal of International Law
ASEAN	Association of South-East Asian Nations
BYIL	British Yearbook of International Law
CYIL	Canadian Yearbook of International Law
ECOSOC	Economic and Social Council
GA	General Assembly
ICJ	International Court of Justice
ICRC	International Committee of the Red Cross
ILA	International Law Association
ILO	International Labour Organization
OAS	Organization of American States
OAU	Organization of African Unity
RCADI	Recueil des Cours de l'Académie de droit international de la Haye
UN	United Nations
UNDP	United Nations Development Programme
UNEPRO	United Nations East Pakistan Relief Operation
UNESCO	United Nations Educational, Scientific and Cultural Organization
UNFICYP	United Nations Peacekeeping Force in Cyprus
UNHCR	United Nations High Commissioner for Refugees
UNICEF	United Nations Children Fund
UNITAR	United Nations Institute for Training and Research

"As the Preparatory Commission foresaw, the Secretary-General in certain circumstances must speak for the Organization as a whole."

Secretary-General Trygvie Lie, in his first Annual Report to the General Assembly, 26 June 1946.

"The Secretary-General . . . has to act for the Organization as a whole, independent of the special interests of any single member nation."

Secretary-General Dag Hammarskjöld, Annual Report to the General Assembly, 21 July 1954.

"The Secretary-General's obligations under the Charter must include any humanitarian action that he can take to save the lives of large numbers of human beings."

Secretary-General U Thant, "The Role of the Secretary-General", UN Monthly Chronicle, No. 9, October 1971.

"I have always regarded it as my duty to exercise my good offices in human rights matters and I shall continue to assist in any way I can."

Secretary-General Kurt Waldheim, Annual Report to the General Assembly, 1980.

PREFACE

Good offices are a valuable part of any system for the promotion and protection of human rights. We live in a world of nation-States co-operating within the framework of international organizations established on the premises of respect for national sovereignty and non-interference in the internal affairs of States. As a result, arrangements for the promotion and protection of human rights often fall short of what is needed to ensure protection of human rights. When cases or situations arise outside of the sessions of human rights organs and where inter-sessional arrangements are either non-existent or inadequate, is the plight of human beings to be ignored? If the international organs concerned cannot agree, or decide, on a course of action because of political differences, is human suffering or human need to go by unheeded? Even if human rights organs do take up a case or situation, should not a reputable and respected international personality such as the head of an international organization or secretariat with competence in the field, do whatever he or she can in order to assist in providing humanitarian relief? In most systems of law it has been found necessary to develop forms of equitable relief in order to render justice to those who are not covered by the specific terms of the law, or who would suffer injustice if the law were to be applied rigidly. Are good offices not a useful medium for this purpose?

While the exercise of good offices for the maintenance of international peace and security has been the subject of some scholarly investigations, the exercise of good offices in the field of human rights has so far been the subject of little study. However, interest in the subject is growing, as is indicated by various resolutions recently adopted in the United Nations on, or related to, the topic. There is also much interest among Member States in utilizing more fully the possibilities open to the Secretary-General under the Charter of the United Nations.[1] It has been suggested for example "that the Secretary-General could maintain a watch-list of potential crisis areas to be reviewed at periodic Security Council meetings, possibly closed, or informal consultations."[2] A related suggestion is that "A body attached to the office of the Secretary-General could be created which could involve itself in research and projection into the future about the potential crisis areas."[3]

In the present work it is proposed to analyze the concept and characteristics of humanitarian good offices in international law with particular reference to the good offices of the United Nations Secretary-General in the field of human rights. As a serving United Nations official I am fully aware of the delicacy involved in entering into an area which is at once sensitive and also close to the Secretary-General himself. I have felt enabled to do so on account of the following factors: (a) The examination will be based exclusively on materials which are in the public domain; (b) I shall confine myself purely to conceptual matters. Examples taken from specific cases or situations will be used merely to illustrate the conceptual discussion; (c) I shall assume a purely academic mantle and therefore all views expressed, even on conceptual questions, will be entirely my own, solely in my personal capacity, and should in no way be associated with the organization I have the great honour of serving, or its Secretary-General, or any of my other colleagues; (d) International officials need to investigate conscientiously the conceptual and substantive issues affecting their work and also need in this regard, to profit from exchanges with their academic colleagues. The Reid Lectures of Acadia University provide a splendid forum for such an exchange on the concept of humanitarian good offices, particularly since Acadia, one of the oldest of the distinguished universities of Canada, is an example of the finest humanitarian tradition and also because Canada has displayed so much interest in the humanitarian good offices of the United Nations Secretary-General, as will become manifest in the ensuing pages; (e) Only materials before 1 January 1982 will be used. In this way there is no possibility of inadvertently touching on matters affecting the current Secretary-General.

NOTES

1. See, e.g., the Report of the Special Committee on the Charter of the United Nations and on the Strenghtening of the Role of the Organization (1980), A/35/33, pp. 61-62.
2. *Ibid.*, para. 28.
3. *Ibid.*, para. 29.

INTRODUCTION

Article 7 of the United Nations Charter established the Secretariat as a principal organ of the United Nations. The purposes of the Organization, according to Article 1, include the achievement of international co-operation in solving international problems of an economic, social and cultural, or humanitarian character, and in promoting and encouraging respect for human rights and for fundamental freedoms for all without distinction as to race, sex, language or religion. Article 2 adds that the Organization and its members shall act in accordance with the principles contained therein "in pursuit of the purposes stated in Article 1." Therefore, the Secretariat, as a principal organ of the United Nations, is enjoined to foster international co-operation for the promotion and encouragement of respect for human rights and fundamental freedoms.

Article 97 of the Charter provides that the Secretariat shall comprise a Secretary-General and such staff as the Organization may require. The Article also provides that the Secretary-General "shall be the chief administrative officer of the organization," while Article 98 adds that the Secretary-General "shall perform such other functions as are entrusted to him" by United Nations organs. Article 99 states that the Secretary-General "may bring to the attention of the Security Council any matter which in his opinion may threaten the maintenance of international peace and security."

The good offices functions of the Secretary-General are not expressly mentioned in the Charter. However, successive office-holders have developed them as an inherent element of the office and this has been acknowledged by the General Assembly, the Security Council and other organs, which have on various occasions mandated the Secretary-General to utilize his "good offices". In recent years United Nations human rights organs have expressly recognized and appreciated the good offices of the Secretary-General in the field of human rights. In resolution

1979/36, the Economic and Social Council expressed its appreciation to the Secretary-General for his efforts in rendering good offices, as envisaged in the Charter of the United Nations, in the field of human rights. In resolution 34/175 adopted on 17 December 1979, the General Assembly "stressed the important role that the Secretary-General can play in situations of mass and flagrant violations of human rights." At its thirty-sixth session in 1980, the Commission on Human Rights by resolution 27 (XXXVI) welcomed the statement of the Secretary-General, in his Report of 1979 on the work of the Organization, that he is continuing to exert his best endeavours on behalf of human rights whenever he considers that his actions may be of assistance to the persons or groups concerned, and "requested the Secretary-General to continue and intensify the good offices envisaged in the Charter of the United Nations in the field of human rights." In resolution 30 (XXXVI), the Commission requested the Secretary-General, in cases where large-scale exoduses of persons become a matter of international concern and solidarity, to consider establishing direct contacts with appropriate governments, to assess the relationships between the situation and full enjoyment of human rights and to make concrete recommendations for ameliorating such situations. The resolution also requested the Secretary-General, where warranted, to submit to the Commission or to the General Assembly, as appropriate, at its next sitting a summary of his findings and recommendations to assist governments in restoring full enjoyment of human rights.[1]

It may thus be seen that the exercise by the Secretary-General, of good offices in the field of human rights, either on his own initiative, or at the request of United Nations organs, is an established part of the efforts of the United Nations for the promotion and protection of human rights.

At the thirty-fourth session of the United Nations General Assembly, in 1979, the Canadian Secretary for External Affairs, Miss Flora MacDonald, urged the United Nations to find better, more certain ways to deal with gross violations of human rights, no matter where they happen and proposed that "the General Assembly should agree to establish a position of Under-Secretary-General for Human Rights, and . . . should appoint an individual of undisputed stature in the international community to that office. This person would exercise the mandate the Secretary-General has under the Charter to use his good offices in the human rights field."[2]

At the same session of the General Assembly, the Canadian Permanent Representative elaborated further upon this proposal as follows: "We are calling for the establishment of a post, at the level of Under-Secretary-General, of a special representative of the Secretary-General for human rights and humanitarian affairs . . . We would view the special representative as concerning himself primarily with the promotion of human rights and with the exercise of good office functions as assigned by the Secretary-General. He would be the Secretary-General's point of liaison with governments on these matters, and would act in a low-key and unpublicized manner in the expectation that a reconciliation between local conditions and international expectations could encourage some improvement in actual conditions."[3]

Eventually, a draft resolution[4] tabled by Canada and proposing the establishment of such a post was not pressed to a vote because it was considered preferable that such a proposal should be adopted by consensus. The following year, however, the new Secretary for External Affairs, Mr. MacGuigan returned to the subject in an address to the plenary during the general debate when he urged "that greater use should be made of the Secretary-General's Charter responsibilities in acting within the authority of his office in situations arising from violations of human rights . . . I urge the Secretary-General to use his good offices where the evidence of human rights violation is sufficiently serious. All States should extend their co-operation to him in order to alleviate difficulties in a non-confrontational manner and to further the interests of international co-operation."[5] Canada therefore tabled in the Third Committee of the Assembly a draft resolution on the good offices of the Secretary-General in the field of human rights.[6]

Speaking on this proposal, the Canadian representative in the Third Committee explained that while the search continued for mutually agreed solutions for improving the effective enjoyment of human rights and fundamental freedoms, the United Nations must concentrate on ensuring that the machinery and procedures already available within the United Nations system are put to the best and most effective use possible.[7] One such procedure, she felt, was the good offices role of the Secretary-General in the field of human rights, as envisaged in the Charter, which had been gradually developed over the years by successive Secretaries-General in response to changing circumstances in the world. It had come to be universally accepted by all Member States of the United Nations as an integral and essential part of the Secretary-

General's functions and had been employed on many occasions. All the Secretaries-General had effectively resorted to their good-offices role in the human rights field and they had all viewed that aspect of their function as constituting an integral part of their mandate. They had all approached it from a strictly humanitarian point of view and the good-offices function had therefore consistently been regarded as non-political. The role had always been performed with the express consent of the countries concerned and had consequently never been regarded as interference in internal affairs. Interesting parallels, she added, could be drawn between the Secretary-General's role in the human rights field and his activities in the area of humanitarian assistance and relief, to which all the considerations she had set forth applied. Her delegation believed that the protection of innocent individuals from flagrant abuses of their human rights was as important a function of the United Nations as the assistance that it provided to persons in distress who were the victims of man-made or natural disasters.

She noted that a similar good-offices role had developed in humanitarian matters or the human rights field over the years in other international organizations such as UNHCR, ILO, UNESCO and ICRC, confirming that it responded to a need of the times. The ILO practice was especially illustrative of the effective use to which resort to the good-offices function could be put: she had in mind such instances as the procedures whereby, subject to the consent of the government concerned, a representative of the Director-General studied directly with the competent government authorities the practical or legal difficulties encountered in the application of a ratified convention or, in co-operation with the country concerned, considered problems raised by complaints concerning infringements of the principle of freedom of association. The results so far achieved in the ILO through that process had amply demonstrated that "quiet diplomacy" in the human rights field could be made to work in practice in resolving a number of situations which would otherwise have developed into unproductive confrontations.

Experience had shown, the Canadian representative continued, that it was appropriate to leave to the discretion of the Secretary-General the precise manner in which he would elect to intercede in any given circumstances. His decision would always be predicated on the assumptions which had prompted the action of Secretaries-General in the past, namely: a determination that a resort to his good-offices function was likely to have beneficial results in improving a given situation; a willingness to provide any assistance which might appear useful from a strictly humanitarian point of view; the consent of the country concerned; and a clear understanding that the Secretary-General's concern related to humanitarian and non-political considerations. Her delegation firmly believed that the informality of the procedure was conducive to the rapid improvement of situations of gross violations of human rights and the alleviation of the sufferings of victims of such situations. It was to be hoped, she said, that the Secretary-General's expression of concern and offers of assistance would receive the most serious consideration on the part of all parties concerned.

With those considerations in mind, she explained, her delegation had submitted the above mentioned draft resolution which aimed at the full development of the good-offices role of the Secretary-General to enable the United Nations system to cope more adequately with the all too frequent situations of mass and flagrant violations of human rights which persisted throughout the world.

During the ensuing debate in the Third Committee, different assessments were expressed as to the need for the proposed resolution. The view was expressed that since good offices in the field of human rights had become traditional, the resolution was not really necessary. To this it was replied that there was merit in the Member States indicating that they valued the use of good offices in the field of human rights and wished to see it enhanced, while leaving it up to the Secretary-General how to go about its implementation, in his discretion. It was also said that the resolution would lend support to the activities of the Secretary-General without in any way dictating to him. Eventually, the Third Committee decided, on a procedural motion, not to vote on the draft resolution. The general view of the Committee was that the Secretary-General should be left free to decide on the manner and modalities of the exercise of good offices and that the function should not be restricted or regulated in any way.[8]

While different views were expressed on some matters of detail, and there was a certain degree of political reluctance to the adoption of the draft resolution, there was no real disagreement of substance on the appropriateness of the Secretary-General interceding at his discretion, on humanitarian grounds, in matters involving violations of human rights. Substantive questions were raised mainly by the Brazilian delegation. However, it stated expressly that "it would not deny the Secretary-

General the possibility of contacting Governments in an attempt to ameliorate human suffering" but cautioned that that would be on his own initiative and at his own risk, subject to the acceptance of the governments concerned.[9] The Brazilian delegation was insistent, however, that in making such humanitarian intercessions the Secretary-General should act in accordance with Article 2(7) of the Charter of the United Nations dealing with the principle of non-intervention in the internal affairs of States. To this the United States delegate replied that the Secretary-General as the head of the Secretariat, a principal organ of the Charter, could do nothing outside of the Charter.

Another point raised by the Brazilian delegate was that good offices were properly used by the Secretary-General "only when his action had a bearing on international peace and security" and that "good offices constituted a means for the settlement of disputes and presupposed at least two parties agreeing to their use." The delegate of the USSR expressed similar views. (These delegates did not deal with the considerable practice of good offices in the humanitarian field which has developed since the establishment of the League of Nations and which has resulted in the evolution and refinement of the concept.) The Brazilian delegate nevertheless admitted the propriety of the Secretary-General's use of "direct contacts" with regard to human rights questions and sought to draw a distinction between "good offices" and "direct contacts" with governments. The relevance and significance of this distinction were not explained. The Brazilian delegate added that his delegation did not share the interpretation that under the Charter the Secretary-General was entitled to assume a good-offices role in the field of human rights and that the Charter in no way instructed the Secretary-General to exercise good offices in the field of human rights.

Essentially, this point involved more semantics than substance. For the Brazilian delegate recognized the propriety of intercessions by the Secretary-General on humanitarian grounds but did not wish to see this labelled "good offices". The practical reasons for his difficulties were not explained and they are hard to discern, for there are no characteristics or attributes of the exercise of good offices, even in their traditional sense, which involve anything more than intercession on humanitarian grounds or could be objectionable in the field of human rights.

Many other delegations, however, supported the enhancement of the good-offices role of the Secretary-General in the field of human rights. The United States delegate believed that the use of the good offices of the Secretary-General was most useful and could be employed more frequently and consistently. He suggested that in the future the General Assembly, or the Commission on Human Rights, should evolve detailed and objective criteria for employing the good offices of the Secretary-General. Such a role could, for example, serve to

"(a) ascertain the facts in a case of gross violation of human rights;
(b) maintain communications and contacts with the government concerned;
(c) send routinely a special representative or working group to the government concerned;
(d) bring to the attention of the government the report of the special representative;
(e) attempt to influence the government to restore respect for human rights;
(f) make available technical assistance or advisory services to help accomplish the task;
(g) raise and report on the issue before the Commission on Human Rights or its Sub-Commission;
(h) convene international conferences to consider the situation, if necessary;
(i) make public comment on the situation; and
(j) refer the matter to appropriate United Nations bodies for public consideration."

The Dutch delegate pointed out that while the good-offices function of the Secretary-General was not specified in so many words in the Charter of the United Nations, the Secretary-General had exercised a good-offices function almost from the inception of his office. For example, on 5 November 1980, a statement by the President of the Security Council had made it clear that members of the Council fully supported the use of good offices by the Secretary-General in seeking to bring about peaceful negotiations between Iran and Iraq. In the field of human rights, the good-offices role of the Secretary-General had generally been recognized for a long time. A United Nations press release issued on 29 April 1967 had stated that the Permanent Representatives of Poland and Czechoslovakia, on behalf of a group of socialist countries, had met with the Secretary-General on 28 April 1967 and had requested him to use his good offices with a view to ending persecutions in Greece and to preventing the possible execution of political leaders who had been detained; in particular, they had requested the Secretary-General to intercede to save the life of Mr. Manolis Glezos.

As far as gross violations of human rights were concerned, the Dutch delegate added, the good-offices role of the Secretary-General had not been as fully developed as it had been in connection with individual cases. However, in 1979 the General Assembly had adopted resolution 34/175 which had not only reaffirmed that mass and flagrant violations of human rights were a special concern of the United Nations but had also stressed the important role that the Secretary-General could play in such situations. The importance of the good-offices role of the Secretary-General had also been recognized in Economic and Social Council resolution 1979/36. He emphasized that all those resolutions had been adopted by consensus. His delegation therefore considered that significant progress could be made if the General Assembly adopted a resolution which would request the Secretary-General, when urgent situations of mass and flagrant violations of human rights arose, to consider establishing direct contacts with the governments concerned. The resolution might also request the Secretary-General, in so far as he might deem it appropriate, to keep the President of the General Assembly, the Chairman of the Commission on Human Rights or the President of the Security Council informed of developments regarding such situations as well as any action which was to be undertaken in relation thereto.[10]

The New Zealand delegate noted that several countries facing human rights problems had received visits from special representatives of the Secretary-General. The precedents for such actions, and their firm basis in terms of the Charter, should, she felt, remove any doubts a government might have of interference in its domestic affairs.[11] The Italian delegate said that there was no doubt that the exercise of good offices in cases of gross human rights violations enabled the United Nations to be speedily informed about the facts of any situation creating international concern, so that it might take timely and effective action on its humanitarian aspects.[12] The Norwegian delegate remarked that the good offices machinery of the United Nations Secretariat and the Commission on Human Rights had been considerably refined over the years and had been used with good results. He therefore felt that further efforts should be made to strengthen that machinery and to make it more efficient in the field of human rights within the entire United Nations system.[13]

The delegate of the United Kingdom recalled that increasing attention had been drawn in recent years by the Secretary-General and various United Nations bodies concerned with human rights to the good-offices role of the Secretary-General in that field. The Commission on Human Rights at its thirty-sixth session had unanimously adopted resolution 27 (XXXVI) requesting the Secretary-General to continue and intensify his good-offices role. The United Kingdom delegation fully supported that call and was appreciative of the Secretary-General's efforts.[14] The Irish delegate also recalled that every Secretary-General of the United Nations had regarded the question of good offices as one of the most important aspects of his role and had emphasized the importance of discretion in its exercise. Secretary-General Waldheim had stated that because of the very nature of the problem of good offices, in many cases little or nothing could be said publicly about the efforts made if those efforts were to have any hope of succeeding. The Secretary-General had also stated that governments were prepared to respond positively to a discreet approach, based on humanitarian grounds, if their own problems and responsibilities were sufficiently understood. It was clear, he added, that the essence of the exercise of good offices was discretion, informality and personal contact. There could be no rigid rules or restrictions for that role.[15]

The French delegate expressed the view that the ruling bodies of the United Nations should use the good offices of the Secretary-General only if there was a sound reason to do so. It was clearly not desirable to expose the Secretary-General to failure in his task. When an individual or an organization acted without legal competence, it must do so with certainty of success, since its influence, credibility, prestige and moral authority were at stake. If the Secretary-General acted in such cases, he would be committing his moral authority, which was that of the United Nations itself. It would therefore be difficult *a priori* to define situations in which his action would be required, and it would be better to request such action on a case-by-case basis.[16]

The following conclusions may be drawn from the consideration of this question by the Third Committee at the thirty-fifth session of the General Assembly:

(1) While the utility of humanitarian intercessions by the United Nations Secretary-General in the field of human rights was widely recognized, there was some political resistance to what was perceived as an attempt to codify or regulate the function.

(2) While a few delegations raised questions regarding the use of the terms "good offices" where were more of a semantic rather than a substantive character, the term has become so widely used in international practice, including the field of human rights that it has become a term of art and serves as an appropriate label for the kind of activity being discussed.

(3) Earlier resolutions of the General Assembly, the Economic and Social Council and the Commission on Human Rights which recognized and appreciated the Secretary-General's exercise of good offices in the field of human rights and requested him to continue doing so, retain full relevance and validity. Indeed, a few days after the Third Committee's consideration of this question, it adopted another draft resolution which as subsequently endorsed by the General Assembly, requested the Secretary-General "to use his best endeavours" in cases where minimum legal safeguards applicable to persons accused of capital offences appear not to have been respected.[17] This provides ample evidence that the debates of the Committee on the Canadian draft resolution, in part, involved more questions of semantics than of substance.

(4) The overwhelming majority of delegations which spoke, wished to see the potential of the good-offices function of the Secretary-General in the field of human rights utilized to even greater advantage.

(5) However, the consensus was that the good-offices function of the Secretary-General in the field of human rights should not be regulated or restricted; that the Secretary-General should not be dictated to as regards the manner or modalities of the exercise of his good offices.

(6) All delegations felt that the Secretary-General should act in accordance with the principles of the Charter in exercising good offices in the field of human rights.

(7) In view of the reluctance of some States to "legislate" on the subject, it follows necessarily that the nature and characteristics of the concept of good offices in the field of human rights must be determined by reference to the relevant international practice and to such rules of international customary law as may have emerged from it. An examination of the relevant rules and practice will be offered in the following pages.

NOTES

1. See on this, Chapter X below.
2. A/34/PV.8, p. 33.

3. Address to the Third Committee by His Excellency Mr. William H. Barton, Ambassador and Permanent Representative of Canada to the United Nations. Taken from text of address provided by the Permanent Mission of Canada to the United Nations.
4. A/C.3/34/L.18.
5. A/35/PV.4, pp. 61-62.
6. A/C.3/35/L.78. See Annex X below.
7. A/C.3/35/SR.62, paras. 27-31.
8. For the records of the discussion, see A/C.3/35/SR.56-62.
9. A/C.3/35/SR.60, para. 12.
10. A/C.3/35/SR.56, paras. 64-65.
11. A/C.3/35/SR.59, para. 4.
12. A/C.3/35/SR.59, para. 34.
13. A/C.3/35/SR.60, para. 28.
14. A/C.3/35/SR.58, para. 24.
15. A/C.3/35/SR.59, paras. 13-14.
16. A/C.3/35/SR.60, para. 39.
17. GA resolution 35/172, para. 2.

Chapter I

THE HUMAN RIGHTS POLICY OF THE UNITED NATIONS SECRETARY-GENERAL

I. Human rights, peace and security

The promotion and protection of human rights are the essential and ultimate *raison d'être* of the United Nations. The reaffirmation of faith in fundamental human rights, in the dignity and worth of the human person, and in the equal rights of men and women is in the forefront of the goals of the United Nations in the Charter. It is significant that among the "ends" enumerated in the Charter's Preamble, the following is placed first, even before the maintenance of international peace and security: "*To practice tolerance* and live together in peace with one another as good neighbours" (emphasis added). In Article 1 of the Charter, the purposes of the Organization are enumerated as being: 1. To maintain international peace and security; 2. To develop friendly relations among nations; 3. To achieve international co-operation in solving international problems of an economic, social, cultural or humanitarian character, and in promoting and encouraging respect for human rights and for fundamental freedoms for all without distinction as to race, sex, language, or religion; 4. To be a centre for harmonizing the actions of nations in the attainment of these ends.

According to some leading commentators on the Charter, "The order of listing, together with the content of subsequent Charter provisions, gives support to the view that the maintenance of peace and security is the prmary purpose of the Organization and takes priority over other purposes."[1] However, as Judge Sir Gerald Fitzmaurice cautioned in the *Expenses Case* "the humanitarian . . . functions of the Organization are . . . hardly less important than its political functions, and may well contribute materially, or even be essential, to the success of the latter."[2] At the San Francisco Conference, the view of the drafters of the Charter was that all provisions of the Charter, being indivisible are equally valid and operative and each therefore is to be construed and applied in function of the others.[3] This intention is fittingly demonstrated in Article 55, which states that: "With a view to the creation of conditions of stability and well-being which are necessary for peaceful and friendly relations among nations based on respect for the principle of equal rights and self-determination of peoples, the United Nations shall promote:

"(a) higher standards of living, full employment, and conditions of economic and social progress and development;
(b) solutions of international economic, social, health, and related problems; and international cultural and educational co-operation; and
(c) universal respect for, and observance of, human rights and fundamental freedoms for all without distinction as to race, sex, language or religion."[4]

At its session of 1947 held in Lausanne, the Institute of International Law, after considering a thoughtful report by the late Professor Charles de Visscher, adopted a resolution entitled "The fundamental rights of man as the basis for a restoration of international law", in which it declared that recognition and respect of the inherent rights of human beings, are closely bound up with the development of international law, and that an effective system of international law is inseparably bound up with respect for the individual within the State. The declaration had been drafted by Professor Charles de Visscher who, in his report to the Institute, pleaded eloquently that "the battle which has . . . been joined over the issue of human freedoms is intimately connected with the establishment of an international order. In making human values the final meeting point of all law and constituting them an autonomous province beyond the reach of political action by the state, the proposed declaration has in view the regeneration of international law on a moral and legal basis acceptable to all civilized states. Put in this way the problem assumes an absolutely fundamental character . . ."[5]

The human dignity or human rights theory of international law has not been given the attention it deserves from international lawyers. However, there have been a few voices cyring in the wilderness. Thus, Professor Myres McDougall has, for a long time, called for the establishment of an international law of human dignity.[6] Judge Haim Cohn of Israel has suggested that efforts be made to develop an overall human rights theory of law.[7] More recently, Professors MacDonald, Morris and Johnston, in the useful introduction to the book which they edited on International Law and Policy of Human Welfare[8] argued the case for an international legal system of human welfare conducive to the satisfaction of the needs (material as well as spiritual) of every human being.

Article 28 of the Universal Declaration of Human Rights proclaims that everyone is entitled to a social and international order in which the rights and freedoms set forth in the Declaration can be fully realized. In addition to adding a dimension of universality to the concept of international concern for human rights, this Article reflects the basic goal of the international order envisaged in the Charter: a life of dignity and well-being for everyone everywhere, and at all times, in a world where human rights and fundamental freedoms prevail and are enjoyed by all without restraint. Serving the interests of mankind by promoting and protecting economic, social, cultural, civil and political rights, and the inalienable rights of peoples and groups, is the *raison d'être* of all human societies and social organizations, whether national, regional, or international. Human rights represent the highest embodiment of the human factor: the respect and welfare of all human beings as subjects and not objects of all human endeavours. They represent mandatory objectives for all societies and social organizations.

The practical implications of the centrality of human rights in the international order envisaged in the Charter of the United Nations were referred to in the current United Nations Medium-Term Plan in the field of human rights, which states that: ". . . in the conception of the Charter, the promotion and encouragement of respect for human rights and fundamental freedoms for all was placed in direct relationship with the maintenance of international peace and security and the creation of conditions for economic and social progress and development. The interdependence between human rights, peace and development means that freedom from fear and freedom from want belong as much to the heart of the concept of human rights as political freedoms. This same interdependence assumes and requires that the wider recognition and acceptance of the human factor be made the central theme in all human endeavours. One of the most important challenges for the United Nations is the elaboration and implementation of approaches to problems and strategies for solving them, which are based on respect for human rights. Along with the new international economic order, the United Nations has to work for a new social and human order enabling peoples and individuals to enjoy the rights which are basic to their existence and development."[9]

The question may be asked, to what extent has the human rights approach been applied in practice to the solution of international problems arising out of present international conditions? This question, and the answer given to it, have deep practical significance. If, for example, international order is perceived purely, or overwhelmingly, in terms of security, this could result in patterns of inter-State behaviour in which security, as the dominant and overriding concern, minimizes the human factor. If, on the other hand, it is perceived in human terms, as aiming first and foremost at realization of the basic rights of all persons and all peoples, the result could be that the promotion and protection of those rights would become the dominant goal and that human rights considerations would become a guiding and integrated factor in the conduct of inter-State relations and policies relating thereto. Such a conception of international order would also influence the approach to security questions, for if we start from the premise that all persons and all peoples are entitled to live in peace, for example, this could lead to intensified efforts to realize this right through consistent steps aimed at putting a halt to the arms race and at disarmament. Moreover, arguments favouring security at all costs would then lose much of their force and it would become increasingly difficult to use security concerns to restrict, limit, or violate human rights and fundamental freedoms.

While the maintenance of international peace and security is, and must remain, a primary objective of the international community and of the United Nations, it should nevertheless be recognized that peace is indivisible in its universal, regional or national dimensions, and that events occurring within a single country – be they internal conflicts or gross violations of human rights – may result in human suffering of as great a magnitude as those stemming from inter-State conflicts. While mindful at all times of the principle of respect for the sovereignty and independence of States, the international order nevertheless should afford enough flexibility to provide ways and means of dealing with situations involving gross violations of human rights which entail great human suffering, for the very notion of international order may be negated, or called into question, when such violations occur without adequate attention from the international community.

There is a great need, at the international as well as at the regional, national and local levels, to follow more deliberate human rights approaches to political, economic, social and cultural questions and to integrate the human rights dimension into policies and programmes pursued in these areas so as to make the basic rights of all persons and all peoples the central objective of such policies. It may be asked whether adequate attention is being given to the human rights dimension in the consideration of national, regional or international questions. To what extent is there an approach which starts from the premise that all human beings are entitled to enjoy their inalienable human rights and fundamental freedoms and that, in all areas, policies at the national, regional or international levels should be inspired in their conception as well as in their execution by the need to promote and protect those rights and freedoms? Often the human rights factor – though present in a broad, general sense – is markedly absent in practical terms. Unless the human rights dimension is taken as the essential starting point, international co-operation in any area may be found wanting. The current international deliberations on questions of peace, disarmament, and development have to be oriented towards the human rights dimensions of the issues which are being discussed. If, for example, deliberations on development questions proceed without adequate consideration of the human rights factor, this could lead to the deleterious result that the consequences of development policies for human beings and their rights and freedoms might be overlooked.

In his Annual Report on the work of the United Nations Organization during 1980-81, former Secretary-General Kurt Waldheim pointed out that: "In the contemporary world, the interrelationship between human rights and questions of peace and security is emerging into sharper focus. The purposes and principles of the Charter are mutually supporting and interdependent. Thus, it is increasingly clear that peace and development are necessary for the full realization of human rights. At the same time, in the absence of respect for human rights, peace and development lose much of their meaning. It is essential therefore that the efforts of the United Nations and its Member States to promote and protect civil and political, as well as economic, social and cultural rights should be accorded the highest importance."[10] Human rights, peace and development are interrelated and interdependent and the fostering of one promotes the enhancement of the other.

Peace is not merely the absence of war. It is also the promotion of a state of harmonious relations within a State, or between States. The promotion of peace at the international level is linked to the achievement of peace within each State. Mass and flagrant violations of human rights are flagrant breaches of international peace and security. Peace has not merely a negative connotation of an absence of war, but is also a positive concept which includes peaceful good-neighbourly and co-operative relations both within a country and among countries. It is basically an attitude of mind which involves both the desire to co-operate for mutual benefit and the desire to solve such problems as might exist in a peaceful spirit free of external influence and without bitterness or acrimony.

Peace is not merely an absence of violence and it requires harmony and should be a just peace. Respect for human rights is a precondition of a just peace. International peace is the creation of a just world order, and national peace the creation of a society where human rights are safeguarded for everyone. This notion is sometimes described as "positive peace" distinct from "negative peace", which is defined as the absence of violence.

If peace is understood as the elimination of threats and the means of facilitating the possibility for societies to live in peace, it can lead to the rebirth of trust, to gradual disarmament and creativity can be unleashed and greater openness emerge. Consequently, a better realization of human rights would become possible. But peace based on deterrence and on the threat to maintain stability by superior force does not allow the realization of human rights. If peaceful coexistence is understood as the right of every nation to live in peace, and to choose its own social and economic system without fear of intimidation from any corner of the world, this would be constructive to global peace.

Let us enumerate rapidly some concrete practical questions requiring attention insofar as the human rights aspects of peace and security questions are concerned:

(i) What do the international human rights standards involve for the content of peace?

(ii) How do violations of human rights affect peace and security? In many instances since the end of the Second World War, violations of human rights occurring within countries have resulted in levels of human suffering far greater than those ensuing from many disputes or conflicts between two or more States. In one country, for example, the United Nations Commission on Human Rights was informed by one of its rapporteurs that over a millon persons had been killed. Reports pertaining to human rights situations in many other countries reveal terrible human suffering, on massive scales.

(iii) Would policies and strategies with human rights orientations speed up the realization of global peace and security?

(iv) How do current patterns of violence and violence-related phenomena affect the realization of human rights? Reference could be made here, for example, to nuclear weapons, the arms race, militarization and the "national security state".

(v) What is the relevance of international human rights standards to situations of armed conflict?

(vi) How are war propaganda and the propagation of doctrines of racial or national superiority or other doctrines which may incite hatred to be combatted?

(vii) How are individuals who object to the use of all of or certain means of arms, usually referred to as "conscientious objectors" to be granted recognition?

(viii) How can resources released through disarmament contribute to the realization of human rights, particularly basic rights such as the rights to food, to work, to health and to education?

(ix) How do the International Covenant on Economic, Social and Cultural Rights and the Declaration on Social Progress and Development feature in global strategies for development and for the realization of a new international economic order?

(x) To what extent have the three United Nations international development strategies elaborated so far taken account of human rights considerations? Is the human rights factor adequately reflected in the latest international development strategy, and, if not, how can the situation be rectified?

Fundamental human rights questions are also raised with respect to the arms race. A primary consequence of the arms race is to divert resources which could otherwise be used for the realization of human rights. In addition, the arms race has a number of direct consequences for human rights. An intensified arms race inevitably leads to a maximization of security concerns and to resulting limitations upon human rights; military alliances and block rivalries often lead to interference in the internal affairs of States, particularly of small States, and denials of their right to self-determination; a concomitant of the arms race and of regional or hemispheric security concerns is the increasing rise of the "national security state", in which security concerns are given the highest priority and individual freedoms are consequently accorded little importance. There is also the question of the right of the people to information about military policies and programmes of their governments and their implications. The updated report of the Secretary-General, entitled "Economic and Social Consequences of the Arms Race and of Military Expenditures" states that the people "have an obvious right to information about the military policies and programmes of Governments and their implications. Much of the secrecy in this field is not justified by military requirements. In some cases, it results from mere tradition, in others it serves such purposes as shielding questionable or unnecessary armaments programmes from public scrutiny and public criticism. Without endangering the security of any country much greater openness of information could and should be applied in this field."[11] Another aspect which is assuming more and more importance is the production of repressive apparatus as a by-product of modern technology in armaments. It has been documented that repressive apparatus produced by the military-industrial complex in certain countries is made available to oppressors in other parts of the world. There is also the question of the human rights and humanitarian aspects of particularly inhumane weapons, including biological chemical weapons.

The environment resulting from the arms race and group rivalries often leads, also, to the strengthening of the role of the army, the police and other administrative powers and to the extension of the possibilities of State interference in the public sphere, thereby hampering the realization of political and civil rights. Militarization as a process whereby military values supersede other political, economic, social and cultural values, poses grave dangers for human rights.

In his address during the general debate at the thirty-sixth session of the General Assembly, Crown Prince Hassan of Jordan stated: "If the human race is to maintain its claim of being civilized, then it is imperative that humanitarian principles be the cornerstone of this claim. An internationally recognized framework of comprehensive humanitarian principles should govern relations among peoples and nations in times of war and of peace. It should have an in-built monitoring system and should become the basis for the solution of problems of refugees and displaced persons, poverty, illiteracy, terrorism and other issues that are detrimental to the progress of mankind.

I should like to propose to this Assembly the promotion of a new international humanitarian order parallel to the efforts being made in the economic and other fields. Before dealing with economics and politics, let man learn to be more human. I believe that just as the 1948 United Nations Declaration on Human Rights became the springboard for a number of international covenants and legal principles, this comprehensive international humanitarian order may offer a new impetus for a code of conduct in human and international relations of which we are so desperately in need."[12]

II. The Secretary-General's human rights policy

In his departure statement to the Commission on Human Rights in February 1982, after five years of distinguished service as Director of the United Nations Division of Human Rights, Theodoor C. van Boven told the Commission that: "The humanitarian policies of the United Nations, particularly in the area of human rights, still offer much room for development, and the role of the Secretariat under the Charter remains to be fully exploited."[13] Earlier, in a statement to the Commission on 2 February 1981, Dr. van Boven had posed the following key issue to the Commission: "In many instances since the end of the Second World War, violations of human rights occurring within countries have resulted in levels of human suffering far greater than those ensuing from many disputes or conflicts between two or more States. In one country, for example, the Commission on Human Rights was informed by an expert rapporteur that over a million persons had been killed. Reports pertaining to human rights situations in many other countries reveal terrible human sufferings on massive scales. When such events occur, without adequate response by the United Nations, can there be any pretence that there is a functioning world order, or that the universal peace which it is one of the purposes of the United Nations to strengthen, still exists? Do not serious violations of human rights, even more than threatening world peace, also violate it manifestly? In its modern concept, peace is a dynamic and indivisible concept and it is impossible to separate the internal, international or universal components."[14]

How have past Secretaries-General of the United Nations seen the human rights component within their overall strategies in leading the Organization? In particular, how have they perceived the interrelationships between human rights questions and questions of international peace and security. In the rest of this chapter we shall look at these issues, using principally the Annual Reports of Secretaries-General Lie, Hammarskjöld, U Thant and Waldheim.

(a) *Trygve Lie*

Secretary-General Lie provided the first broad insights into his thinking in his Annual Report for the period 1948-49. His view was that the main reason for the existence of the United Nations was to prevent a new world war from breaking out, but he recognized that other developments were adding to the importance of the United Nations. He referred in this regard to the rise of many peoples in Asia and Africa from a position of dependency towards one of equality and the growing strength of the movement to extend the observance of human rights everywhere in the world. "I believe", he said, "that the rise of dependent peoples and the human rights movement will, in the long run, have far more significance and give rise to greater events in the second half of the twentieth century . . ."[15] Referring to the Universal Declaration of Human Rights which had recently been adopted on 10 December 1948, Secretary-General Lie observed that "the Declaration . . . is only the first, although the most important of the steps being taken by the United Nations to extend respect for human rights more widely in the world. The essential role of the United Nations in these great developments is now becoming more clearly defined. On the one hand, the United Nations is assisting the movements towards greater equality of opportunity between the peoples of Asia and Africa and the peoples of the Western world, and between the more highly developed countries and those which are less developed. It is also giving a powerful impetus to winning human rights for all peoples, wherever they live. On the other hand, the United Nations is making it possible for these fundamental changes to be carried out with far less violence than would otherwise be the case."[16]

The following year, Secretary-General Lie added to this picture: "The interdependence of all continents and areas does, in fact, require a series of bold acts, beginning at the earliest possible moment and extending over many years, to replace the widespread misery and poverty of the under-developed areas by a steadily increasing prosperity and improved social organization which, in turn, will prove of benefit to the whole world."[17] In the intervening period, he had launched his famous, ten-point programme for achieving peace which, he said, represented an overall approach to the problem of peace based on the spirit and intentions of the Charter of the United Nations.[18] The eighth point of this programme called for vigorous and continued development of the work of the United Nations for wider observance and respect for human rights and fundamental freedoms throughout the world.[19]

In the introduction to his Annual Report for 1950-51, Secretary-General Lie emphasized that the United Nations must never forget that its functions were not only "peace-keeping" but "peace-creating", and that the creation of conditions of peace would, in a large measure, be the result of providing the economic and psychological framework within which the majority of mankind could find life liveable and worthwhile. He added that it was important to recall that the establishment of the United Nations was motivated by a fundamental and lasting concept that the peace and well-being of all nations and peoples had become in the present age so intimately inter-related that it was necessary for them, despite all their differences, to join in a world-wide organization looking towards security from war, freedom and independence for the peoples and mutual economic and social progress. In the field of social welfare and human rights he found that there had been an increasing recognition of the solemn obligations imposed by the Charter: "The Universal Declaration of Human Rights stands as a beacon of hope and progress for peoples everywhere. Its potentially vast effect upon the future of mankind has as yet only begun to make itself manifest, but the trend is already apparent."[20]

(b) *Dag Hammarskjöld*

Secretary-General Hammarskjöld gave a detailed view of his own perceptions, after only two and a half months in office. In his first Annual Report, submitted on 15 July 1953, Hammarskjöld pointed out that the efforts of the governments to control and moderate those conflicts that constitute an immediate danger to world peace must command first attention in day-to-day decisions of the Organization. However, side by side with those conflicts, or underlying them, he detected two fundamental trends in human society which must determine the long-term direction of its efforts. One trend was directed towards wider social justice and equality for individuals. The other was directed towards equality and justice between nations, not only politically but also in the economic and social sense. Of human rights, Hammarskjöld stated: "The development of social justice is closely connected with the problem of human rights. Such international legal instruments as the proposed covenants on human rights are parts of a concerted effort that is, in fact, proceeding on a much wider basis. Fundamentally, the rate of progress will be determined by the degree to which the developing social conscience of the peoples of the world is able to find expression not only in national legislation and in international treaties, but in the climate of opinion in the various regions of the world. The Universal Declaration of Human Rights should set a standard of achievement that will guide opinion in this field, which is so essential to the ultimate success of the United Nations."[21]

In his Annual Report, the following year, Hammarskjöld, recalling that the Economic and Social Council and the General Assembly had laid down, as an overriding objective of the total economic and social programme of the United Nations, the promotion of the economic and social development of under-developed countries, declared his intention of making this aim a guiding principle in the elaboration of programmes and projects within the Secretariat and underscored that "this could and should be accompanied by continued efforts to achieve wider respect for and promotion of human rights and fundamental freedoms."[22]

In his Annual Report dated 8 July 1955, Hammarskjöld, reviewing the activities of the United Nations during its first ten years (1945-55), said of human rights: "The consolidation and extension of human rights throughout the world continue to be a solemn obligation of the United Nations. It is perhaps in this field that future lines of action are most difficult to define. International instruments embodying the principles contained in the Universal Declaration of Human Rights do not yet appear to meet with general acceptance, and it is doubtful whether the technical assistance approach, which has proved so fruitful in other fields, could contribute significantly to the promotion of human rights.

"It should not be surprising that, having laid down universal standards in an area where cultural differences are so wide and fundamental, the United Nations should experience some difficulties in finding practical methods to enhance the adoption and implementation of these standards on a world-wide basis. These inevitable difficulties should not generate a sense of frustration, nor should they prompt the Organization to actions with doubtful implications. In carrying out its obligations under the Charter in the field of human rights, the Organization should favour initiatives leading forward without introducing the risk of sterile and endless controversy."[23] Hammarskjöld appeared to be opting for a cautious approach to the implementation of human rights. It is significant in this regard that in his next Annual Report he registered his doubts regarding the establishment of three proposed new commissions, two of which had been proposed by the Commission on Human Rights and the third by the Economic and Social Council: one to conduct a survey of the status of the right of peoples and nations to permanent sovereignty over their natural wealth and resources; the second to examine any situation resulting from alleged denial or inadequate realization of the right of self-determination, to provide its good offices for the peaceful rectification of any such situation and, if no adjustment could be effected, to report the facts, with appropriate recommendations, to the General Assembly; the third to conduct a thorough study of the concept of self-determination.[24]

The pressures for measures of implementation in the field of human rights were, however, building up. In 1956, a topic was included in the agenda of the General Assembly at the request of Greece as to whether, pending the entry into force of the covenants on human rights, then under preparation, the United Nations should not take interim measures with respect to violations of the human rights set forth in the Charter of the United Nations and the Universal Declaration of Human Rights. During the discussion of the item in the Third Committee, it was proposed that the General Assembly should request the Commission on Human Rights to consider the possibility of establishing a committee to examine any complaint made by a Member State against another Member State concerning violations of human rights. It was also proposed that the Commission should be requested to consider the possibility of appointing a High Commissioner or establishing a special organ to receive or deal directly with individual petitions concerning violations of human rights. The General Assembly decided eventually to transmit the official records and other documents relating to the question of interim measures to the Commission on Human Rights for discussion in the Commission.[25]

The pressure for activities within the United Nations to foster the implementation of human rights continued to increase. As Hammarskjöld reported on 22 August 1957, hitherto the human rights programme had been concerned primarily with the establishment of general standards and broad definitions. However, he detected that in the course of the year 1956-57 "the United Nations has directed its attention toward the application of the standards, toward the making of inquiries into principles and practices in respect of specific rights, and toward the development of the means for nations and peoples to enter into a free exchange of experience in the protection of human rights. This 'action programme' calls upon Governments to submit reports on human rights . . . directs the Commission on Human Rights to make intensive studies of specific rights . . . and authorizes the Secretary-General to organize seminars on human rights, preferably on a regional basis. The positive objective of this programme, which is still in an experimental stage, is to enable nations and peoples to learn from one another of the results obtained and the difficulties encountered in the promotion of human rights and to benefit thereby. It seems likely that by such means gains will be consolidated and new progress rendered possible."[26]

The picture which has so far emerged from Hammarskjöld's approach is that while he did see the human rights programme as being of importance, he nevertheless approached it in a compartmentalized manner, insofar as practical action by the Organization was concerned. He did not appear to perceive human rights as part of the core activities of the Organization insofar as implementation was concerned. This conclusion is rendered further plausibility when it is taken into account that in the Annual Report just referred to, Hammarskjöld made a wide-ranging review of the "Role of the United Nations", no part of which mentioned human rights. He viewed the United Nations as an indispensable instrument of nations in working for a peaceful evolution towards a more just and secure world order: "The greatest need today is to blunt the edges of conflict among the nations, not to sharpen them. If properly used, the United Nations can serve a diplomacy of reconciliation better than other instruments available to the Member States. All the varied interests and aspirations of the world meet in its precincts upon the common ground of the Charter . . . the tendency in the United Nations is to wear away, or break down, differences, thus helping toward solutions which approach the common interest and application of the principles of the Charter."[27] No mention was made of human rights or humanitarian issues in this core strategy.

The same approach continued during the remaining years of Hammarskjöld's term of office. In his Annual Report of 31 August 1960, he reviewed the special need and the special possibilities for preventive United Nations diplomacy and drew particular attention to the entrusting of wide executive tasks to the Secretary-General on the basis of mandates of a general nature. But he continued to demonstrate no awareness of the potentialities of these developments in the human rights field, although he recognized a role for preventive diplomacy in the economic sphere.[28] Hammarskjöld concluded this Annual Report by observing that the United Nations had increasingly become the main platform – and the main protector of the interests of those nations which felt themselves strong as members of the international family but who were weak in isolation: "Thus, an increasing number of nations have come to look to the United Nations for leadership and support in ways somewhat different from those natural in the light of traditional diplomacy. They look to the Organization as a spokesman and as an agent for principles which gave them strength in an international concert in which other voices can mobilize all the weight of armed force, wealth, an historical role and that influence which is the other side of a special responsibility for peace and security."[29] But of weak and vulnerable persons *within* nations he had little to say. In his last Annual Report, Hammarskjöld provided a re-statement of his understanding of the purposes and principles of the Charter: "In the Preamble to the Charter, Member nations have reaffirmed their faith 'in the equal rights of men and women and of nations large and small', a principle which also has found many other expressions in the Charter. Thus, it re-states the basic democratic principle of equal political rights, independently of the position of the individual or of the Member country in respect of its strength, as determined by territory, population or wealth. The words just quoted must, however, be considered as going further and imply an endorsement of as well as a right to equal economic opportunities."[30]

There can be no doubt of Hammarskjöld's commitment to human rights and to humanitarian principles. But he had so much on his shoulders, and he built up so much that was new in the area of international peace and security that it would be unrealistic to have expected him to be simultaneously creative on all fronts. He placed his energies into the historic movement for de-colonization; he pleaded for equality of opportunity and he urged a structural approach to economic and social progress. In an address at the celebration of the 180th anniversary of the

Virginia Declaration of Rights (1776-1956) at Williamsburg, Virginia, on 14 May 1956, he pleaded: "What is the right to security? Is it not the right to the free development of individual and national life within the limits set by the right of other parties to the same security? What is the right of freedom from attack? Is it not the right to freedom from fear? Thus, we see how close the links are between the philosophy reflected in the recognition of the rights of individuals and the basic principles which may decide the issue of war and peace."[31] Similarly, in an address at the fiftieth anniversary dinner of the American Jewish Committee, on 10 April 1957, he again developed this theme: "We know that the question of peace and the question of human rights are closely related. Without recognition of human rights we shall never have peace, and it is only within the framework of peace that human rights can be fully developed.

In fact, the work for peace is basically a work for the most elementary of human rights: the right of everyone to security and to freedom from fear. We, therefore, recognize it as one of the first duties of a government to take measures in order to safeguard for its citizens this very right. But we also recognize it as an obligation for the emerging world community to assist governments in safeguarding this elementary human right without having to lock themselves in behind the wall of arms."[32]

(c) *U Thant*

U Thant's tenure as Secretary-General saw a flowering of the human factor in the perceptions of the Secretary-General. As he reported on 15 September 1969, "There is now a general realization that concern for the 'human factor' should inspire and penetrate all activities of our Organization whether they deal with political disputes affecting large populations or with the economic and social development of all mankind. Very properly, the Commission on Human Rights and the Economic and Social Council have recalled that, in the United Nations conception, the final objective of development is to ensure the dignity of all human beings, the simultaneous and joint enjoyment of all civil political, economic, social and cultural rights."[33] As he left office, U Thant made the finest statement of his philosophy: "I feel more strongly than ever the worth of the individual human being is the most unique and precious of all our assets and must be the beginning and the end of all our efforts. Governments, systems, ideologies and institutions come and go, but humanity remains. The nature and value of this most precious asset is increasingly appreciated as we see how empty organized life becomes when we remove or suppress the infinite variety and vitality of life of the individual."[34]

During U Thant's period of office, the pressure which had been building up for the United Nations to act against violations of human rights continued to grow. Indeed, in the Declaration on the Occasion of the Twenty-Fifth Anniversary of the United Nations, Member States of the Organization, noting that, despite some progress achieved, serious violations of human rights were still taking place, solemnly pledged themselves to a continued and determined struggle against all violations of the rights and fundamental freedoms of human beings by eliminating the basic causes of such violations, by promoting universal respect for the dignity of all peoples without regard to race, colour, sex, language or religion, and in particular through greater use of the facilities provided by the United Nations in accordance with the Charter.[35]

U Thant made valiant efforts to utilize the possibilities available to him under the Charter to the fullest extent. This may be seen in relation to the crisis in East Pakistan (now Bangladesh) to which we will refer in chapter VI below. In his later years in office, he articulated the possibilities of his good offices in the humanitarian field and left office with the following distress call: "I feel obliged to mention a problem which has been almost daily in my mind during my time as Secretary-General. I refer to the violation of human rights within the frontiers of a State . . . I myself have privately done the best I could in many such situations . . . But this can never be enough, and the time has surely come when Governments in the United Nations must make a determined effort to give justice a world-wide dimension."[36] In a speech delivered on 16 September 1971, U Thant shared some more of his preoccupations: "I sometimes think that the drafters of the Charter were overly obsessed with political and military conflicts . . . Much more could be done through the United Nations if its Members paid as much attention to relatively non-controversial, but nonetheless appalling threats to humanity as they do to political conflicts which may become threats to the peace. Then there are the great humanitarian emergencies which the United Nations is still not equipped to meet. I am glad that steps are now being taken to fit the Organization to deal with natural disasters. The next step is to expand its capability to cover *unnatural* disasters."[37]

(d) *Kurt Waldheim*

In a book published in 1977, Secretary-General Waldheim stated his approach to the role of the United Nations as follows: "Toutes les activités de l'organisation mondiale visent au fond, à resoudre un même problème: comment concilier l'intérêt nationale de chaque pays avec ses responsabilités internationales et les intérêts à long terme de la communauté mondiale dans son ensemble? A l'intérieur de ce cadre fondamental, on peut discerner dans l'oeuvre des Nations Unies trois composantes principales. La première est le maintien de la paix et de la sécurité internationales, sans lequel toutes les autres taches ne tarderaient pas à perdre leur sens . . . La seconde composante de l'oeuvre des Nations Unies et leur rôle de moteur du changement pacifique . . . La troisième grande composante de l'action des Nations Unies est la tentative en cours pour planifier dès aujourd'hui le devenir de l'homme dans une perspective de coopération globale."[38] It will be seen that human rights do not feature in this statement of the core approach; however, a separate chapter on human rights does exist in the book. An earlier statement of the core perspective was as follows: "The original concept of the United Nations as an organization of which the primary function was to maintain, and if necessary, impose international peace and security has long been replaced by a more pragmatic approach. At the risk of over-simplification, the present efforts of Governments within the United Nations framework may be summarized under three forms of activity which proceed simultaneously:

There is the day-to-day effort to maintain peace and security, to deal with and if possible prevent, conflict and to face immediate international problems in the political or other fields, as for example in emergency relief operations. There is the middle term activity, which represents the vast proportion of the Organization's effort in terms of manpower and money. This deals with urgent problems requiring sustained efforts over a longer period such as disarmament, development, trade, population, environment and natural resources, as well as preparing for the future in such questions as the sea-bed and outer space. Finally, there is the long-term goal for which these activities are the workshop, preparation and experimental ground. This is the process through which the present association of States in the United Nations may develop by practical experience into a more reliable instrument of world order and co-operation, accepted and respected by all Governments and capable of safeguarding the common interests of mankind in a crowded world of increasingly interdependent but sovereign States.''[39] The same document stated in another chapter, however, that the protection of human rights is an area where the credibility of the United Nations is especially at stake. Over the past years, the international community had been faced with a number of matters affecting human rights, which had posed – sometimes in a very acute form – the difficulty of reconciling the sovereign jurisdiction of Member States with the principles laid down in the Universal Declaration of Human Rights. The United Nations had been active in attempting to improve fundamental human rights and freedoms in some areas but had proved unable to act in other cases. This had provoked considerable criticism. It had been possible for the Secretary-General to exercise his good offices in certain humanitarian situations, but it was clearly necessary that Member States continue to address themselves to the problem of developing more effective action by the Organization on problems of human rights wherever they occurred.[40]

While human rights did not feature in the statement of his core strategies, Waldheim did, in other contexts, repeatedly stress the importance of human rights and he also referred occasionally to the centrality of human rights. Thus, in his Human Rights Day message on 10 December 1973, he stated that ''among the global problems which beset us, a profound and constant concern for the individual human rights and freedoms of all humanity should have the highest priority. If we fail in our approach to this absolutely basic challenge, our successes in other fields will be hollow indeed.''[41] Certain other themes also recurred in the approach of Secretary-General Waldheim. First, he insisted often that human rights are a legitimate subject for international concern. Thus, in his Annual Report in 1977 he asserted: ''The fundamental principle . . . that respect for individual human dignity is based on universally accepted values and that therefore abuses of human rights, wherever they may occur, are a legitimate subject for international concern. This concept, touching as it does on the sovereignty of Member States as well as on the relationship between human rights and the individual's duty to his community, confronts us with the most challenging problem of putting principles into action and of achieving an effective balance between national and international concerns.''[42] In a statement which he made at the opening of the World Conference to Combat Racism and Racial Discrimination on 14 August 1978, he spoke in similar terms: ''. . .

there is now developing an acceptance of the principle implicit in the Charter and the Universal Declaration, that the recognition and promotion of the worth and dignity of every human being is a legitimate concern of the world community.

There is an inescapable link between respect for human rights and the maintenance of international peace and security, and no nation can justifiably claim immunity, under Article 2(7) of the Charter, from international scrutiny and expression of concern about flagrant and systematic abuses of the human rights of its citizens."[43]

A second recurrent theme of Waldheim was the primary responsibility of governments in human rights matters. His statement on human rights day in 1978 provides an example of a point which he repeatedly made: "In the final analysis we can make headway only with the political will and active co-operation of the Member States of the United Nations. Their commitment is basic to the world-wide promotion and protection of human rights through the rule of law, which is the promise of the Declaration."[44]

A third recurrent theme was his drawing of attention to the gap between principle and practice. As early as 1973 he had warned that "the protection of human rights is an area where the credibility of the United Nations is especially at stake" and he called upon Member States "to continue to address themselves to the problem of developing more effective action by the Organization on problems of human rights wherever they occur."[45]

Regarding his perception of the role of the United Nations in the field of human rights, Waldheim stated in his Annual Report in 1976: "The responsibilities of the United Nations in the field of human rights grow daily, while international public opinion follows our actions with attention, concern and hope – and sometimes with a large degree of frustration and disappointment. It is of primary importance for the Organization and for the world community that we continue to try to respond adequately to this challenge, in the full knowledge both of the immense difficulties involved and of the fundamental importance of this task for all peoples of the world."[46] "The basic aim of United Nations actions in this field," Secretary-General Waldheim felt, "is not to accuse or to provoke acrimonious debate, but to develop a common consciousness in the international community and to encourage improvement in respect for individual dignity and fundamental freedoms."[47]

III. Conclusion

From the above survey, can it be said that the first four Secretaries-General of the United Nations perceived the need to include human rights within their core strategies? With the exception of U Thant, the answer appears to be in the negative. Secretaries-General Lie and Hammarskjöld served during the formative years of the Organization and it would be unrealistic to have expected them to go further. Hammarskjöld's contribution to the development of methods of action for dealing with political crises is legendary. U Thant continued Hammarskjöld's work in handling political crises, sought to utilize his good offices in dealing with humanitarian crises and left office openly pointing out the need for the Organization to face up to humanitarian crises, including violations of human rights. U Thant came nearest to including human rights questions within his core strategy. Secretary-General Waldheim was certainly mindful of the need to deal with humanitarian crises and also used innovative methods for dealing with them, but the evidence suggests that he approached human rights more in a compartmentalized than an integrated manner.

NOTES

1. L.M. Goodrich, E. Hambro and A.P. Simons, Charter of the United Nations (1969), pp. 25-26.
2. ICJ Report 1962, pp. 214-215.
3. Goodrich, *et al., op. cit.*, p. 21.
4. See generally, the report of the United Nations Seminar on Human Rights, Peace and Development, ST/HR/SER.A/10; the report of the UN Secretary-General on present international conditions and human rights, A/36/462 and the Annual Report of the UN Secretary-General, 1981, A/36/1, Section VIII on human rights. In the Section that follows the author draws liberally from these documents, with all of which he has been closely associated personally.
5. Report of the Institute, 1947, reproduced in UN doc. E/CN.4/40, p. 4.
6. See, e.g., M.S. McDougall and associates, Studies in World Public Order (1960), chapter 12: Perspectives for an International Law of Human Dignity. See also the book by Prof. McDougall and associates on Human Rights and World Public Order: The Basic Policies of an International Law of Human Dignity, published by Yale University Press in 1980.
7. H. Cohn, "A Human Rights Theory of Law," in: René Cassin Amicorum Discipulorumque Liber IV (1972), pp. 31-60.
8. (1978).

9. A/33/6/Rev.1, para. 1-31.
10. A/36/1, Section VIII.
11. UN Publication Sales No. E.78.IX.1, para. 179.
12. A/36/PV.15, pp. 56-57.
13. T.C. van Boven, "People Matter" (1982), p. 8.
14. *Ibid.,* p. 73.
15. A/930, p. xii.
16. *Ibid.,* p. xiii.
17. Annual Report, 1949-1950, A/1287, p. xiii.
18. *Ibid.,* p. xii.
19. T. Lie, "In the Cause of Peace" (1954), p. 281.
20. A/1844/Add.1, pp. 4, 7.
21. A/2404, pp. xi, xv.
22. A/2663, p. xiv.
23. A/2911, p. xvi.
24. A/3137, p. 51.
25. A/3594, p. 81.
26. A/3594/Add. 1, pp. 6-7.
27. *Ibid.,* p. 3.
28. A/4390/Add.1, pp. 3, 4, 5.
29. A/4800/Add.1, p. 5.
30. *Ibid.,* p. 1.
31. W. Foote (ed.), Servant of Peace: A Selection of Speeches and Statements of Dag Hammarskjöld (1962), pp. 103-107, at p. 107.
32. *Ibid.,* p. 127. See further, E. Kelen, Hammarskjöld: The Political Man (1968), chapter 4, Peace and Human Rights.
33. A/7601/Add.1, p. 17.
34. A/8401/Add.1.
35. GA resolution 2627 (XXV), para. 8.
36. Concluding remarks in the Introduction to his Annual Report (1970-71).
37. U Thant, "The Role of the Secretary-General," UN Monthly Chronicle, No. 9 (October 1971).
38. Un métier unique au monde (1977).
39. Annual Report, 1973, A/9001/Add.1, p. 2.
40. *Ibid.,* p. 5.
41. Press release SG/SM/232, 3 December 1973. For other similar statements, see A/9601/Add.1, p. 8; press release SG/SM/269, 3 December 1974; press release SG/SM/297, 9 December 1975; A/31/1/Add.1, p. 9; A/32/1, p. 6; OPI/622, p. 16; press release SG/SM/338, 5 December 1977; press release SG/SM/366, 8 December 1978.
42. A/32/1, p. 6.
43. Press release RD/23, 14 August 1978, p. 5. See also OPI/622, p. 16; press release SG/SM/366, 8 December 1978.
44. Press release SG/SM/366, 8 December 1978.
45. See also press release SG/SM/315, 7 December 1976; press release SG/SM/366, 8 December 1978.

46. A/31/1/Add.1, p. 9.
47. A/32/1, p. 6. For Waldheim's perception of the role of the Secretary-General, see Un métier unique au monde (1977), pp. 99-101.

Chapter II

HUMANITARIAN GOOD OFFICES IN INTERNATIONAL LAW

I. Introduction

The exercise of good offices with respect to human rights or humanitarian matters is quite extensive in present-day international organizations, such as the United Nations, the United Nations High Commissioner for Refugees (UNHCR), ILO, UNESCO and the International Committee of the Red Cross (ICRC). In many of these organizations, good offices with respect to human rights or humanitarian matters are exercised at various levels: by the head or by other members of the secretariat; by organs as well as by their presidents, chairmen or members. In some instances there are express mandates to exercise such good offices, while in others they are grounded in the doctrine of inherent or implied competence.

In their traditional meaning, good offices "consist in a third party – Government, international organization, individual – attempting to bring conflicting parties to a negotiating table without interfering in the negotiation themselves."[1] Good offices as a means of settling international disputes have a long history among the instruments of diplomacy. In more recent times the concept may be traced in the Hague Conventions of 1899 and 1907 on the Pacific Settlement of Disputes, Article 2 of which provided that the contracting powers agreed to have recourse, in case of serious disagreement or dispute and as far as circumstances allowed, to the good offices or mediation of one or more friendly powers. Article 3 added that, independently of such recourse, the contracting powers deemed it expedient and desirable that strangers to the dispute should, on their own initiative, and as far as circumstances allowed, offer their good offices or mediation to States at variance and that the exercise of that right could never be regarded by any of the parties in a dispute as an unfriendly act.

As a method for furthering peaceful solutions of international disputes, the good offices of the Secretary-General have been defined by Pechota as "the informal contacts and friendly suggestions made as far as circumstances allow by the Secretary-General, which are designed to facilitate the settlement of a dispute between two or several of the Organization's Member States."[2] The same writer classifies the good offices of the Secretary-General into: (i) forms of diplomatic assistance such as informal contacts and consultations with parties to a dispute; (ii) diplomatic action designed to express international concern, to induce the parties into talks before a favourable atmosphere fades away or before they reach a point of no return, and to assist them in finding a suitable framework for settlement; (iii) mediation, conciliation and co-ordination; (iv) enquiries, fact-finding, the supervision of plebiscites, elections or referenda and the determination of legal rights and duties in a specific issue. Within the third category, namely mediation, conciliation and co-ordination, the author includes "various activities aimed at assisting the parties in alleviating human sufferings or easing other burdens such as refugee problems entailed in certain conflicts" but adds that "such activities can hardly be described as good offices in the usual meaning of the term."[3] Perhaps he meant the "traditional" rather than the "usual" meaning of the term for he himself acknowledges among the categories of involvement by the Secretary-General in the exercise of good offices, "humanitarian problems" including the situation of minorities within some States.[4]

In some instances, humanitarian good offices are expressly mandated by the relevant constitutional instruments or organs, be it in regard to specific cases or, occasionally, in general terms. In a great number of cases, however, good offices have been carried out by the heads of international organizations or by other such personages as an inherent element of their offices or in virtue of the positions which they hold.

International practice has shown that as far as the methods or modalities of humanitarian good offices are concerned, there is, for the most part, little practical difference whether the exercise of good offices is expressly mandated or is an exercise of inherent competence: in practice the methods and modalities are the same. Therefore, in the present study, while mindful that a specific mandate could occasionally indicate particular methods or modalities, we will, generally, not distinguish between "expressly-mandated" and "implied-competence" humanitarian good offices. We will, instead, seek to identify models of action in the exercise of humanitarian good offices in general.

The practice of good offices in the field of human rights within organizations such as the League of Nations, the United Nations, the UNHCR, the ILO, the UNESCO, the ICRC, the Council of Europe and the OAS shows that among the purposes for which such good offices have been exercised were:

(a) To promote human rights generally, including the ratification of human rights treaties,
(b) To facilitate the establishment or restoration of an attitude of respect for human rights;
(c) To alleviate situations of gross violations of human rights,
(d) To ease tensions and facilitate the movement of refugees,
(e) To initiate consultations to help reach solutions to human rights problems,
(f) To assist individuals or groups,
(g) To assist in the drafting of legislation or the establishment of national or local institutions for the promotion and protection of human rights,
(h) To resolve practical or legal difficulties encountered in the application of a human rights convention,
(i) To provide for contingencies, cases or situations outside regular mandates or to provide *ad hoc* protection which lack specific authorization,
(j) To support the activities of human rights organs through discreet facilitative action behind the scenes,
(k) To fill gaps left by human rights organs, particularly in responding to urgent situations,
(l) To bring about friendly settlements to complaints,
(m) To provide equitable relief in cases where the strict application of rules might result in lack of justice,
(n) To perform fact-finding, diplomatic, mediatory or conciliatory activities,
(o) To respond to human needs generally, particularly in situations of emergencies or entailing human suffering.

Good offices have, in most organizations, been tackled in a flexible manner and few attempts have been made to rationalize them or to legislate in advance for possible scenarios for the exercise of good offices. However, in some instances, such as in the ICRC, some efforts have been made to elaborate criteria to guide the organization in deciding whether to act.

It has been firmly established in international law and practice that intercession on humanitarian grounds by heads of State, Secretaries-General or Directors-General of international organizations do not constitute intervention into internal affairs. This was well brought out in a UNESCO study: "First of all a distinction has to be made between the concept of intercession and that of intervention. Under both the Charter of the United Nations (Article 2 (7)) and the Constitution of UNESCO (Article I, paragraph 3), international organizations are prohibited from intervening in matters which are essentially within the domestic jurisdiction of Member States. The same applies as regards relations between States where, according to a principle reaffirmed in the Declaration on Principles of International Law concerning Friendly Relations and Co-operation among States in accordance with the Charter of the United Nations (resolution 2625 (XXV)), 'no State or group of States has the right to intervene, directly or indirectly, for any reason whatever, in the internal or external affairs of any other State.'

Considering, however, that it is also a constitutional principle of the United Nations as well as of UNESCO that Member States should act, together and individually, in order to further universal respect for, and observance of, human rights and fundamental freedoms, such action cannot be un-affected by what occurs within States. It is, then, within the context of respect for the two principles of non-intervention and the promotion of human rights that the concept of intercession should be viewed, a concept that reflects the idea of request and entreaty on behalf of someone, an idea which is in no way implied by the concept of intervention.

According to a very widespread diplomatic practice a head of State – or another State authority – may intercede, either on his own initiative or at the behest of a third party or organization, with his counterpart in another State in order to draw his attention to the desirability of improving the lot of any individual or group. The extent to which he is entitled to press the matter may vary considerably between one State and another and between one case and another. As long as the interest taken does not exceed the limits of intercession, it is firmly established and accepted practice in relations between States."[5]

International practice is also quite convincing. Thus, at the 2301st plenary meeting of the United Nations General Assembly in 1974, the

President, Mr. Bouteflika of Algeria, responding to statements requesting the intercession of the President of the General Assembly and of the Secretary-General in order to save human lives said to be endangered in Ethiopia, made the following statement: "I should like to summarize the situation to make sure that I have correctly understood what action is being called for from the Secretary-General of the United Nations and the President of the twenty-ninth session of the General Assembly.

I infer from this short debate . . . that the General Assembly would wish both the Secretary-General of the United Nations and the President of the twenty-ninth session of the General Assembly acting in accordance with the United Nations Charter, and with the principles set forth in the Universal Declaration of Human Rights, to do all they can to save the human lives now in danger and provide them with a minimum of protection through what the Minister of Foreign Affairs of Ethiopia has referred to as a fair trial under normal judicial processes.

It is quite clear, therefore, that in the minds of members of the General Assembly, collectively and individually, the action does not in any way represent interference in the domestic affairs of a Member State.

Is there any objection to my interpretation? Since there is none, I take it that I have correctly understood the significance of the action."[6]

II. League of Nations

In the League of Nations system for the international protection of minorities, resolutions of the League Council had provided for the handling of "exceptional and extremely urgent cases"[7] and had stipulated that in such cases the Secretary-General of the League should simultaneously inform the State concerned and the Members of the Council of the matter.[8] Minorities Committees, for their part, had made it their practice to try to settle questions raised in communications by means of informal negotiations with the State concerned. Barros also reports that "in certain serious cases the Secretariat had found it possible, privately, to draw the governments' attention to the seriousness of the accusations made and that the charges made did not seem without foundation. By doing so the Secretariat had put an end to the abuse or effected a change for the better, even before the Committee of Three was faced with the petition."[9]

The report of a Committee instituted by a Council resolution of 7

March 1929 disclosed that because in the majority of cases the information at the disposal of the Committee did not allow it to reach a clear-cut decision either to refer the matter to the Council or simply to shelve it, the Committee endeavoured "to obtain favourable consideration of the minorities' wishes by approaching the Government concerned in an informal and friendly manner. The Committee then, acting through the Minorities Section [of the Secretariat], enters into informal negotiations with that Government with a view either to obtaining further information or to securing a satisfactory settlement of the matter . . . A system of genuine and friendly co-operation has thus grown up between the League, acting through the Committee of Three, and the Governments concerned, with a view to the equitable and satisfactory settlement of such cases."[10]

III. ILO

In ILO practice, it has become established that the Director-General should do whatever he can to facilitate the achievement of the objectives of the organization, the smooth and effective operation of ILO procedures and of the work of ILO organs. The Director-General often acts discreetly behind the scene and may have quiet discussions with governments or other parties concerned, prior to, or at the same time as formal procedures are in motion. His aim in such situations may be to facilitate the operation of the procedures or to promote contacts between the parties concerned. The Director-General or a representative may even visit the country and then report to the organ concerned.

Interviews with retired high-ranking ILO officials have confirmed that the Director-General and his staff often intercede discreetly in order to save lives or to protect the security, liberty or freedoms of trade unionists. In some instances, representatives have been sent to the countries concerned in order to try to obtain the release of trade unionists from prison. The writer was informed of a certain case some years ago in which trade unionists were reportedly being liquidated *en masse*. Complaints were made by international trade union organizations under the pertinent ILO procedures but it would have taken some months for these complaints to go through the various stages. In view of the urgent humanitarian nature of the situation, the Director-General invited representatives of the government concerned, and representatives of the complainants to meet urgently under his chairmanship. They agreed, and out of these meetings, undertakings were given by the government that they would protect the lives and freedoms of trade unionists; that they would ratify the relevant ILO conventions and that they would permit the ILO to monitor the implementation of these undertakings. Thousands of lives were thus spared by this timely intercession of the Director-General.

There are also elements of good offices in the procedure of direct contacts introduced in 1968 for the purpose of permitting a representative of the Director-General of the ILO to examine directly with the competent government services, practical or legal difficulties encountered in the application of a ratified Convention. The procedure has since been extended to cover, in particular, obstacles to the ratification of a given Convention. Resort to this procedure is subject to the consent of the government concerned. It has been used on several occasions to examine questions relating to human rights conventions. Depending on the question at issue the direct contacts are carried out either by an official of the Office or by an independent person appointed by the Director-General. Direct contacts have also been used under the Governing Body freedom of association procedure to examine with officials of the country concerned problems raised by complaints alleging infringements of the principles of freedom of association. In accordance with the rules governing the procedure of direct contacts, the representative of the Director-General in all cases makes contact with the national organizations of employers and workers in order to keep them informed of the topics discussed and to elicit their points of view.[11]

Recently a new development has occurred in this procedure. Normally, direct contacts are undertaken either at the request of an ILO organ or of the government concerned. In the case of Bolivia, in 1980, the Director-General himself after consulting the Chairman of the Committee on Freedom of Association, proposed to the Government of Bolivia that a representatve of the Director-General should visit Bolivia. The Government accepted and a visit was carried out.[12] The background to the case provides a good idea of the role of the Director-General of the ILO.

In July 1980, ILO Director-General Francis Blanchard notified the Government of Bolivia by cable that complaints of violations of workers' rights in Bolivia had been lodged by several international and regional trade union groups. The complaints, he said, expressed profound concern at the death and detention of union leaders, occupation of union premises and repression of the labour movement in Bolivia. They also voiced fears for the life of union leader Juan Lechin. In view of the gravity of the allegations he asked the Government for an urgent reply. This was received in Geneva within two days. On 28 July 1980, the Government of Bolivia was asked by the Director-General to receive urgently a visit by a high-ranking ILO official to discuss the situation. "I have taken this step because of the exceptionally serious nature of the complaints," Mr. Blanchard commented the same day. He added: "The on-the-spot mission by a senior representative, if it materializes as I hope, will transmit to the authorities the concern that has arisen over the situation. It will also explain to the authorities the principles of freedom of association involved and seek to obtain their initial reaction to the complaints."[13] Subsequently, a high official of the International Labour Office, Mr. Ian Lagergren, visited Bolivia to discuss the situation of the country's trade unions and trade union leaders.[14]

The role of the Director-General with respect to the labour situation in Poland in 1980 is also revealing. According to press reports on 20 August 1980, the suggestion had been made that ILO Director-General Francis Blanchard should head a delegation to visit Warsaw to help resolve the labour conflict there in accordance with the principles of the ILO. In response to questions which he received, Mr. Blanchard recalled that the ILO had a major responsibility for the promotion of freedom of association for trade union purposes. He reaffirmed his conviction that the free exercise of trade union rights for the exclusive protection of workers is essential in modern societies and should be scrupulously assured irrespective of the political régimes concerned, and announced that he "wishes to place his good offices and those of the International Labour Office at the disposal of the authorities concerning the framing of legislation assuring the free exercise of trade union rights."[15]

During subsequent months, the ILO followed with close attention the evolution of the trade union situation in Poland. In particular, several ILO missions – including one led by the Director-General – visited Poland to examine the situation on the spot.

When the situation became graver, Director-General Francis Blanchard on 14 December 1981 cabled the Polish Prime Minister to express "his deep concern" over the restrictions imposed on trade union rights in Poland. The telegram addressed to General Wojciech Jaruzelski read as follows:

"Have noted with deep concern latest developments trade union situation in Poland. Express keen hope that your country will return as rapidly as possible to respect for trade union rights and civil liberties and that the detained trade unionists will be freed in the near future. In this perspective International Labour Office is ready to provide, as it has already done, all assistance which your Government may judge useful with a view to re-establishment of trade union freedoms and contribution to social peace in the country."[16]

IV. UNESCO

In a study submitted to the Executive Board of UNESCO in 1977,[17] the Director-General of UNESCO, noting that "it is common knowledge that the Secretary-General of the United Nations uses the right of intercession in his conversations and correspondence with heads of State and government and their representatives, on humanitarian grounds," added that "The action of the Director-General of UNESCO has always been inspired by the same concern, and the General Conference has had occasion, in one particular case, to encourage him to act along these lines.[18] Following these efforts by the Director-General, the Executive Board reiterated its entire confidence in the continuation of the Director-General's actions to ensure that human rights are better known and observed throughout the world . . ."[19] It is with this in mind that the Director-General, in his introduction to the general policy debate of the General Conference at its nineteenth session,[20] asked that he might in future be given the necessary moral means to enable him to act more effectively in safeguarding human rights within UNESCO's spheres of competence. The General Conference noted this request in its resolution on the subject.[21]

In UNESCO decision 104/Ex.3.3 adopted by the Executive Board in 1978, which established new procedures to be followed in the examination of cases and questions submitted to UNESCO concerning the exercise of human rights in the spheres of its competence, expressly recognized the important role of the Director-General in (a) seeking continually to strengthen the action of UNESCO in the promotion of human rights, both through the settlement of cases and the elimination of massive systematic or flagrant violations of human rights and fundamental freedoms and (b) initiating consultations, in conditions of mutual respect, confidence and confidentiality, to help reach solutions to particular problems concerning human rights and "invite(d) the Director-General to pursue this role."[22] In a report which he submitted to the twentieth session of UNESCO's General Conference in 1978, the Director-General observed that the above decisions had consolidated his role "in respect of intercessions on humanitarian grounds and representations of a conciliatory nature" and that his role had been "extended, since his role is no longer confined solely to individual cases but also covers questions."[23]

V. UNHCR

In the Office of the United Nations High Commissioner for Refugees, the General Assembly of the United Nations, by its resolution 1388 (XIV) of 20 November 1959, had "authorize(d) the High Commissioner, in respect of refugees who do not come within the competence of the United Nations, to use his good offices in the transmission of contributions designed to provide assistance to the refugees."[24] The following year, the General Assembly, noting with satisfaction the efforts made by the High Commissioner in his various fields of activity for groups of refugees for whom he lent his good offices, again requested the High Commissioner to pursue his activities on behalf of those for whom he extends his good offices.

These and subsequent resolutions of the General Assembly enabled the High Commissioner to intervene on behalf of marginal groups and later to assist masses of refugees who could not individually be verified for eligibility but could be presumed to be eligible for help collectively. Nowadays, however, they all come within the general category of refugees and displaced persons, and there is no longer any need for the device of good offices in order to help them. With its expanded and unified framework of competence, the High Commissioner's Office is now equipped to take action needed to deal with the various situations resulting from man-made disasters where the Office's assistance may be called for. This led a former High Commissioner to ask: "should the notion of good offices be completely abandoned and dropped altogether from the day-to-day language of the High Commissioner's Office?" If that happened, he said, "it would be a dis-service to the institution of good offices as constantly interpreted in international life. The institution remains as useful as ever for contingencies and situations on the fringe of the normal activities of the High Commissioner's Office. These may relate more to diplomacy and the role of 'intermediary of good will' which the High Commissioner is sometimes called upon to play. For example, discreet approaches are sometimes made by the UNHCR in the hope of easing a situation involving refugees or displaced persons. Similarly, using the tool of 'quiet diplomacy' the High Commissioner is often required to ease the tensions that arise inevitably between the country of origin and the country of asylum. His task then consists in depoliticizing refugee situations and putting them into a purely humanitarian context so that they do not continue to be contentious. In Africa, for example, the removal of refugees from border areas is one of the practical methods used for this purpose. Similarly, maintaining good relations with both countries of origin and the countries of asylum, in the context of universalization of its humanitarian vocation, enables the UNHCR to 'contain' a refugee situation. This atmosphere also promotes eventually with the evolution of circumstances the voluntary repatriation of refugees which is, by far, the happiest of permanent solutions."[25]

In his report to the United Nations General Assembly in 1980, the High Commissioner gave some glimpses into good offices or related exercises undertaken by his Office. He reported for example that "when measures of intended réfoulément have come to the High Commissioner's notice in due time it has been possible for him to approach the authorities of the country concerned with a view to preventing réfoulément. In other cases, however, the measure of réfoulément was brought to his attention only after the event. Where this occurred, the High Commissioner nevertheless registered his serious concern."[26] Also, "as in previous years, the High Commissioner was required to approach the authorities of certain States to request the stay of an expulsion order in respect of a refugee or group of refugees while efforts were made by his office to secure admission to another country."[27] "During the reporting period," the High Commissioner stated further, "a number of cases in which the personal safety of refugees was placed in serious danger again made it necessary for the High Commissioner, pursuant to the mandate entrusted to him by the international community, to make appropriate representations to the Governments concerned."[28] "In several other instances," the High Commissioner added, he "was obliged to make appropriate representations" where refugees were subjected to systematic measures of harassment by the authorities of their countries of asylum.[29]

VI. ICRC

The International Committee of the Red Cross (ICRC) has, among the tasks assigned to it by the Geneva Conventions, that of offering its good offices to facilitate the institution of hospital zones and localities (Article 23 of the third Convention) and safety zones and localities (Article 14 of the fourth Convention). Under the Geneva Conventions, the International Committee of the Red Cross also has a right of initiative, that is to say, it may propose to the parties to a conflict to agree that it should discharge general humanitarian tasks in cases of non-international armed conflicts (Article 3 common to the four Geneva Conventions of 1949) and of international armed conflicts (Article 9 of the first, second and third Conventions, and Article 10 of the fourth Convention). Attempts at protection without specific authorization in international law are also based on Article 4 of the Statutes of the ICRC which state that: "The special role of the ICRC shall be . . . (d) to take action in its capacity as a neutral institution, especially in case of war, civil war *or internal strife*: . . . and to serve, in humanitarian matters, as an intermediary between the parties;" (emphasis added). "The ICRC may also take any humanitarian initiative which comes within its role as a specifically neutral and independent institution and consider any question requiring examination by such an institution."

The organization also engages in what has been termed *ad hoc* protection, that is to say protection attempts which lack specific authorization. It has been predicted that this type of activity may be expected to increase in the future: "Conflicting parties frequently refuse to accept that the law of armed conflicts applies. There is frequent disagreement over which law applies and to what extent. Great humanitarian need exists in situations not falling under the law of armed conflict. In all of these cases, Red Cross *ad hoc* protection is the most important and often the only means of responding to the need."[30]

In 1973 and 1974, the ICRC developed a series of criteria to be taken into consideration in determining whether the ICRC *ad hoc* protection should be attempted. In situations of "domestic troubles" the ICRC is to see whether (1) the trouble is serious, involving acts of violence; (2) events are prolonged rather than occasional; (3) there is a struggle among one or more organized groups; (4) there are victims in need. In situations of lesser domestic instability, the ICRC listed another set of criteria, any of which could trigger its involvement: (1) the aftermath of civil war or other serious domestic troubles; (2) existence of a serious state of political, religious, racial or social tension; (3) suspension of judicial due process, introduction of emergency laws, or disrespect of national laws; (4) administrative detention or expulsion and deportation; (5) excessive penalties; (6) *prima facie* evidence of inhumane treatment.[31]

Two illustrative cases of the exercise of humanitarian good offices by the ICRC may be examined. In a press release of 13 December 1973, the ICRC announed that in view of the serious breaches of the Geneva Conventions of which the Governments of the Arab Republic of Egypt and the Syrian Arab Republic on the one hand, and the Government of Israel on the other, had accused one another, it had sent a note to the three Governments on 12 December, declaring its willingness to lend its good offices with a view to setting up, under its own auspices or those of some other organization approved by the parties, an *ad hoc* procedure for the constitution of bipartite commissions of enquiry into the alleged violations. The commissions' terms of reference would be to investigate the materiality of facts of the alleged violations or interpret Convention provisions which were the subject of disagreement between the parties. The commissions' conclusions would be communicated to the Governments concerned.

Each commission would have three members: one appointed by each of the parties, the third by the ICRC or any other organization approved by the parties, chosen from prominent citizens of neutral States. The ICRC said that if it were called upon to nominate the neutral member it would choose a person outside the ICRC, in keeping with its practice and principles, for the ICRC itself does not conduct enquiries, this not being its task laid down in the Geneva Conventions.[32]

Another model of ICRC good offices is provided in a resolution (No. XXI) adopted at Istanbul in September 1969. In this resolution, the XXIst International Conference of the Red Cross recommended that in cases of armed conflicts or of situations which are a threat to peace, the ICRC should, if necessary, ask the representatives of the National Societies of the countries concerned to meet together or separately with the ICRC to study the resolution of humanitarian problems involved and in agreement with the governments concerned to examine what contribution the Red Cross could make to preventing the outbreak of the conflict or achieving a cease-fire or cessation of hostilities. The Conference recommended to the National Societies to comply with the request of the ICRC and give it all desirable co-operation in this field.

VII. Other instances

With respect to human rights organs, Article 28 of the European Convention on Human Rights requires the European Commission to place itself at the disposal of the parties concerned with a view to securing a friendly settlement of complaints on the basis of respect for human rights. A similar provision exists in Article 48 (1) (f) of the American Convention on Human Rights. Article 41 of this Convention could also be the basis of good-offices functions of the Inter-American Commission on Human Rights. Article 41 (1) (e) of the International Covenant on Civil and Political Rights requires the Human Rights Committee to make available its good offices to the States parties concerned in an inter-State complaint with a view to a friendly solution of the matter on the basis of respect for human rights and fundamental freedoms. A similar provision exists in Article 42 (1) (a) of the Covenant.

Good offices are occasionally exercised by the heads or other members of the secretariats of regional inter-governmental organizations such as in the OAS or the Council of Europe, but the practice is not as extensive as in other organizations and the evidence is not readily accessible. From interviews conducted it appears that occasionally a case or situation is taken up with the permanent mission of the country concerned or with the government in question. In other instances, representatives of the Secretary-General may be sent to the country concerned for discussions or to mediate. This has been done in the OAS for example, in certain situations where hostages were taken by armed opposition forces.

Human rights organs established in the Inter-American and European regions sometimes engage in "friendly settlement" which has elements of good offices. Good offices or functions akin thereto are sometimes also exercised by the Secretaries of the European and Inter-American Commission on Human Rights. This may take the form of intercessions to obtain the release of persons from custody. It is a matter of record that the Chairman of the UN Commission on Human Rights also occasionally exercises his good offices.

Article 90 of the First Additional Protocol (1976) to the Geneva Conventions on humanitarian law of 1949 includes among the competence of the International Fact-Finding Commission provided for under that Article the task of facilitating through its good offices the restoration of an attitude of respect for the Conventions and the Protocol.

VIII. Conclusion

The foregoing survey shows the broad scope and variety of types of good offices exercised in the human rights and humanitarian field. In essence they all have in common a basic rationale: what is the humanitarian need, and how can it be addressed?

Good offices in the field of human rights have certain characteristics which distinguish them from traditional good offices or which may not even exist in contemporary good offices in the settlement of international disputes generally. Among these the following may be mentioned: (i) There may be only one government involved; (ii) the matter may be internal to a State (though not within its exclusive domain); (iii) the consent of the State concerned is not necessarily a pre-requisite to the good offices initiative though its co-operation will be esential to its success; (iv) good offices may be exercised with respect to situations as well as to individual cases.

NOTES

1. V. Pechota, The Quiet Approach: A Study of the Good Offices Exercised by the Secretary-General in the Cause of Peace. A Unitar Study (1972), p. 13. See similarly, H.G. Darwin, "Mediation and Good Offices," in International Disputes: The Legal Aspects, Report of a Study Group of the David Davies Memorial Institute of International Studies (1972), pp. 83-92 at p. 83. Cf. chapter III (Good offices) of the Second Report on the Peaceful Settlement of International Disputes, submitted to the ILA at its New Delhi Conference in 1974 by the Committee on the Charter of the United Nations: Article 10(1): "In any dispute which it has not been possible to settle by direct negotiations, any party to the dispute may invite one or more States not parties to the dispute, or an international body, the Secretary-General of the UN, or another international official, or an eminent personality of international reputation, to use good offices to bring the parties together so as to make it possible for the parties to reach an adequate solution between themselves."
2. Pechota, *op. cit.*, p. 2.
3. Pechota, *op. cit.*, p. 17.
4. *Ibid.*, p. 17. Cf. also Articles 41(1)(e) and 42(1)(a) of the International Covenant on Civil and Political Rights which refer to the good offices of the Human Rights Committee in dealing with human rights complaints.
5. UNESCO doc. 102 EX/19, paras. 28-29.
6. A/PV.2301, pp. 16-17.
7. Council resolution of 27 January 1921.
8. Until 1929, meetings of minorities committees were usually held during the sessions of the League Council, and exceptionally between sessions. In order to expedite the

procedure, it was decided in 1929 that meetings should be held in the interval between Council sessions whenever the committees deemed it advisable. The time which elapsed between the beginning of a committee's consideration of a question and its decision varied greatly. It depended on the importance and complexity of the question, on whether or not additional information was required and on whether or not the question gave rise to negotiations with the government concerned.

9. J. Barros, Office without Power: Secretary-General Drummond 1919-1933 (1979), pp. 194-195.
10. See UN doc. E/CN.4/Sub.2/6 of 7 November 1947: The International Protection of Minorities under the League of Nations, pp. 27-32. See also, P. de Azcarate, League of Nations and National Minorities – An Experiment (1945). J. Barros, Office without Power, *op. cit.*, pp. 97-98.
11. See ILO doc. GB/205/21/7: Past practice concerning special inquiries with particular reference to human rights questions, paras. 27-29.
12. For materials on the carrying out of direct contacts or similar missions in the ILO, see:

    Argentina: 189th Report of Freedom of Association Committee, consultation between Chairman of Committee and Minister of Labour, followed by visit by independent person, paras. 24-25 ff.

    Bolivia: 162nd Report, paras. 8-10 ff. Visits to Bolivia.

    Dominican Republic: 190th Report, para. 40 ff. Direct contacts.

    Chile: 185th Report, paras. 9 ff and 77 ff. Visit to Chile.

    Poland: 202nd Report (G-B 213/8/13) – Direct contacts.

    Tunisia: 181st Report, para. 224 – Visit by Bolin (DD-G); 202nd Report (G-B 213/8/13), para. 118 – Visit by Director-General.

    Uruguay: 153rd Report, paras. 159-160 ff. – Direct contacts; 170th Report – Direct contacts (full text of Chairman report).

    UK – Antigua: 187th Report, para. 198 ff. – Direct contacts.
13. ILO press release 36/80, 28 July 1980.
14. ILO press release 41/80, 9 September 1980.
15. ILO press release 38/80, 21 August 1980.
16. ILO press release 45/81, 14 December 1981.
17. Study of the Procedures which should be followed in the examination of cases and questions which might be submitted to UNESCO concerning the exercise of human rights in the spheres of its competence, in order to make its action more effective, UNESCO doc. 102 Ex/19, para. 30.
18. See 18 C/Resolution 11.3, para. 3 and 19 C/Resolution 14.1, para. 3. The Executive Board has also expressed itself similarly, for example in 93 EX/Decision 8.2, para. 13.
19. 100 EX/Decision 9.1.
20. 19 C/INF.12.
21. 19 C/Resolution 12.1, Part II, final paragraph of the Preamble.
22. 104/EX/Decision 3.3, paras. 8 and 9.
23. UNESCO doc. 20/C/14, 28 September 1978, para. 84.
24. GA resolution 1499 (XV) of 5 December 1960 also called upon States Members of

the United Nations to consult with the High Commissioner in respect of measures of assistance to groups of refugees who do not come within the competence of the United Nations. See A. Grahl-Madsen, The Status of Refugees in International Law (1966), vol. I, pp. 107-108.

25. S Agha Khan, "Legal Problems Relating to Refugees and Displaced Persons," 149 RCADI (1976, I), pp. 287-350, at p. 349.
26. Report of the United Nations High Commissioner for Refugees, General Assembly Official Records: Thirty-Fifth Session, Supplement No. 12 (A/35/12), para. 25.
27. *Ibid.,* para. 26.
28. *Ibid.,* para. 28.
29. *Ibid.,* para. 30.
30. D. Tansley, Final Report: An Agenda for the Red Cross. Re-appraisal of the Role of the Red Cross (1975), p. 72. See also, D.P. Forsythe, Present Role of the Red Cross in Protection. Background Paper No. 1 of the Joint Committee for the Re-appraisal of the Role of the Red Cross (1975), chapter IV, pp. 30-48: Protection through *Ad Hoc* Diplomacy.
31. Forsythe, *op. cit.*, p. 33.
32. ICRC press release 1189 B, 13 December 1973.

Chapter III

THE GOOD OFFICES OF THE UNITED NATIONS SECRETARY-GENERAL IN THE FIELD OF HUMAN RIGHTS

I. Introduction

The need for the exercise of good offices in the field of human rights by the United Nations Secretary-General was well stated by U Thant in a passage to which we have already referred before: "I sometimes think that the drafters of the Charter were overly obsessed with political and military conflict. No doubt that obsession was justified in the situation prevailing at the time. In the world of today, it might be useful to add an Article 99(a) which would authorize the Secretary-General to bring to the attention of the membership global threats to human well-being other than those to peace and security. . . . There are the great humanitarian emergencies which the United Nations is still not equipped to meet. I am glad that steps are now being taken to fit the Organization to deal with natural disasters. The next step is to expand its capability to cover *unnatural* disasters. . . . In an effort to do something about some disasters, I have, on my own initiative and without any supporting resolution from any United Nations organ, launched two relief operations which are concerned with millions of people and expenditures of hundreds of millions of dollars. I have felt that an initiative on my part was esential to fill the gap until more regular arrangements can be made, and that the Secretary-General's obligations under the Charter must include any humanitarian action that he can take to save the lives of large numbers of human beings. The political aspects of such situations, on the other hand, must obviously fall, as far as the United Nations is concerned, primarily within the competence of the Security Council."[1]

In his last Annual Report as Secretary-General, U Thant stated, as we have had occasion to mention before: "I feel more strongly than ever the worth of the individual human being is the most unique and precious of all our assets and must be the beginning and the end of all our efforts. Governments, systems, ideologies and institutions come and go, but humanity remains. The nature and value of this most precious asset is increasingly appreciated as we see how empty organized life becomes when we remove or suppress the infinite variety and vitality of the individual. In this connexion, I feel obliged to mention a problem which has been almost daily in my mind during my time as Secretary-General. I refer to the violation of human rights within the frontiers of a State. Theoretically the United Nations has little standing in such situations – and they are all too common. Legally, the membership has done an admirable job on human rights. The necessary texts exist. But practically where does an individual or a group of individuals find recourse against oppression within his own country? World public opinion has become an increasingly important factor in such problems. I myself have privately done the best I could in many such situations, knowing full well the weakness of my own position, and I know that many national leaders have done the same. But this can never be eough, and the time has surely come when Governments in the United Nations must make a determined effort to give justice a world-wide dimension."[2]

II. Legal bases for the United Nations' Secretary-General's exercise of good offices in the field of human rights

The United Nations Secretary-General's exercise of good offices in the field of human rights may have one or more of four possible bases: First, he may receive a specific mandate for this purpose. Recent examples were requests to the Secretary-General to use his good offices in cases of enforced or involuntary disappearances of persons[3] or to ensure full enjoyment of human rights by United Nations staff members.[4] Secondly, the Secretariat, as a principal organ of the United Nations is enjoined in the Charter to foster international co-operation for the promotion and encouragement of respect for human rights. As Gordenker has noted, "although Article I has only sporadically been cited as an important basis for the development of the office of Secretary-General, it does provide the concept of a prestigious and important legal position."[5] This could provide the basis for the doctrine which U Thant propounded that the "Secretary-General's obligations under the Charter must include any humanitarian action that he can take to save the lives of large numbers of human beings."[6] Similarly, Secretary-General Waldheim stated in his Annual Report in 1980: "I have always regarded it as my duty to exercise my good offices in human rights matters and I shall continue to assist in every way that I can."[7]

Thirdly, the doctrine of inherent or implied competence has frequently been invoked as a basis for the exercise of good offices. Indeed, the practice is so extensive that it may be said that the competence of the Secretary-General has solidified into a rule of customary law within the United Nations. Secretary-General Hammarskjöld formulated his conception of the office of Secretary-General as justifying action on his part, without any mandate from an organ of the United Nations "should this appear to him necessary in order to help in filling any vacuum that may appear in the systems which the Charter and traditional diplomacy provide for the safeguard of peace and security."[8] An insight into the legal bases which Hammarskjöld relied upon is provided by Urquhart. It may be recalled that, following the Sharpeville massacre on 21 March 1960, the Security Council, on 1 April 1960, had passed a resolution requesting the Secretary-General, in consultation with the Government of the Union of South Africa, "to make such arrangements as would adequately help in upholding the purposes and principles of the Charter and to report to the Security Council whenever necessary and appropriate." Urquhart reports: "Since the South African Government held that the UN had no competence in what it regarded as a purely internal affair, Hammarskjöld decided to use once again the Peking formula which had been the basis for his talks with Chou En-Lai on the release of the American airmen. This formula was not merely a face-saving device for reluctant Governments; it also provided a means by which the United Nations, through the physical presence and activities of the Secretary-General, could move into situations where other UN organs would not be acceptable. The essence of this formula was as follows: the Secretary-General functions on the basis of his authority under the Charter. Any challenge to his authority must therefore be either because he is acting *ultra vires* or because the party concerned refuses to acknowledge the Charter itself, which had been recognized even in 1955 by the Peking Government as a universally valid instrument. Thus a member state of the United Nations cannot reject an initiative of the Secretary-General except on the basis that he is exceeding his authority under the Charter. Article 2, paragraph 7 of the Charter, which safeguards the domestic jurisdiction of States against international interference, is not a limitation if the Security Council has found, as it had done in the case of the Sharpeville massacre, that a domestic situation is also a threat to international peace and security. 'Neither Chou nor South Africa,' Hammarskjöld said later, 'considered that discussion with the Secretary-General activated Article 2(7). Any Government can do this (i.e., talk with the Secretary-General) as an act of sovereignty. The next step is what you can do with it. That I don't know. My first care was to establish a working relationship with South Africa.'

Hammarskjöld told the permanent representative of South Africa in New York that his action would be 'limited to consultation rendered necessary by the instructions addressed to me for certain action to be undertaken on the basis of the authority of the Secretary-General under the Charter and that his actions would not require the prior recognition by South Africa of the United Nations' authority in the question of *apartheid*.' Eric Louw, the South African Foreign Minister, replied that this formulation removed South Africa's difficulty of appearing, by consenting to talks with the Secretary-General, to recognize the United Nations' right to intervene in South Africa's internal affairs."[9]

In recent years several governments, including those of India,[10] Canada,[11] Ceylon,[12] Netherlands, Sweden, the Federal Republic of Germany[13] and the United Kingdom[14] have urged the Secretary-General to exercise his good offices in the field of human rights. A draft resolution moved by the Netherlands in the Third Committee in 1972, proposed that the Secretary-General be requested to continue to offer his good offices in humanitarian problems and that governments be requested to make use of the Secretary-General's good offices in situations where human rights are a matter of special concern.[15] A similar draft resolution moved by Canada in 1980, which was referred to in the introductory chapter to this work, also received support from many governments.

It is submitted that the Secretary-General has, on the basis of Article 98 of the Charter, now been granted a general mandate to exercise his good offices in the field of human rights. Policy-making organs, including the General Assembly, the Economic and Social Council and the Commission on Human Rights have repeatedly stressed the importance of the role of the Secretary-General in the field of human rights. The following aspects have been specifically mentioned in recent resolutions of these organs: intensifying the good offices of the Secretary-General in the field of human rights; enhancing the role of the Secretary-General in situations of gross violations of human rights; developing a role for the Secretary-General in assessing the relationship between situations of large-scale exoduses of persons and full enjoyment of human rights; and the strengthening of direct contacts with governments encountering difficulties in the field of human rights.

United Nations human rights organs have, as we have seen before, expressly recognized and appreciated the good offices of the Secretary-General in the field of human rights (see resolutions 1979/36 of the Council, 34/175 of the General Assembly and 27 (XXXVI) of the Commission). The latter resolution, for example, "requested the Secretary-General to continue and intensify the good offices envisaged in the Charter of the United Nations in the field of human rights."

Fourthly, good offices may be exercised in the context of the competences of the Secretary-General under Article 99 of the Charter, which states that the Secretary-General of the United Nations may bring to the attention of the Security Council any matter which, in his opinion, may threaten the maintenance of international peace and security. At the San Francisco Conference in 1945, "the majority agreed that the right should be exercised at the discretion of the Secretary-General and should not be made a duty."[16] The view of the Preparatory Commission was that "the responsibility it confers upon the Secretary-General will require the exercise of the highest qualities of political judgment, tact and integrity."[17]

That a "good offices" component is inherent in the competences of the Secretary-General under Article 99 of the Charter was supported by the views of some representatives in the Special Committee on the Charter of the United Nations and on the Strengthening of the Role of the Organization. Thus, it has been suggested that any texts recommended by the Committee on the authority of the Secretary-General to discharge his responsibilities under Article 99 should make it clear "that he had authority to conduct good offices, mediation and fact-finding with the approval of the parties concerned."[18] It was also suggested that "The General Assembly should reaffirm, by its resolution or some other means, that each time an important dispute or situation arises, the Secretary-General, under the competence that he possesses as a prerequisite to carrying out his functions provided for in Article 99, may, for example, station his representative, for a certain period, in the area concerned, and ask him to investigate the facts of the situation and to report the outcome to him from time to time. All States Members should cooperate to the maximum extent with the Secretary-General in his carrying out such tasks."[19]

In so far as violations of human rights are concerned, however, Article 99 could only be expressly invoked if such violations are so serious as to threaten or breach international peace and security. It would, in the normal course of things, be only in exceptional situations that one could envisage an invocation of Article 99 by the Secretary-General with reference to a situation of violations of human rights. Cases or situations outside of these would usually be dealt with under the various other Charter-based or treaty-based procedures. The requirement of the element of a threat or breach to international peace and security was pointed out by the late Professor Hersch Lauterpacht who took the view "that Article 99 presents 'considerable potentialities' for bringing to the Security Council's attention 'violations of human rights so grave that they threaten the maintenance of international peace and security'." Moreover, he felt, "The clause of domestic jurisdiction of Article 2, paragraph 7, presents no impediment in the way of the exercise of this particular function of the Secretary-General. The matters referred to in Article 99 are not, by definition, essentially within the domestic jurisdiction of any State."[20]

According to Cordier and Harrelson, U. Thant, "before accepting a second term . . . sought to clarify the role of the Secretary-General by spelling out his understanding that he would have the right to bring to the attention of the Security Council and other United Nations organs basic issues confronting the Organization and disturbing developments in any part of the world. The Council accepted this interpretation of the Secretary-General's role, which in effect was an extension of Article 99 of the Charter. Article 99 simply states that the Secretary-General may bring to the attention of the Security Council 'any matter which in his opinion may threaten the maintenance of international peace and security'. U. Thant felt that this Article should be invoked sparingly, but that the Secretary-General should have the unquestioned right to address the Council and the General Assembly without the formality implicit in Article 99 . . ."[21]

In a recent instance, the question was raised whether the Secretary-General should invoke Article 99 in situations involving serious violations of human rights. On 8 April 1979, Mr. Martin Ennals, Secretary-General of Amnesty International, addressed the following telegram to the Secretary-General: "Amnesty International Executive Committee urges you to use your Excellency's authority under article 99 of the Charter to convene a meeting of Security Council to consider urgent measures to stop current wave of political executions and murders across world. UN Resolution 31/62 reaffirmed its view on the desirability of abolishing capital punishment and requested the Sixth UN Congress on the Prevention of Crime and the Treatment of Offenders to consider this matter. Amnesty International has called for international moratorium on execution. We are disturbed at imminence of further executions in Pakistan, Iran, USA, Trinidad, USSR, Kampuchea, both of political and convicted criminal offenders. Amnesty International urges your Excellency to use your prerogative of office to call upon governments to halt executions."

On 10 April 1979, the Secretary-General sent the following reply to Mr. Ennals: "I have carefully examined your telegram containing the suggestion that I propose a meeting of the Security Council under Article 99 of the Charter in connexion with the current executions across the world.

As you may know, I made both public and private appeals for clemency in connexion with several recent cases. However, these appeals and numerous others were to no avail. It was because of this disturbing fact that I issued a press statemnt on 8 April indicating my concern at the increased evidence of failure to give due regard to expressions of international opinion on matters where the most fundamental human rights are involved.

Having said this, and despite the seriousness of the problem and my distress at the increased number of executions, you will no doubt understand my conclusion that invocation of Article 99 is not the most appropriate way to deal with the problem since that article deals explicitly and exclusively with matters involving international peace and security."

In a telegram dated 3 May 1979, Amnesty International informed the Secretary-General that: "While understanding the inhibitions you feel in invoking Article 99 of the Charter, we do not interpret that as indicating that under no circumstances could Article 99 be invoked to bring serious violations of human rights, particularly where executions are pending, before the Security Council." It may be noted in this respect that the Secretary-General did not go as far as saying that under no circumstances could Article 99 be invoked to bring serious violations of human rights before the Security Council. However, his statement that Article 99 "deals explicitly and exclusively with matters involving international peace and security" left the question somewhat open.

Some observations may be made about these exchanges between Amnesty International and the Secretary-General:

First, it has long been recognized in international law that serious violations of human rights could involve threats to the maintenance of international peace and security. They could therefore be proper grounds for the invocation of Article 99 by the Secretary-General; whether the violations do actually give rise to a threat to international peace and security is a question to be determined in each case.

Second, Amnesty did not claim that the situations or acts about which it complained involved an actual or potential threat to international peace and security. Rather, as stated in the second telegram, it asserted that Article 99 could "be invoked to bring serious violations of human rights, particularly where executions are pending, before the Security Council." Unless the element of an actual or potential threat to international peace and security is present, it is difficult to envisage the Secretary-General bringing the matter to the attention of the Security Council under Article 99. This does not, however, preclude the possibility of other forms of humanitarian action by the Secretary-General.

It is significant that the right of the Secretary-General to bring a matter which, in his opinion, threatens international peace and security, to the attention of the Security Council has been generally recognized to carry with it the right to take preliminary steps necessary to determine whether he should act. As Secretary-General Lie once stated, the Secretary-General must reserve his right to make such enquiries or investigations as he may think necessary in order to determine whether or not he should consider bringing any aspect of this matter to the attention of the Council under the provisions of the Charter. This competence of the Secretary-General may certainly be exercised in situations involving gross violations of human rights. Whether it should be or not is a matter of political judgment.

It is also very significant that on a number of occasions the Secretary-General has designated persons to represent him, with the consent of the receiving States, in situations of tension for the purpose of keeping him informed regarding developments. In his Annual Report for 1980, the Secretary-General stated that in several instances governments had received special representatives designated by him to enter into contacts on human rights matters.[22]

In recent years, the scales of violations of human rights *within* some countries have attained proportions to make them at least as grave for the international community as situations *between* two or more countries. As we have mentioned earlier, in one country, for example, the

United Nations was informed by one of its expert rapporteurs that over a million persons had been killed; in another, 300,000-500,000 persons had lost their lives. In both cases the loss of life was far greater than in any recent armed conflict between two or more nations. The provisions of the Charter should be viewed in dynamic perspectives and applied in such a manner as to meet the needs of changing times. It cannot have been in the intention of the framers of the Charter that a situation involving massive violations of human rights should be ignored by the United Nations simply because it takes place *within* a country, whereas a less serious situation *between* two countries may evoke the competence of the United Nations.

There are precedents when the United Nations has acted in response to serious violations of human rights in a country, even though there has been no suggestion that the difficulties affected any other country. The basis for such action was that the seriousness of the violations of human rights in the countries concerned had given rise to international concern to the point where it became akin to a threat to international peace and security.

From the foregoing, there is little doubt that the Secretary-General has the competence to invoke Article 99 to bring to the attention of the Security Council situations of serious violations of human rights. However, as a matter of policy, the question is more complex. The following considerations may be mentioned. First, is the situation one of such gravity that the Secretary-General should seize the Security Council *ab initio* so as to bring the attention of the United nations to the problem, or is the situation one where the Secretary-General may be able to do more through humanitarian action in virtue of his good offices? As a general principle, it may be said that the Secretary-General should seek to employ his good offices before deciding to invoke Article 99 of the Charter. It may be noted in this connection that in some instances when United Nations organs were seized with situations involving violations of human rights they turned to the Secretary-General and asked him to exercise his good offices.

Secondly, if the Secretary-General does employ the humanitarian approach in the first place, and it becomes apparent that his efforts are not very successful, or that he has very little impact on the situation, at what stage should he then seize the Security Council of the situation? This indicates the need for the "highest qualities of political judgment, tact and integrity" which was foreseen by the founding fathers of the United Nations Charter.

III. The practice of good offices in the field of human rights by Secretaries-General of the United Nations

Pechota reported that "the requests pouring into the Secretary-General's office include many in the field of human rights, which is not surprising if we take into account a tendency to look to the United Nations as a focal point for action on behalf of the international community to ensure respect for universal standards of human rights. The Secretary-General cannot shun such issues, especially if some expectation of assistance had been encouraged by the United Nations' resolute stands on the principles involved. There is reason to expect that discreet facilitative action in the area may soon become one of the major fields in which good offices are exercised."[23]

The first four Secretaries-General of the United Nations have all engaged in good offices in human rights or humanitarian matters. According to Gordenker, "in 1949, Secretary-General Trygvie Lie implied that the Secretary-General had a good-offices function when he offered such services to the great powers to facilitate consultations among them. Furthermore, he enunciated in a primogenital way the doctrine that the Secretary-General could, as part of preventive diplomacy, desptach representatives on fact-finding missions. He flatly claimed during the Security Council debate on the Greek frontier question in 1946, that if the Council did not act to investigate the situation, he had the right to do so in order to determine whether he should bring any aspect of the dispute to the attention of the Council. This was a claim, according to Schwebel, that he had not 'merely the right to make inquiries or investigations without authorization from United Nations organs, but the right to initiate such investigations even in cases where the Security Council has decided not to look into the matter'."[25] Trygvie Lie disclosed in his memoirs some of the efforts which he had undertaken on behalf of Greek children taken to communist countries during the guerrilla war in Greece. He reported that he had discussed the matter during visits to Marshal Tito, of Yugoslavia,[26] Foreign Minister Siroky of Czechoslovakia,[27] and General Stalin of the USSR.[28] He also reported on the conversations he had had with Marshal Tito concerning Bishop Aloysius Stepinac: " 'Bishop Aloysius Stepinac is still in prison,' I began. 'If anything could be done to effect his release, such a step would be highly regarded throughout the . . . world . . .'."[29]

As was mentioned earlier, Dag Hammarskjöld addressed the human rights problems in South Africa during meetings with South African leaders. In one instance, "he suggested the appointment by the South African Government of some kind of ombudsman who would receive, review and act upon complaints concerning human rights, could deal with Ministers or initiate court actions, and could report to the South African Parliament or even to the Secretary-General."[30] During a visit to Pretoria in 1961, he sought to find arrangements for safeguarding human rights in accordance with United Nations principles. Urquhart reports that "in his meetings with Verwoerd, Hammarskjöld began by criticizing both the theory and the practical application of the Union Government's Bantu 'homelands' policy . . . As to the segregation policy, he expressed himself as frankly shocked both at the South African legislation itself and at its application."[31]

In his Annual Reports on the work of the Organization, Hammarskjöld provided information concerning persons who claimed to have been victims of so-called scientific experiments in Nazi concentration camps. Up to May 1960, 584 of such cases had been brought to the attention of the Federal Republic of Germany.[32]

In a speech to the Royal Commonwealth Society on 15 June 1970, on the "Role of the Secretary-General", U. Thant recounted some of his experiences in exercising good offices. As far as humanitarian cases were concerned, he stated that in August 1963, he was requested by the Governments of Malaya, Indonesia, and the Philippines to ascertain, prior to the establishment of the Federation of Malaysia, the wishes of the people of Sabah (North Borneo) and Sarawak and to ensure that recent elections in those areas had been truly representative of the inhabitants' wishes and had been properly conducted. Although this very delicate mission was not wholly successful and two of the governments concerned did not formally accept its findings, it had helped, U Thant felt, to pave the way for the inclusion of the two territories in the Federation of Malaysia. U Thant added that he had also exercised his good offices in two cases of hijacking, one of an El Al plane to Algiers and one of a TWA plane to Damascus, in which there had been difficulties and delays in extricating the crew and passangers and, later on, the aircraft. "Securing the release of a hijacked aircraft provides a particularly difficult problem," he said, adding, "It is only natural that the Governments, families, and companies concerned should wish to get their relatives, crews and aircraft back as soon as possible and at almost any cost."

In 1969, U Thant further stated, he had sent a representative to Equatorial Guinea to help solve difficulties which had arisen over the presence of Spanish troops and the status of Spanish citizens in that country. With his help, what had been a threatening and even violent situation was resolved within a month to the satisfaction of both governments, thus forestalling the necessity for more drastic moves.[33]

In *View from the United Nations*, U Thant gave a further glimpse into some of the good offices in which he engaged: "Regarding the problem of Soviet Jews, Mr. Tekoah[34] had been in touch with me, on a personal and confidential basis, since the middle of 1969. From time to time, he brought with him dozens of signed petitions from Soviet citizens of the Jewish faith who wanted to leave the Soviet Union. When I first mentioned the matter to Yakov Malik, the Soviet delegate, asking if I could use my good offices to facilitate the exit of Soviet Jews from Russia, he told me that it was a very sensitive matter in his country and advised me not to take any action on the petitions. I tried to convince him that I was fully aware of the juridical aspects of the matter, and that it was an internal affair, but that I wanted to pursue the matter on a purely humanitarian basis. He was insistent that I should not take up the matter with him.

I then decided that I would utilize the good offices of my two Russian aides – Leonid N. Kutakov, Under-Secretary for Political and Security Council Affairs, and Victor M. Lessiovski, my Special Assistant – as channels of communication between myself and Moscow. Whenever I received petitions from Mr. Tekoah, I passed them on to one of them for transmission to Moscow. Even my closest colleagues did not know the procedure I was employing, since I felt that complete discretion alone would bear results.

Later in 1971, Mr. Tekoah informed me that out of over eight hundred petitioners, more than four hundred had already arrived in Israel, and he conveyed his government's appreciation to me for my personal efforts to facilitate the exit of those Soviet Jews. It may be recalled that the Soviets had allowed ten thousand Russian Jews to go to Israel from 1961 through 1970, an average of only a thousand a year. In 1971, according to reliable reports, about five thousand Soviet Jews had arrived in Israel. Mr. Tekoah asked me what methods I had employed in transmitting the petitions to the Soviet Government. I told him that I was sorry that I could not disclose the methods."[35]

U Thant reported that he applied "some general rules . . . to any exercise of good offices. Obviously efforts of this kind must be fully in accordance with the general principles of the United Nations Charter.[36] Then the Secretary-General must reach a considered judgement as to whether his intervention is likely to be helpful, or whether, on the contrary, it will be ineffective, or even positively harmful. On this basis he must himself decide whether or not to accede to a request to take an initiative to exercise his good offices in a particular situation." "Once the Secretary-General has decided to act," he added, "some other ground rules apply . . . confidence, mutual respect and absolute discretion are vital to success, and the less publicity there is, the better . . ."

The exercise of humanitarian good offices by Secretary-General Waldheim is well-documented.

Individual cases

A review of the policy of Secretary-General Waldheim discloses that in dealing with individual cases in the context of the exercise of good offices, he acted, *inter alia*, on the following principles:

1. He was guided mainly by the welfare of the persons concerned.
2. He acted mainly on humanitarian grounds, mindful as a general rule of the injunction against intervention in internal affairs.
3. He took into account the circumstances and responsibilities of the government(s) concerned.
4. He normally acted confidentially and discretely but on occasions he spoke out publicly when necessary.
5. He occasionally sent a representative to consult with the government concerned.
6. *Ratione materiae*, he interceded in cases involving (i) danger of loss of life; (ii) torture or other serious abuses against the physical or mental integrity of persons; (iii) victims/prisoners of conscience, where there were special reasons for acting; (iv) cases arousing widespread concern at the international level; and (v) cases where there were other, strong humanitarian grounds for acting.
7. To qualify for action by the Secretary-General, certain elements were usually required, such as a denial of justice, for example, a deliberate bypassing of the regular judicial processes or political subversion of these processes. In other words, the Secretary-General

should not be expected to act where someone has, for example, been sentenced to death after having been found guilty through fair process of law. In every case the Secretary-General should also have enough evidence to demonstrate cause for legitimate concern on his part.

8. Among the types of action taken by Secretary-General Waldheim were: (i) Where there was evidence giving cause for concern but the facts were not sufficiently clear, the Secretary-General might indicate his concern by asking for information as to the well-being of the person(s) concerned; (ii) in appropriate cases he might ask the government to take measures to guarantee the safety or well-being of the person concerned; (iii) in other types of cases he might ask for a stay of execution pending further review of the case; (iv) in some cases, where he had enough facts and there were reasons for doing so, he might ask the government to exercise clemency or to grant a pardon; (v) in appropriate cases he might in co-ordination with the High Commissioner for Refugees, ask the government to consider allowing a person to leave instead of executing him.

In his first Annual Report, in 1972, Secretary-General Waldheim stated: "The Secretary-General faces a recurring dilemma whenever and wherever large-scale military conflict or civil strife within a State results in massive killings of innocent civilians. In the latter case, the Secretary-General has to reconcile Article 2, paragraph 7 of the Charter with the moral principles, and especially those concerning the sacredness of human life, which the Charter embodies.

No matter what criticisms or setbacks may arise, the unwritten moral responsibility which every Secretary-General bears does not allow him to turn a blind eye when innocent civilian lives are placed in jeopardy on a large scale."[37] In the same Annual Report, the Secretary-General also reported that he had dispatched a humanitarian mission to Burundi in the wake of the disastrous events in that country.

In his Annual Report in 1974 he stated: "It is essential that all appropriate measures be taken for the protection of human rights, whenever they may be threatened, but it is necessary to approach this most delicate of problems in such a way as to ensure to the fullest extent possible that the conditions of those oppressed are in fact improved."[38] Giving an idea of how he viewed his good-offices role he said: "It is in the very nature of the problem that in many cases little or nothing can be said publicly about the efforts made, if those efforts are to have any hope of succeeding. I have found in many instances, however, that Governments are prepared to respond positively to a discreet approach on humanitarian grounds if their own problems and responsibilities are sufficiently understood.''[39]

In 1976 he reported that ''attempts to alleviate particular problems of human rights by various means, usually of a discreet and confidential nature, are a major and continuous task of the Secretary-General and his staff.''[40] He reported again in 1977: ''For my part, I have continued to exercise my good offices in specific human rights cases. I have usually found my efforts to be most effective when undertaken confidentially, although I have not hesitated to speak out when I felt that this was necessary and in the general interest. In most cases, however, little or nothing can be said publicly about particular efforts without jeopardizing their success. In practical and urgent cases, in the present circumstances of international affairs, I feel that my actions must be governed by one overriding criterion – namely what approach will best serve the welfare of the individuals concerned.''[41].

In 1978, he continued to report in similar terms: ''My own efforts in the field – in the exercise of my good offices in specific humanitarian cases – have met with some success. To secure the maximum benefit for the individuals involved, past experience has demonstrated that it is best to proceed on purely humanitarian grounds, and usually with the utmost confidentiality. Not only does this approach work to the advantage of the victims, but it also avoids the political sensitivity often associated with such cases. I shall continue these efforts whenever and wherever they best serve the welfare of the individuals concerned.''[42] Similar statements appeared in his Annual Reports in 1979, 1980 and 1981.

In a book published in 1977, Secretary-General Waldheim re-stated his good-offices approach: ''. . . je dispose d'une certaine marge de manoeuvre me permettant d'exercer mon influence dans la défense des droits de l'homme. Pour cela, je me conforme à un critère fondamenal: le bien-être de la personne ou des personnes concernées. Le plus souvent, j'offre mes bons offices, à titre officieux, en me plaçant sur un terrain purement humanitaire. J'intercède pour assurer la vie sauve à un condamné à mort, pour favoriser la réunion de familles, pour obtenir des 'clarifications' sur les conditions de détention de prisonniers ou sur le traitement réservé à une minorité nationale. J'assure toujours le gouvernement concerné de mon souci de ne pas m'ingérer dans ses affaires intérieures, tout en lui faisant valoir qu'un geste positif de sa part ne manquerait pas de relever son prestige dans l'opinion mondiale. Toute publicité à ma démarche risquerait de faire avorter l'entreprise. Aucun Etat, en effet, ne tient à donner l'impression qu'il a cédé à une quelconque sollicitation étrangère.

Cependant, j'ai aussi recours aux interventions publiques quand j'estime que celles-ci sont nécessaires. Ainsi ai-je lancé, par exemple, un appel public au gouvernement ougandais pour lui demander d'autoriser une enquête impartiale sur les circonstances de la mort de l'archevêque Janani Luwum et de deux ministres. Cela ne m'a pas empêché de poursuivre des contacts confidentiels dans cette affaire."[43]

At a press conference in Geneva on 19 May 1977, Waldheim, in response to a question on the situation then existing in Uganda, gave a glimpse of a specific good-offices mission: "I am," he said, "in contact with the authorities in Uganda and one of my representatives has been there to discuss the human rights aspects with the appropriate authorities. I want to tell you that I am continuing to do all I can."[44] In an earlier press conference, on 1 Marh 1977, he had disclosed that "he was continuing his contacts with the country's delegation to the United Nations in connection with his request for an impartial international investigation of the recent deaths of the Anglican Archbishop and two Government Ministers in Uganda."

Situations of gross violations of human rights

The role of the Secretary-General in dealing with situations of gross violations of human rights has not been developed as much as his good-offices role in dealing with individual cases. In its resolution 34/175, the General Assembly "stressed the important role that the Secretary-General can play in situations of mass and flagrant violations of human rights," while the Commission on Human Rights, in its resolution 27 (XXXVI) welcomed the statement of the Secretary-General in his Report on the work of the Organization (1979), that he is continuing to exert his best endeavours on behalf of human rights whenever he considers that his actions may be of assistance to the persons or groups concerned. In another resolution (30 (XXXVI)), the Commission requested the Secretary-General in cases where large-scale exoduses of persons become a matter of international concern and solidarity, to consider establishing direct contacts with appropriate governments to assess the relationships between the situation and full enjoyment of human rights and to make concrete recommendations for ameliorating such situations. The resolution also requested the Secretary-General, where warranted, to submit to the Commission or to the General Assembly, as appropriate, at its next sitting a summary of his findings and recommendations to assist governments in restoring full enjoyment of human rights.

The above-mentioned resolutions demonstrate the search for an enhanced role for the Secretary-General in dealing with situations involving gross violations of human rights. Over the years, various suggestions have been made which could assist the Secretary-General. It has been proposed, for example, that the United Nations should establish an office of United Nations High Commissioner for Human Rights, but political agreement has so far eluded this proposal. A related proposal has been that the Secretary-General should designate an Under-Secretary-General for Human Rights. As we saw in the Introduction to this work, a draft resolution to this effect was debated at the thirty-fourth session of the General Assembly but was not pressed to a vote. Pending the realization of any such proposals the role of the Secretary-General in this field needs, therefore, to be considered within the existing possibilities and structure of the Secretariat.

The following objectives of the Secretary-General in discharging a role in this field may be suggested:

- to ascertain the facts in a situation of gross violations of human rights.
- to maintain communications and contacts with the government concerned.
- to try to influence the government concerned to adopt measures which could lead to cessation of violations and restoration of human rights and, in this regard, to utilize whatever possibilities of assistance may be available in the United Nations, such as technical assistance, advisory services.
- to express, if necessary, the conscience of the international community regarding the situation in question, particularly in the face of an unco-operative or recalcitrant government.[45]

United Nations organs have sometimes specifically requested the Secretary-General to exercise his good offices in relation to situations.

Thus, paragraph 5 of General Assembly resolution 3219 (XXIX), adopted in 1974, requested the President of the twenty-ninth session of the General Assembly and the Secretary-General to assist in any way they might deem appropriate in the re-establishment of basic human rights and fundamental freedoms in Chile. The action taken by the Secretary-General under this resolution was described in a report which he submitted to the thirtieth session of the General Assembly.[46] The Secretary-General stated that in consultation with the President of the twenty-ninth session of the General Assembly, he had continued to exercise his good offices towards the re-establishment of basic human rights and fundamental freedoms in Chile. In that respect, following the adoption of resolution 3219 (XXIX) on 6 November 1974, the Secretary-General, or the Under-Secretary-General for Political and General Assembly Affairs on his behalf, had held frequent meetings with the Permanent Representative of Chile to the United Nations. The Secretary-General had also met with the Minister for External Relations of Chile.

During these discussions it was urged that basic human rights and fundamental freedoms in Chile, including *inter alia*, full respect for the right of *amparo (habeas corpus)*, provided for in the Constitution of the Republic of Chile, be restored and safeguarded. In addition, the attention of the Government of Chile was drawn to the names of individuals who had been reported to be held in detention without charge or solely for political reasons, with a view to securing their release or fair trial. Deep concern was also expressed to the Government of Chile about frequent and persistent allegations of violations of human rights which had been brought to the Secretary-General's attention. Those included reports of torture and other cruel or inhuman punishments, of the absence of information concerning a number of individuals whose whereabouts have been unknown for an extended period of time, of poor conditions in places of detention and of other reported denials of basic human rights.

Within the framework of paragraph 5 of resolution 3219 (XXIX), the Secretary-General, after consulting with the President of the twenty-ninth session of the General Assembly, requested the Under-Secretary-General for Political and General Assembly Affairs to visit Chile in response to an invitation from the Government of Chile. This visit took place between 23 and 28 February 1975.

During the course of his visit to Chile, the Under-Secretary-General was received by the President of the Republic of Chile and had several meetings with the Minister for External Relations. The Under-Secretary-General also met with other members of the *Junta de Gobierno*, with the President of the Supreme Court, with members of the Government, and with other public officials. During these discussions the Under-Secretary-General raised those matters which had been the subject of concern expressed during the debates at the twenty-ninth session of the General Assembly and which had resulted in the adoption of resolution 3219 (XXIX).

The Under-Secretary-General also had the opportunity during his stay in Chile to meet with a number of individuals not associated with the Government. He visited certain detention camps for the purpose of meeting and speaking with individuals who were being held under detention. During discussions with the Chilean authorities, it was pointed out that exile of a citizen constituted the denial of a human right under Article 9 of the Universal Declaration of Human Rights.

In light of the information received, the Secretary-General stated in his report to the General Assembly that he was unable to report that the objectives identified by the General Assembly in paragraph 3 of resolution 3219 (XXIX) had been achieved.[47]

IV. Conclusion

The following concluding observations may be recapitulated:

(1) The good offices of the United Nations Secretary-General in the field of human rights have become a fully established part of, to use the words of Hammarskjöld, the "common law of organized international co-operation" and therefore of international customary law.[48]

(2) Good-offices initiatives must be in accordance with the general principles of the United Nations Charter. However, the requirements of the international human rights norms must also be taken in account. Good offices should be carried out in a spirit of mutual respect and with discretion.

(3) The exercise of good offices by the United Nations Secretary-General is always discretionary. No element of compulsion or automaticity can or should be injected in this function.

(4) In practice, a Secretary-General, in dealing with individual cases

in the context of the exercise of good offices, may act *inter alia*, on the following principles:

a. He may use his personal judgement as to whether an intercession on his part would be appropriate or would be helpful.
b. He is guided mainly by the welfare of the persons concerned.
c. He acts mainly on humanitarian grounds, mindful as a general rule of the injunction against intervention in internal affairs.
d. He takes into account the circumstances and responsibilities of the government(s) concerned.
e. He normally acts confidentially and discretely but on occasions he may speak out publicly when necessary.
f. He may on occasions send a representative to consult with the government concerned.

(5) In dealing with situations of gross violations of human rights the Secretary-General may *inter alia*, adopt the following approaches:

a. He may establish contacts with the governments concerned.
b. He may send a representative for discussion with the government concerned.
c. He may personally make a visit on-the-spot.
d. He may designate a special representative to deal with the situation.
e. He may seek to provide international humanitarian assistance, e.g. through the office of the United Nations High Commissioner for Refugees.
f. He may offer United Nations technical assistance.
g. He may convene an international conference to consider the situation.
h. He may establish an inquiry into the situation.
i. He may, if he considers it necessary, comment on the situation publicly or express his concern about it.

(6) The Secretary-General could invoke Article 99 to bring situations of serious violations of human rights to the attention of the Security Council.

NOTES

1. U Thant, "The Role of the Secretary-General," UN Monthly Chronicle, VIII, No. 9 (October 1971), pp. 178-187 at p. 185. See also U Thant, View from the United Nations (1978), pp. 27 and 32; Cf. Secretary-General Lie: "Article 99 is an atomic bomb or at least a 32-inch gun . . . Why can't I use the smaller rifles? Why just on world peace?" cited in S. Schwebel, The Secretary-General of the United Nations, his political powers and practice (1952), p. 205.
2. U Thant, "The Role of the Secretary-Genral," *loc. cit.*
3. General Assembly resolution 33/173.
4. Commission on Human Rights resolution 31 (XXXVI).
5. L. Gordenker, The United Nations Secretary-General and the Maintenance of Peace (1967), p. 65.
6. See p. 52 above.
7. A/35/1, Section IX.
8. A/PV.690, paras. 72-73.
9. B. Urquhart, Hammarskjold (1972), pp. 494-496.
10. E/CN.4/AC.21/L.1, para. 83.
11. A/35/PV.4, p. 61.
12. A/C.3/SR.1809, para. 7.
13. A/10235, paras. 179-181.
14. A/C.3/SR.2168, para. 6.
15. A/C.3/L.1932.
16. L.M. Goodrich, E. Hambro and A.P. Symons, The Charter of the United Nations (1969), p. 589.
17. *Ibid.*, see also, S. Schwebel, "The Origins and Development of Article 99 of the Charter," XXVIII BYIL (1952), pp. 371-382.
18. A/35/33, p. 19, para. 53.
19. *Ibid.*, p. 22.
20. H. Lauterpacht, International Law and Human Rights (1950), p. 187.
21. A.W. Cordier and M. Harrelson, Public Papers of the Secretaries-General of the United Nations, Vol. VIII, U Thant 1968-1971 (1977), p. 380.
22. A/35/1.
23. V. Pechota, *op. cit.* on p. 49 above, p. 61; see also pp. 49-50.
24. Secretaries-General of the League of Nations also made intercessions on humanitarian matters. See, for example, on the humanitarian efforts of Secretary-General Drummond, J. Barros, Office without Power. Secretary-General Sir Eric Drummond 1919-1933 (1978), pp. 105-106.
25. Gordenker, *op. cit.*, p. 80.
26. T. Lie, In the Cause of Peace (1954), p. 243. In his famous ten-point memorandum, Lie had advocated: "8. Vigorous and continued development of the work of the United Nations for wider observance and respect for human rights and fundamental freedoms throughout the world." He added: "It is becoming evident that the Universal Declaration of Human Rights, adopted by the General Assembly in 1948 without a dissenting vote, is destined to become one of the great documents of history. The United Nations is now engaged on a program that will extend over

the next twenty years – and beyond – to secure the extension and wider observance of the political, economic and social rights there set down. Its success needs the active support of all Governments." *Ibid.*, p. 281.

27. *Ibid.*, p. 289.
28. *Ibid.*, p. 304.
29. *Ibid.*, pp. 242-243.
30. B. Urquhart, Hammarskjöld (1972), pp. 496-497. See also, on Hammarskjöld's exercise of good offices in general, pp. 308-314.
31. *Ibid.*, p. 497.
32. A/4390, p. 49.
33. See UN Monthly Chronicle, VII (July 1970), pp. 122-131.
34. Israeli Ambassador.
35. View from the United Nations (1978), pp. 351-352.
36. Hammarskjöld also felt that the Secretary-General should not be asked to act unless guidance can be found either in the Charter or in a decision of a major organ – Gordenker, *op. cit.*, p. 75. See also Urquhart, *op. cit.*, p. 309: "Hammarskjöld normally undertook 'good offices' missions only at the request of governments and he refused to take initiatives if he believed that either his right to do so or his chances of success were seriously in doubt."
37. A/8701/Add.1, Section IX.
38. A/9601/Add.1, p. 8. See generally, B. Urquhart, Hammarskjöld (1972), pp. 308-314. U Thant, View from the United Nations (1978), pp. 351-352.
39. A/9601/Add.1, p. 8.
40. A/31/1/Add.1, p. 9.
41. A/32/1, pp. 6-7.
42. DPI/622, pp. 16-17.
43. K. Waldheim, Un métier unique au monde (1978), p. 102.
44. Press release SG/SM/321, p. 6.
45. In his Annual Report for 1980, the Secretary-General stated: "Increasingly, I have been requested by various United Nations bodies dealing with human rights to enter into direct contacts with Governments of countries facing problems. In several instances, such Governments have received visits from special representatives designated by me." In a resolution adopted by the Sub-Commission on Prevention of Discrimination and Protection of Minorities at its thirty-third session, in 1980, it was suggested that due consideration be given to the avenues open to the Secretary-General in responding to reports of mass and flagrant violations of human rights of an urgent nature by, for example, bringing a United Nations presence to bear on situations through the exercise of his good offices, through personal contacts, the use of special representatives, members of the United Nations Secretariat, United Nations field officers, other emissaries, or through other appropriate discreet methods. – Resolution 25 (XXXIII), para. 5, reproduced in annex III below.
46. A/10295.
47. For further instances of good offices with respect to the situation of human rights in Chile, see A/C.3/32/227.
48. Cf. D.P. Forsythe, Present Role of the Red Cross in Protection, Background paper

No. 1 of the Joint Committee for the Reappraisal of the Role of the Red Cross (1975), p. 31: "It can be argued on the basis of innumerable factual situations, though not legally proven at the moment, that beyond armed conflict the ICRC's right of initiative in humanitarian matters has become part of customary law certainly of customary international practice."

Chapter IV

CHARTER-BASED RESPONSIBILITIES AND EXPRESS HUMANITARIAN MANDATES OF THE UNITED NATIONS SECRETARY-GENERAL

I. Practice

As we have already seen, in recent years some cases have occurred in which the Secretary-General has been specifically requested by human rights organs such as the General Assembly, the Economic and Social Council and the Commission on Human Rights, to exercise good offices, or to engage in direct contacts with governments, or to carry out fact-finding activities in relation to cases or situations involving breaches of human rights. In this chapter, we will discuss how such mandates relate to the Charter-based responsibilities of the Secretary-General.

(a) *General requests*

A general request to the Secretary-General was made in resolution 27 (XXXVI) of the Commission on Human Rights, which requested him "to continue and intensify the good offices envisaged in the Charter of the United Nations in the field of human rights." Earlier, the Economic and Social Council by its resolution 1979/36, had "expressed its appreciation to the Secretary-General for his efforts to continue rendering the good offices as envisaged in the Charter of the United Nations in the field of human rights." In its resolution 34/175, on effective action against mass or flagrant violations of human rights, the General Assembly stressed "the important role that the Secretary-General can play in situations of mass and flagrant violations of human rights."

In its resolution 31 (XXXVI) adopted on 11 March 1980, the Commission on Human Rights requested "the Secretary-General to use his good offices to ensure the full enjoyment of human rights by United Nations staff members and the enjoyment of rights conveyed under the Convention on the Privileges and Immunities of the United Nations."

With respect to certain categories of persons, the General Assembly, in its resolution 33/173 adopted on 20 December 1978, urged the Secretary-General "to continue to use his good offices in cases of enforced or involuntary disappearances of persons, drawing, as appropriate, upon the relevant experience of the International Committee of the Red Cross and of other humanitarian organizations." Related requests to the Secretary-General to appeal to all governments to co-operate with and assist the Commission on Human Rights' working group on the question of missing and disappeared persons in the performance of its tasks were adopted by the Commission on Human Rights at its 36th, 37th and 38th sessions.

In its resolution 30 (XXXVI), adopted on 11 March 1980, the Commission on Human Rights, *inter alia*, requested the Secretary-General, in cases where large-scale exoduses become a matter of international concern and solidarity, to consider establishing direct contacts with the appropriate governments, to assess the relationships between the situation and full enjoyment of human rights and to make concrete recommendations for ameliorating such situations. In paragraph 5 of the same resolution, the Secretary-General was requested, where warranted, to submit to the next session of the Commission or General Assembly, as appropriate, a summary of his findings and recommendations to assist governments in restoring full enjoyment of human rights. Pursuant to this resolution the Secretary-General submitted a report to the 37th session of the Commission on Human Rights.[1]

(b) *Specific situations*

On various occasions, United Nations organs have addressed requests to the Secretary-General with respect to alleged situations of violations of human rights in particular countries. Indeed, at its 34th session, in 1978, the Commission on Human Rights adopted decision 6 (XXXIV) in which "the Commission, having regard to the decisions it took at its thirty-third session concerning alleged situations of violations of human rights in particular countries, decided to express its appreciation to the Secretary-General for responding to the requests addressed to him by the Commission."

(i) *Telegrams/urgent cases*
On some occasions the Commission on Human Rights has requested the Secretary-General to intercede in urgent cases involving threat to life. In every such case, the Secretary-General has interceded with the government concerned and transmitted the Commission's concern or made an appeal on behalf of the persons in question. As an example, reference may be made to decision 2 (XXXIII) adopted by the Commission on 15 February 1977, in which the Commission requested the Secretary-General "to employ in all urgency, whatever means he may deem most appropriate to save the lifes of" two members of SWAPO facing danger of death before the law courts of South Africa. In response to this decision, the Secretary-General addressed the following reply to the Commission: "I have received your message of 15 February drawing to my attention the apprehensions of the Commission on Human Rights for the fate of Aaron Mushimba and Hendrik Shikongo of SWAPO. I fully share the Commission's concern in this regard and have immediately contacted the South African authorities. You may be assured that I shall continue to follow the developments in this matter closely and take whatever action I appropriately can within the possibilities of my office."[2]

(ii) *Chile*
In its resolution 3219 (XXIX), adopted in 1974, the General Assembly requested the President of the twenty-ninth session of the General Assembly and the Secretary-General to assist in any way they might deem appropriate in the re-establishment of basic human rights and fundamental freedoms in Chile. The action taken by the Secretary-General under this resolution was described in chapter III above.[3]

(iii) *Arab-occupied territories*
In resolutions adopted at its thirty-third, thirty-fourth, thirty-fifth, thirty-sixth, thirty-seventh and thirty-eighth sessions, the Commission on Human Rights requested the Secretary-General "to collect all relevant information concerning detainees, such as their number, identity, place and duration of detention, and to make this information available to the Commission." In response to these requests the Secretary-General has usually sent notes to governments, specialized agencies, regional intergovernmental organizations, non-governmental organizations in consultative status, as well as to recognized liberation movements solic-

iting relevant information. Material thus provided has been made available to the Commission (see, e.g., E/CN.4/1307 submitted to the thirty-fifth session of the Commission; E/CN.4/1352 and Add.1 submitted to the thirty-sixth session of the Commission; E/CN.4/1418 and Add.1 submitted to the thirty-seventh session of the Commission, and E/CN. 4/1481 submitted to the thirty-eighth session of the Commission).

(iv) *Kampuchea*

By its decision 9 (XXXIV) of 8 March 1978 on the human rights situation in Democratic Kampuchea, the Commission on Human Rights decided to request the Secretary-General to transmit to the Government of Democratic Kampuchea the documents and summary records of the thirty-fourth session of the Commission relating to the human rights situation in that country, with a view to inviting that Government to send its comments and observations, and to transmit the response of the Government of Democratic Kampuchea, together with all the information that might be available about the situation, to the Commission at its thirty-fifth session, through the Sub-Commission on Prevention of Discrimination and Protection of Minorities. A report of the Secretary-General containing information solicited from governments, specialized agencies, regional intergovernmental organizations, non-governmental organizations in consultative status with the Economic and Social Council and individuals was submitted to the Sub-Commission at its thirty-first session in 1978.[4]

Subsequently, in 1981, the Commission on Human Rights, in its resoluion 11 (XXXVII) on the situation of human rights in Kampuchea, requested the Secretary-General "to appoint a special representative to assist him in the implementation of General Assembly resolution 35/6."

(v) *Nicaragua*

In its resolution 14 (XXXV), adopted on 13 March 1979, on the situation of human rights in Nicaragua, the Commission on Human Rights requested the Secretary-General "acting through the appropriate channels, to keep under continuing review the development of the situation in Nicaragua, and in particular violations of human rights and fundamental freedoms and to submit a report, based on all relevant sources, to the Commission on Human Rights at its thirty-sixth session through the Sub-Commission on Prevention of Discrimination and Protection of Minorities." In his reports submitted to the Sub-Commission and to the Commission in accordance with this request, the Secretary-General transmitted information received from governments, specialized agencies, regional intergovernmental organizations and non-governmental organizations in consultative status with the Economic and Social Council.[5]

(vi) *Guatemala*

In its resolution 32 (XXXVI) adopted on 11 March 1980, the Commission on Human Rights decided to keep the situation of human rights and fundamental freedoms in Guatemala under review at its thirty-seventh session on the basis of information received from all relevant sources, and to that end requested "the Secretary-General to bring this resolution to the attention of the Government of Guatemala and report on the results of this contact to the Commission at that session." At the thirty-seventh session of the Commission the Secretary-General submitted a report on the situation of human rights in Guatemala reproducing information received from governments, specialized agencies, regional intergovernmental organizations and non-governmental organizations in consultative status with the Economic and Social Council.[6] At the same session, the Commission, having noted the report of the Secretary-General requested "the Secretary-General to continue his efforts to establish direct contacts with the Government of Guatemala on the human rights situation prevailing in that country and to collect information thereon from all relevant sources." The Secretary-General was requested to present an interim report of his contacts with the Government of Guatemala to the General Assembly at its thirty-sixth session and a final report to the Commission at its thirty-eighth session. The interim report of the Secretary-General which was submitted to the General Assembly at its thirty-sixth session[7] outlined the efforts made by the Secretary-General up to that point to establish substantive contacts with the Government of Guatemala. In a follow-up report to the Commission at its thirty-eighth session, the Secretary-General reported that the substantive contacts had not yet materialized. The exchanges between the Government of Guatemala and the Secretary-General in this instance raised some issues of principle which were commented upon at the General Assembly, during its thirty-sixth session. These issues will be referred to below.

(vii) *Poland*

At its thirty-eighth session in 1982, the Commission on Human Rights adopted resolution 26/1982 on the situation of human rights and fundamental freedoms in Poland, in which, *inter alia*, it decided "to request the Secretary-General or a person designated by him, to undertake a thorough study of the human rights situation in Poland based on such information as he may deem relevant, including comments and materials the Government of Poland may wish to provide and to present a comprehensive report to the Commission at its thirty-ninth session."

(viii) *Iran*

In resolution 27/1982 on the situation of human rights in Iran, adopted on 11 March 1982, the Commission on Human Rights requested the Secretary-General "to establish direct contacts with the Government of Iran on the human rights situation prevailing in that country and to continue his efforts to endeavour to ensure that the Baha'is are guaranteed full enjoyment of their human rights and fundamental freedoms." The Secretary-General was requested to submit to the Commission at its thirty-ninth session "a report compiled on the basis of all available information, including information on any direct contacts which he may have established with the Government of Iran concerning the general human rights situation prevailing in that country."

From the foregoing practice, it may be seen that the Secretary-General has on various occasions been specifically requested by human rights organs to: engage in good offices generally; engage in good offices with respect to specific categories of persons (missing persons and UN staff); intercede on behalf of specific individuals; to engage in direct contacts with governments generally (mass exoduses); to engage in fact-finding into certain situations (Arab-occupied territories, Nicaragua, Guatemala, Poland and Iran); to engage in an admixture of fact-finding and direct contacts (Chile, Guatemala and Iran), and to appoint a special representative to assist him in dealing with a particular human rights situation (Kampuchea). It may be noted that in relation to Guatemala, the Secretary-General, while endeavouring to establish direct contacts with the Government, at the same time communicated to the Commission information received from various sources on the situation of human rights in that country. An express request to this effect was also contained in Commission resolution 27/1982 on the situation of human rights in Iran.

The practice shows that pursuant to requests of human rights organs, the Secretary-General has: acted urgently to try to save the lives of persons under threat of death; has collected and transmitted to human rights organs information regarding specific situations from governments, specialized agencies, regional inter-governmental organizations, non-governmental organizations and even, on occasions, from individuals; has visited or arranged for visits to countries concerned by his staff; and has carried out contacts with governments concerned either with their representatives at one of the seats of the Organization or in the countries concerned.

The term "direct contacts" is a term of art which has a long-standing practice in organizations such as the ILO and which also has a considerable practice within the framework of the procedures established under resolution 1503 (XLVIII) of the Economic and Social Council. From the United Nations practice, as well as from the practice of the ILO, it may be concluded that there is considerable flexibility in carrying out direct contacts. They may be undertaken at a seat of the Organization or in the country concerned itself. Direct contacts may be carried out personally by the Secretary-General, or by a member of his staff, or by someone designated by him from outside of the Organization. Cases of such designation of outside personalities are quite common in the practice of the ILO.

In the case of Guatemala, however, the report of the Secretary-General to the thirty-sixth session of the General Assembly on his efforts to establish direct contacts with the Government of Guatemala reproduced a letter dated 11 September 1981 from the Government of Guatemala in which the Government informed the Secretary-General that: "it considers that the contacts referred to in the resolution must be established by you through a member of the Secretariat, as has been the practice in all past similar cases known to us, rather than by a member of the Commission on Human Rights, much less a member of the Human Rights Committee established under the International Covenant on Civil and Political Rights, to which Guatemala is not a party. In our opinion, the contact established by the Secretary-General must be consistent with the impartial, objective and apolitical line followed by the Secretariat under your able guidance. The opposite would mean accepting the appointment of a special rapporteur." This led the representative of Ghana to comment (during a meeting of the Third Committee on 27 November 1981) that "in establishing direct contacts and carrying them out, the

Secretary-General was at liberty to use the Secretariat or to call on qualified outside experts. The principle had been employed, for example, by the International Labour Organization (ILO) and the United Nations Educational, Scientific and Cultural Organization (UNESCO). Ghana," he said, "reaffirmed the fundamental principles concerning the Secretary-General's discretionary power to call on experts outside the Organization to assist him.[8] The comments of the representative of Ghana were endorsed by the representative of The Netherlands. No other representative referred to this point expressly. The debate on this question at the thirty-sixth session of the General Assembly was not extensive enough to enable a definitive conclusion to be drawn on the matter and therefore the question must be resolved by reference to the international practice which has developed, particularly within the ILO.[9] This practice leaves no doubt whatsoever that the Secretary-General is at liberty to designate for the purpose of carrying out such direct contacts either a member of his staff or a person outside of the Organization.

II. General principles applicable

To a certain extent, guidance may be obtained from what the Secretary-General has done in complying with the requets of the Commission regarding the situations in Nicaragua, Guatemala and the Occupied Territories (which were recounted above). Nevertheless, in view of the increasing number of such requests, it would seem necessary to have a clearer idea of the general principles which should be applied by the Secretary-General in responding to such requests. Such general principles may be based on the relevant provisions of the Charter affecting the role and competence of the Secretary-General and may also be based in conscious policy decisions adopted by the Secretary-General in dealing with requests by human rights organs having regard to other duties of the Secretary-General vis-à-vis the Organization at large.

The first principle which appears to be relevant relates to the duality of competences. The Secretary-General, as the Chief Administrative Officer of the Secretariat, a principal organ of the United Nations under the Charter, as well as in virtue of certain provisions of the Charter, is vested with certain competences, including competence to exercise, on his own volition and as he deems fit, his good offices in the field of human rights.[10] At the same time, the Secretary-General, under Article 98 of the Charter, is also required to "perform such other functions as are entrusted to him" by United Nations organs. The duality of competences may be demonstrated by reference to two cases which have occurred. In 1977 the Secretary-General was utilizing, of his own volition, his good offices vis-à-vis the situation then prevailing in Uganda, when he was seized with a request by the Commission on Human Rights to carry out certain tasks relating to the same situation.

In a communication which the Secretary-General forwarded to the Commission on that occasion, he emphasized the independence of his own competences vis-à-vis the competences of United Nations human rights organs. The Commission was informed that "the Secretary-General has met twice with the Permanent Representative of Uganda at United Nations Headquarters. He formally requested the Government of Uganda to accept any impartial international investigation of the circumstances surrounding the death of the three individuals which occurred last week in Uganda. He has acted on his own initiative and under the powers conferred upon him under the Charter. He does not consider that he requires any authority in this regard from the Commission on Human Rights. It is his view that the Commission on Human Rights as a competent body in the field of human rights should decide on the measures it considers necessary within the framework of its activities. The Secretary-General is therefore already acting within the sphere of competence of his Office. He believes the Commission on Human Rights should assume its own responsibilities under its terms of reference and the relevant resolutions." Similarly, in 1982, prior to the Commission's request to the Secretary-General to undertake certain duties regarding the human rights situation in Poland, the Secretary-General had publicly disclosed that he was in contact with the Polish authorities regarding the situation of human rights in that country and was requesting information and clarification thereon. The duality of competences can, therefore, as was recognized by Secretary-General Waldheim in 1976, give rise to potential conflict of competences and in this regard the principle stated by Secretary-General Waldheim in 1977 would be a crucial one, namely, that the Secretary-General may wish to act within the sphere of competence of his office while leaving United Nations organs to assume their own responsibilities.

It would follow from this that the Secretary-General possesses some discretion as to how he wishes to go about the implementation of a request. It may be stated as a general principle that the carrying out of such duties requested by United Nations organs should not conflict with the Secretary-General's other duties and responsibilities under the Charter.

It would also follow from the preceding considerations that the Secretary-General may need to utilize care and discretion regarding the content of any report which he may decide to submit to human rights organs pursuant to their requests to him to take action vis-à-vis specific cases or situations. This principle was relied upon by the Secretary-General in the report which he submitted to the thirty-seventh session of the Commission pursuant to resolution 30 (XXXVI) of the Commission on the question of mass exoduses and human rights. The Secretary-General stated that "there are doubtless many situations in which mass exoduses are caused by denials of human rights, and the Secretary-General does not fail to point this out in his contacts and consultations with the parties concerned. However, the Secretary-General often finds that considerable caution needs to be exercised in the public disclosure of the precise substance of his contacts with the Governments concerned . . . so as to avoid prejudicing future contacts and closing the possibility of his being of assistance in the future to the victims of such situations."

III. Conclusions

To recapitulate the following general principles may be posited:

(1) The competence of the Secretary-General to exercise his good offices in relation to any case or situation is independent of the competence of human rights organs to address such cases or situations. It goes without saying, however, that the Secretary-General would need to take account of what a UN organ may be doing in deciding upon his own actions;
(2) In the event of potential conflict between the duties and responsibilities of the Secretary-General under the Charter and a request addressed to him by a human rights organ, the Secretary-General has discretion in deciding how to implement the mandate;
(3) In carrying out any such requests by human rights organs the Secretary-General is entitled to take into account the need to ensure that his other duties and responsibilities to the Organization under the Charter are not prejudiced;

(4) The Secretary-General has discretion with regard to the content of any report which he may decide to submit to an organ on a particular situation or question.

NOTES

1. E/CN.4/1440.
2. Reproduced in the report of the Commission on its 33rd session, E/5927/Annex IV.
3. See pp. 69-70.
4. E/CN.4/Sub.2/414 and Adds. 1-7.
5. E/CN.4/Sub.2/426 and E/CN.4/1372.
6. E/CN.4/1438.
7. A/36/705.
8. See GA press release GA/SHC/2482 of 27 November 1981, pp. 3-4. See similarly A/C.3/36/SR.64, paras. 1-4.
9. See G. von Potobsky, "On-the-Spot Visits – An important cog in the ILO's supervisory machinery," 120 International Labour Review (1981), pp. 581-596 at pp. 585-587.
10. See on this, B.G. Ramcharan, "The Good Offices of the United Nations Secretary-General in the Field of Human Rights," 76 American Journal of International Law, No. 1 (January 1982), pp. 130-141.

Chapter V

MODELS OF HUMANITARIAN ACTION

In the present chapter, some additional examples will be presented in order to demonstrate the variety of approaches and methods of humanitarian action applied.

I. Action to protect life or liberty

On 29 April 1967 a United Nations spokesman announced that on behalf of the group of socialist countries, the Permanent Representatives of Poland and Czechoslovakia had met with Secretary-General U Thant at 11.15 p.m. on Friday 28 April 1967 at his residence and had requested him to use his good offices with a view to stopping the persecution and averting the possible execution of political leaders then under detention in Greece. They had particularly requested the Secretary-General to intercede to save the life of Manolis Glezos. The Permanent Representative of Poland saw the Secretary-General again on Saturday 29 April at 12.00 noon and conveyed a personal message from the Foreign Minister of Poland to the same effect. The Secretary-General then met with the Permanent Representative of Greece and requested him to convey his personal appeal on humanitarian grounds, on behalf of the political detainees. He expressed his confidence that, in keeping with the noble traditions of Greece, the usual judicial processes of democratic countries would be followed in dealing with the political leaders in detention.[1]

On 1 May 1967 a second statement was issued by a United Nations spokesman announcing that the Permanent Representative of the Soviet Union had called on the Secretary-General on Sunday 30 April, at his residence to convey the concern of his Government in regard to the treatment of political detainees in Greece. His Government had expressed particular concern with regard to Manolis Glezos. The Secretary-General had again met with the Permanent Representative of

Greece on 1 May and had conveyed to him the concern of the Government of the Soviet Union, and also his personal appeal on humanitarian grounds, on behalf of the political detainees.[2]

On 3 May 1967, it was announced that the Permanent Representative of Greece, acting on instructions from his Government, had called on the Secretary-General that day in connection with the latter's personal appeal on behalf of political detainees in Greece. The Greek Ambassador had informed the Secretary-General that the life of neither Manolis Glezos nor of any other detainee had been in danger. The Ambassador further assured the Secretary-General that due legal judicial processes would be followed in dealing with the detainees. The Secretary-General expressed his thanks to the Ambassador for the prompt and positive reply given by his Government to his personal appeal.[3]

II. Discreet expression of concern

In a letter dated 29 October 1980 to the Secretary-General, the President of Bolivia referred to a talk which Secretary-General Waldheim had had with the Minister of Foreign Relations of Bolivia on 9 October 1980 and informed the Secretary-General that "bearing in mind that . . . [human rights] was one of your concerns, I wish to state that my Government is ready to fix a date on which a delegation from the Commission on Human Rights may visit Bolivia so as to dispel once and for all the distorted picture which biased informants are seeking to give of Bolivia in an effort to do harm to my country."[4] It is significant that the Secretary-General's discreet expression of concern in this instance led to an invitation for a visit to Bolivia by the Commission on Human Rights.

III. Public appeals

On 15 March 1979 a United Nations spokesman made a statement on behalf of Secretary-General Waldheim in which the Secretary-General noted with deep concern that summary executions continued to be carried out in Iran without due process of law and that such a fate might also be meted out to former Prime Minister Amir Abbas Hoveida. The Secretary-General announced that he was gratified that the then Prime Minister of Iran had himself publicly expressed opposition to a continuation of this practice. Without in any way wishing to interfere in the internal affairs of Iran, the Secretary-General strongly urged on humanitarian grounds that all concerned assure full respect for the human rights of political prisoners in Iran and that summary executions without due process be ended immediately.[5]

In relation to another situation a spokesman on behalf of Secretary-General Waldheim announced on 23 April 1980 that the Secretary-General had learned with deep concern of the executions which had recently taken place in Liberia. Without in any way wishing to intervene in matters of domestic jurisdiction, the Secretary-General reiterated on humanitarian grounds his appeal to the Liberian authorities that all concerned should receive a fair trial and strongly urged that summary executions without due process of law cease.[6]

With regard to a third situation on 12 July 1979, Secretary-General Waldheim appealed urgently to governments and international organizations to contribute to an emergency programme of humanitarian assistance to Uganda. The Secretary-General was said to be gravely concerned over the human suffering and material destruction that had occurred in Uganda and emphasized the vital importance of international assistance in that situation. An Emergency Programme of Humanitarian Assistance to Uganda was drawn up by the United Nations High Commissioner for Refugees (UNHCR), in response to a request from the Government of Uganda for international assistance to deal with the problems of returning refugees and displaced persons in that country. The programme gave details of the most immediate requirements based on an on-the-spot assessment by a UNHCR mission. The needs included food, transport, tools and seeds for agriculture and restoration of certain basic facilities.[7]

IV. Urgent action

On 6 November 1979 a United Nations spokesman announced that Secretary-General Waldheim had called in Jamal Shemirani, Chargé d'affaires of Iran, with whom he had met for 40 minutes, and had asked him to convey urgently to the Ayatollah Khomeini and the Government of Iran his grave concern about the situation at the United States Embassy in Tehran. The Secretary-General, it was said, had also been in touch with a number of other delegations on this question. The spokesman said that in view of the delicate nature of the problem, further details could not be given. However, he stressed, the Secretary-General was sparing no effort to contribute to a solution of the problem.[8]

V. Visits on the spot

From 14 June to 26 June 1977 a group of 26 persons organized a hunger strike on the premises of the Economic Commission for Latin America. The aim of this action was to draw international attention to the fate of the "missing persons" in Chile. Following efforts by the Secretary-General to contribute to the solution of the problem, the Government of Chile promised *inter alia* to transmit information on the fate of the relatives of this group of persons who had participated in the hunger strike. In addition, the Government stated that it would take no action against the members of that group. It had been agreed that the Executive Secretary of the Economic Commission for Latin America (ECLA) would transmit the list of missing relatives – totalling 36 – to the Ministry of Foreign Affairs, which would forward it to the Ministry of the Interior for further information. The reverse procedure would be followed for the communication of the information requested.

On 23 September 1977, the Ministry of Foreign Affairs delivered to the Executive Secretary of ECLA a document concerning the information available on the fate of the 36 persons. This document was then transmitted to the Secretary-General.

After considering this information, the Secretary-General, during a meeting with the Minister of Foreign Affairs of Chile on 29 September, expressed disappointment with the outcome of the investigation. In an endeavour to continue his good offices, the Secretary-General proposed to the Minister of Foreign Affairs that Mr. Eric Suy, the Legal Counsel, in the course of a working visit to ECLA might hold talks with the Chilean authorities in order to explore ways of obtaining more information on the fate of the missing persons. The Minister of Foreign Affairs agreed to this proposal.[9]

Mr. Eric Suy, the Legal Counsel, paid a visit to Santiago from 27 to 31 October 1977. He had a thorough and frank exchange of views with the following authorities: the Minister of Foreign Affairs, the Deputy Minister of Justice, the Comptroller-General, the Chairman of the Constitutional Committee, members of the Council of State, the President of the Supreme Court, the Minister of the Interior, the Director-General and other senior officials in the Ministry of Foreign Affairs. He also spoke with representatives of the Intergovernmental Committee for European Migration (ICEM) and the *Vicaria de la Solidaridad.* He twice had talks with a delegation representing those who had participated in the hunger strikes.

On Friday 28 October 1977, the Government of Chile transmitted to the Legal Counsel a supplementary memorandum concerning the situation of relatives of the 26 persons who had participated in the hunger strike. In this memorandum the Government stated that all the supplementary information referred to proceedings pending before the courts.

During his talks, the Legal Counsel also drew the attention of the Chilean authorities to the question of the safety of United Nations staff members in Chile. The Legal Counsel emphasized to the Minister of the Interior that precise instructions should be given to the police regarding the tranquility and security of international officials in Chile.

VI. Denunciations

On 5 December 1980, a United Nations spokesman declared on behalf of Secretary-General Waldheim that the Secretary-General was deeply shocked and grieved to learn about the killing of innocent people in El Salvador, including the brutal murder of three nuns. As the Secretary-General had already done three times before, he once again appealed that these senseless acts of terrorism and the loss of life that flowed from them must be stopped. The Secretary-General again appealed to all concerned to stop the violence, and he extended his heartfelt condolences to the families of the victims.[10]

VII. Conclusion

The foregoing cases provide good examples of the skill and finesse with which humanitarian good offices need to be exercised. The Secretary-General can be seen addressing personal appeals "on humanitarian grounds"; expressing concern to a foreign minister confidentially about the situation of human rights in the minister's country; expressing "disappointment" to another foreign minister about the outcome of an investigation into alleged violations of human rights; appealing to governments "without in any way wishing to interfere in internal affairs". At the same time, when the occasion required it, the Secretary-General was prepared to express his "shock and grief" about the killing of innocent people.

NOTES

1. UN press release SG/SM/699, 29 April 1967.
2. UN press release SG/SM/700, 1 May 1967.
3. UN press release SG/SM/705, 3 May 1967.
4. A/C.3/35/9, Annex.
5. UN press release SG/SM/2685, 16 March 1979.
6. UN press release SG/SM/2910, 23 April 1980.
7. UN press release SG/SM/2756, 12 July 1979.
8. UN press release SG/SM/2826, 6 November 1979.
9. This account is based on the report of the Secretary-General submitted to the thirty-second session of the General Assembly, A/C.3/32/227.
10. UN press release SG/SM/3010, 5 December 1980.

Chapter VI

CASE STUDY: HUMANITARIAN GOOD OFFICES IN EAST PAKISTAN (BANGLADESH) (1971)

The events leading to the establishment of the State of Bangladesh out of what was formerly East Pakistan are well-known and, for our purposes, do not need repetition here. Briefly, following the occurrence of some natural disasters, there was a situation of internal conflict in East Pakistan resulting in widespread human suffering and the outflow of millions of refugees and these were in turn followed by a war between India and Pakistan. The United Nations eventually provided humanitarian assistance in Bangladesh (East Pakistan), in Pakistan (West Pakistan) and to refugees in India.

As the events unfolded, there is no doubt that there was a serious situation of gross violations of human rights in East Pakistan which was raised to no avail in United Nations human rights organs. As one writer has described it: "The United Nations never deliberately considered the massacre of at least several hundred thousand persons and the perpetration of other forms of gross violations of human rights in Bangladesh, formerly East Pakistan, from March to December 1971. The United Nations' non-response to these tragic events represents a serious omission in the exercise of its responsibility to promote human rights. Prompt consideration of the human rights violations when they were first reported might have prevented further violations as well as the secession of Bangladesh from Pakistan and the hostilities between India and Pakistan."[1] Despite behind-the-scenes urgings of the Secretary-General, as we shall see presently, the Security Council was only convened months after the events were in progress, after the outbreak of war between India and Pakistan. Even then, the Security Council was unable to come to a decision and decided to refer the question to the General Assembly for its consideration. On 6 December 1971 the General Assembly adopted a resolution (2790 (XXVI)) appealing to governments, intergovernmental agencies and non-governmental organizations to intensify their efforts to assist in relieving the suffering of the refugees in India and of the people of East Pakistan. Eventually, the Security Council did manage, on 21 December 1971, to adopt resolution 307 (1971) calling upon all those concerned to take all measures necessary to preserve human life and for the observance of the Geneva Conventions of 1949 and to apply in full their provisions as regards the protection of the wounded and sick, prisoners of war and civilian population. The Council also called for international assistance in the relief of suffering and the rehabilitation of refugees and their return in safety and dignity to their home.

It had, however, taken from March to December 1971, for these organs to act and in the meantime the human drama was being played out with terrible consequences. As Ambassador Lazar Mojsov of Yugoslavia said on 7 December: "All of us together, as Member States of the United Nations, also bear our share of responsibility for insufficient engagement and commitment in defining and ascertaining the real causes of the crisis, and for failing to take effective measures to overcome them in time."[2] Faced with this situation, Secretary-General U Thant decided to draw upon his good offices in an attempt to fill the void. His exercise of humanitarian good offices in this case has been acknowledged for its daring and innovative features and provides many examples of action which have lasting significance. As U Thant himself characterized it: "The United Nations' effort in East Pakistan is an unusual – even an unprecedented – form of activity for the Organization. I initiated this operation, even without any supporting resolution from any United Nations organ, because I felt that my obligations under the Charter must include any humanitarian action which I could take to save the lives of large numbers of human beings."[3] One commentator has remarked that U Thant's actions led to "an important development in the authority of the Office of Secretary-General under the Charter . . . it restores the Secretary-General's leadership in humanitarian matters."[4]

I. The Secretary-General's Initiative

Preoccupied with developments in East Pakistan and the adjacent Indian States and their consequences, or possible consequences, U Thant expressed his concern over the situation to President Yahya Khan shortly after the events of March 1971 and was in continuous touch with the

Governments of Pakistan and India, both through their Permanent Representatives at the United Nations and through other contacts. In these exchanges, he later told the Security Council, he had been "acutely aware of the dual responsibility of the United Nations, including the Secretary-General, under the Charter, both to observe the provisions of its Article 2, paragraph 7, and to work, within the framework of international economic and social co-operation, to help promote and ensure human well-being and humanitarian principles."[5] With this latter responsibility in mind, he appealed for assistance both for the refugees from East Pakistan in India and for the population of East Pakistan. In order to channel the assistance given in response to those appeals, he designated the United Nations High Commissioner for Refugees as the focal point for assistance to the refugees in India and appointed, with the agreement of the Government of Pakistan, a representative in Dacca, in order to make as effective use as possible of the international assistance made available for the relief of the population of East Pakistan.

In a letter dated 20 September 1971 to the President of Pakistan, General Agha Muhammad Yahya Khan, the Secretary-General put on record his understanding of the principles upon which the United Nations East Pakistan Relief Operation (UNEPRO) was based, as follows:

"Now that the United Nations relief operation is established and functioning in East Pakistan, I should like to put on record my understanding of the principles on which this United Nations effort is based.

As Your Excellency knows, this operation was initiated because it seemed imperative to act with speed in order to forestall by a strictly humanitarian action the possibility of famine and related disasters which might cost the lives of vast numbers of human beings in East Pakistan.

This meant that the operation had to be launched solely on the basis of Your Excellency's acceptance of my offer of humanitarian assistance by and through the United Nations for the relief of the distressed people of East Pakistan, and of the assurances given by Your Excellency to my Personal Representative, Mr. Ismat Kittani, during his visit to Islamabad in June of this year. On that occasion, as Your Excellency will recall, you welcomed and gave your full support to the United Nations operation being set up in such a way as to enable me to give contributors and donors the requisite assurances that the relief provided by and through the United Nations was reaching those for whom it was destined, the people of East Pakistan.

The United Nations effort in East Pakistan is an unusual – even an unprecedented – form of activity for the Organization. I initiated this operation, even without any supporting resolution from any United Nations organ, because I felt that my obligations under the Charter must include any humanitarian action which I could take to save the lives of large numbers of human beings. The operation is, as Your Excellency knows, entirely dependent on the response by governments and other donors to my various appeals for help and is based exclusively on voluntary contributions. I need not emphasize here that this is a purely humanitarian operation unrelated to economic assistance of a more long-term nature.

Especially in view of the unusual nature of this operation, it is now necessary for its smooth functioning that we fill in the legal and other details which are normally required in an undertaking of this kind and which were omitted during the initial phase because of the speed with which the emergency had to be met. The arrangements outlined below are designed to put the operation on a more customary and regular basis without, of course, affecting any standing agreements or arrangements the various organizations or agencies engaged in the operation may have with Your Excellency's Government.

In sending this message to Your Excellency, I have in mind, first, the necessity of a good working relationship on the ground between United Nations personnel and all those with whom they will have to deal in East Pakistan. Second, I am very conscious of my obligations to those governments and agencies who have made voluntary contributions to this relief operation and their desire to be assured as to the use of the relief provided. Thirdly, I am anxious to clarify the record so as to avoid any possible misunderstandings between the Government of Pakistan and the United Nations concerning the way in which this operation is to be run."[6]

On the basis of this letter, discussions were held at UN Headquarters with the Permanent Representative of Pakistan, resulting in an agreed statement of "Conditions for the effective discharge of the functions of the United Nations East Pakistan Relief Operation". The agreement was finalized by an exchange of letters between the Secretary-General and the Permanent Representative of Pakistan dated 15 and 16 November 1971. The agreed text of the "Conditions for the effective discharge of the functions of UNEPRO" is reproduced in annex VI below.

The President of the Security Council was kept continuously informed of the action of the Secretary-General relating to his offer of good offices. Copies of all the messages addressed by the Secretary-General in this regard to the Prime Minister of India or the President of Pakistan were immediately communicated to the President of the Security Council for his information.

As the weeks passed since March, U Thant became increasingly uneasy and apprehensive at the steady deterioration of the situation in the region in almost all its aspects. On 20 July 1971, he had submitted a memorandum to the President of the Security Council recounting some of the above matters and adding: "In the light of the information available to me, I have reluctantly come to the conclusion that the time is past when the international community can continue to stand by, watching the situation deteriorate and hoping that relief programmes, humanitarian efforts and good intentions will be enough to turn the tide of human misery and potential disaster. I am deeply concerned about the possible consequences of the present situation, not only in the humanitarian sense, but also as a potential threat to peace and security and for its bearing on the future of the United Nations as an effective instrument for international co-operation and action. It seems to me that the present tragic situation, in which humanitarian, economic and political problems are mixed in such a way as almost to defy any distinction between them, presents a challenge to the United Nations as a whole which must be met. Other situations of this kind may well occur in the future. If the Organization faces up to such a situation now, it may be able to develop the new skill and the new strength required to face further situations of this kind.

It is for these reasons that I am taking the unusual step of reporting to the President of the Security Council on a question which has not been inscribed on the Council's agenda. The political aspects of this matter are of such far-reaching importance that the Secretary-General is not in a position to suggest precise courses of action before the members of the Security Council have taken note of the problem. I believe, however, that the United Nations, with its long experience in peacekeeping and with its varied resources for conciliation and persuasion, must, and should, now play a more fortright role in attempting both to mitigate the human tragedy which has already taken place and to avert the further deterioration of the situation.

The Security Council, the world's highest body for the maintenance of international peace and security, is in a position to consider, with the utmost attention and concern, the present situation and to reach some agreed conclusions as to measures which might be taken. Naturally, it is for the members of the Council themselves to decide whether such consideration should take place formally or informally, in public or in private. My primary purpose at this stage is to provide a basis and an opportunity for such discussions to take place and to express my grave concern that all possible ways and means should be explored which might help to resolve this tragic situation."[7]

On 17 September 1971, in the Introduction to his Annual Report to the twenty-sixth session of the General Assembly, he brought this problem in all its aspects to the Assembly's attention. He concluded his report with the following observation: "In a disaster of such vast proportions, the international community has a clear obligation to help the Governments and peoples concerned in every possible way. But, as I have indicated, the basic problem can be solved only if a political solution based on reconciliation and the respect of humanitarian principles is achieved.[8] With this end in view, I have used my good offices in various ways ever since the events of March in East Pakistan. For obvious reasons I did this with complete lack of publicity. Because of the special importance of the problem, I made an exception to this rule with regard to the case of Sheik Mujibur Rahman, in connexion with which I had the following statement issued on 10 August 1971:

'The Secretary-General feels that it is an extremely sensitive and delicate matter which falls within the competence of the judicial system of a Member State – in this case, Pakistan. It is also a matter of extraordinary interest and concern in many quarters, from a humanitarian as well as from a political point of view. The Secretary-General has received and is still receiving almost every day expressions of serious concern from representatives of Governments about the situation in East Pakistan and there is a general feeling that the restoration of peace and normalcy in the region is remote unless some kind of accommodation is reached. The Secretary-General shares the feelings of many representatives that any developments concerning the fate of Sheik Mujibur Rahman will inevitably have repercussions outside the borders of Pakistan.' "

As we have already seen, on 6 December 1971, the General Assembly unanimously adopted resolution 2790 (XXVI) in which it endorsed the designation by the Secretary-General of the United Nations High Commissioner for Refugees to be the focal point for the co-ordination of assistance to East Pakistan refugees in India from and through the United Nations system, as well as the Secretary-General's initiative in establishing the United Nations East Pakistan Relief Operation (UNEPRO). The Assembly also requested "the Secretary-General and the High Commissioner to continue their efforts to co-ordinate international assistance and to ensure that it is used to the maximum advantage to relieve the suffering of the refugees in India and of the people of East Pakistan."

On 21 December, the Security Council adopted resolution 307 (1971) in which, among other things, the Council:

"3. *Calls upon* all those concerned to take all measures necessary to preserve human life and for the observance of the Geneva Conventions of 1949 and to apply in full their provisions as regards the protection of wounded and sick, prisoners of war and civilian population;

4. *Calls for* international assistance in the relief of suffering and the rehabilitation of refugees and their return in safety and dignity to their homes and for full co-operation with the Secretary-General to that effect;

5. *Authorizes* the Secretary-General to appoint if necessary a special representative to lend his good offices for the solution of humanitarian problems."

Even before the adoption of General Assembly resolution 2790 (XXVI), the situation in the area had undergone grave deterioration, culminating in the outbreak of large-scale hostilities between India and Pakistan on 3 December 1971. Immediately following the adoption of the resolution, the Secretary-General informed the Assembly, at its 2001st plenary meeting, that the humanitarian activities of the United Nations in East Pakistan had had to be suspended, since it was impossible to move supplies in a situation of active hostilities and there was no practical possibility of ensuring the reasonable safety of the international staff; nor was he any longer in a position to assure the donors that the relief supplies would reach those for whom they were intended. The Secretary-General added in this connection that he planned to evacuate the remaining personnel of UNEPRO, but that the necessary arrangements were being made for the United Nations to be in a position to resume its humanitarian operations in the area as soon as conditions permitted, in compliance with the wish unanimously expressed by the General Assembly.

The retention of a small volunteer group of United Nations personnel in Dacca had, however, been decided upon by the Secretary-General on 7 December, because he considered that, in the increasingly chaotic situation prevailing in the city, certain humanitarian functions must continue to be carried out by the United Nations. On that day, as the fighting increased in intensity, the Secretary-General made a statement to the General Assembly, at its 2003rd plenary meeting, in which he appealed to all the parties to the conflict, no matter what their allegiance, to take every possible measure to spare the lives of the innocent civilian population, which was afflicted and threatened by the hostilities. In this connection, the Secretary-General indicated that he was maintaining close contact with the International Committee of the Red Cross which, in its traditional humanitarian role, would endeavour to implement as fully as possible the terms of the Geneva Conventions. The Secretary-General appealed to all parties to observe the terms of those Conventions and to do their utmost to ensure that the above developments did not give rise to yet another senseless sacrifice of human lives on a vast scale. He went on to say that he had instructed his representative in Dacca to examine urgently, in full co-operation with the International Committee of the Red Cross, what practical measures could be taken to this end.

The following day the Secretary-General informed the Governments of India and Pakistan that he hoped that it would be possible to set up neutral zones in Dacca at the local United Nations headquarters and other suitable places in order to establish a base of operation for the United Nations and the International Red Cross, in pursuance of the objectives mentioned in his statement of 7 December, and also to provide a temporary safe haven for the stranded evacuee groups. The Secretary-General requested the two Governments to take all necessary measures to help the United Nations and the International Red Cross in its endeavour for the duration of the hostilities. Eventually, four neutral zones were established in Dacca under the protection of the United Nations and the International Red Cross.

II. Special Representative of the Secretary-General

In paragraph 5 of resolution 307 (1971) the Security Council had authorized the Secretary-General "to appoint if necessary a special representative to lend his good offices for the solution of humanitarian problems."

In the light of developments in the sub-continent, and after consultation with the Secretary-General designate, Secretary-General U Thant decided, on 23 December, to appoint Mr. Vittorio Winspeare-Guicciardi, Under-Secretary-General and Director-General of the United Nations Office at Geneva, as his Special Representative. The Secretary-General so informed the Permanent Representatives of India and Pakistan on the evening of 23 December and asked for the concurrence and co-operation of their Governments in the mission of the special representative.

The Permanent Representative of Pakistan signified the concurrence of his Government in Mr. Winspeare's mission. The Permanent Representative of India informed the Secretary-General that the Indian Government would extend its co-operation to the special representative within the limits of its legal and practical possibilities.

In view of the urgent nature of some of the humanitarian problems in the sub-continent, the Secretary-General instructed Mr. Winspeare to proceed to the sub-continent immediately.[9] On 17 January 1972 the new Secretary-General, Mr. Waldheim, submitted a report to the Security Council on the good-offices mission of his Special Representative. According to this report, Mr. Winspeare decided to travel first to Delhi with a view to making the necessary arrangements for his onward journey to Dacca. He proposed to go to Islamabad after visiting Dacca. He departed on 27 December and arrived in Delhi the following morning.[10] After his arrival in India and during the following three days, Mr. Winspeare met senior officials of the Indian Government: the Foreign Minister, Mr. Swaran Singh; the Foreign Secretary, Mr. T.N. Kaul; the Principal Secretary to the Prime Minister, Mr. P.N. Haksar, and Mr. D.P. Dhar in his capacity as special envoy of India to "Bangladesh". Mr. Winspeare also had discussions with the Ambassador of Switzerland (in the role of Switzerland as protecting power for Pakistan interests in India) and met with United Nations officials in Delhi, including representatives of the High Commissioner for Refugees as focal point, UNICEF and others.

In the course of his initial talks, which were maintained at an exploratory level, Mr. Winspeare stressed that his function as Special Representative appointed under Security Council resolution 307 (1971) was to offer to the Governments and other authorities involved the services of his good-offices mission. It was for the parties concerned to decide how best to avail themselves of this particular instrument.

The background to the situation, as then seen from Delhi, emerged from these conversations, as did an indication of those problems which, in the Indian view, came within the scope of the mission. As had originally been communicated to the Secretary-General in the official response to his proposed appointment, the Government of India was willing to assist the mission within its legal and practical possibilities, but the limits of such assistance were governed by official insistence that India was not and should not be considered either an "occupying" or a "protecting power" in Bangladesh. Indian troops remained where they were at the invitation of the Dacca authorities and would remain there only so long as their presence was requested. The Government of India had recognized Bangladesh as an independent sovereign State. In consequence, the Indian Government did not presume to speak for the Dacca authorities, nor could it accept their responsibilities or pre-empt their right to decide; insofar as there were humanitarian problems in the region, the Bangladesh Government was the sole authority with which to confer.

In the light of this position and having been authorized by the Secretary-General to consult on an *ad hoc* basis with any authorities relevant to the situation in Dacca, Mr. Winspeare, as a practical matter, made the necessary arrangements for his onward travel through the representative of the Dacca authorities in Delhi. Mr. Winspeare flew, in the United Nations aircraft which had been placed at his disposal especially for the mission, via Calcutta to Dacca on 31 December.

In his meetings with the authorities in Dacca, Mr. Winspeare emphasized the humanitarian nature of his mission and stated explicitly that neither the mission as such nor his meetings with the authorities should or could possibly be interpreted as having implications for political recognition on the part of the United Nations since such questions laid within the exclusive competence of the Member States acting according to the Charter through the appropriate organs of the United Nations. The Secretary-General subsequently reported that this point was well understood.

On the evening of his arrival in Dacca Mr. Winspeare met the Foreign Minister, Mr. Abdus Samad. He also conferred with the Foreign Secretary, Mr. F.M.A. Fateh, and the Minister for Relief and Rehabilitation, Mr. A.H.M. Quamaruzzaman, and the Minister's senior advisers. In addition he had extensive meetings with United Nations personnel belonging to the United Nations relief operation in Dacca, representatives of UNICEF and the High Commissioner for Refugees, as well as the principal delegates of the Red Cross (Mr. Laurent Marti of the ICRC and Mr. Sven Lampell of the League of Red Cross Societies).

From these meetings in Dacca various points emerged relating to the issues covered by the terms of reference derived from the Security Council resolution 307 (1971) and to the letters submitted by the Government of Pakistan. With regard to the non-Bengali minorities, principally the inhabitants of Mohammadpur and Mirpur, it was stated that although isolated personal vendettas and criminal acts might still be taking place, the situation was rapidly returning to normal. While no one attempted to deny the tragic events which had taken place the Dacca authorities gave their assurance that under their auspices water and electricity were being supplied to Mohammadpur and Mirpur, and food was being distributed. As proof that there was nothing to hide, the authorities decided to invite the International Red Cross to visit the areas concerned and to report on conditions, and the following day they issued to the press an official communiqué to this effect.

Having been assured that he was free to observe the situation for himself, Mr. Winspeare, accompanied only by an aide, unescorted and in one case without previous warning, visited in a United Nations car both Mohammadpur and the Mirpur complex. He was able to satisfy himself that conditions at the time of his visit were tolerable, water and electricity supplies were functioning and some food distribution taking place. Protective measures by the very small number of military personnel stationed at check points along the road were evidently designed not to control movement out but to prevent trouble-makers from entering the non-Bengali enclaves; however the inhabitants of these areas clearly felt insecure about leaving. Representatives of the Red Cross also visited these and other non-Bengali areas. They confirmed Mr. Winspeare's impressions of the problems, but reported that conditions generally were acceptable.

With regard to Dr. Malik, the head, and other officials of the former régime, the Dacca authorities gave assurances that they were being correctly treated. This was confirmed by a visit undertaken by the principal delegates of the ICRC and the League of Red Cross Societies during Mr. Winspeare's stay in Dacca. It was the intention of the Dacca authorities to establish at the national level and at the sub-divisional level tribunals under which "collaborators" would be tried. For these tribunals judges were being sought who were to be men of eminence and international acceptability. Assurance was given that there would be no summary justice, and that the due process of law would be fully respected.

For their part, the Dacca authorities maintained that a humane solution to the difficulties of the non-Bengali minorities and other problems was related to certain specific issues. The first point concerned the release of Sheikh Mujibur Rahman. It was not merely a question of his release, but of his very early return to Dacca. The second point concerned Bengali civil servants employed by the Government in Islamabad; on the one hand these were needed for the new administration in Dacca, and on the other, there was concern for their position in West Pakistan. The third point concerned the Bengali minority in West Pakistan, a group said to number some 400,000. The fourth point concerned other Bengalis living in the West, especially students. Mr. Winspeare was specifically requested to transmit these concerns to Islamabad.

Finally, the Dacca authorities drew attention to the plight of their country. It was expected that the refugees who would return shortly from India, together with the many displaced persons in the country itself, would bring the total of those needing assistance to some 30 million. Aid from both bilateral and multilateral sources would be welcome. However, the authorities were most anxious to avoid the distribution of relief as such, since it tended to instil a sense of dependence in those receiving it. They wished to concentrate on rehabilitation and reconstruction. They asked Mr. Winspeare to convey to those concerned their hope that potential aid givers, both within the United Nations system and without, would respect their sovereignty and contribute assistance in response to requests from Dacca and through the appropriate Dacca authorities. Mr. Winspeare agreed to transmit these views to those within whose competence such matters lay.

On 3 January 1972, Mr. Winspeare returned from Dacca to Delhi before continuing to Islamabad. While in Delhi, he met again Mr. D.P. Dhar, who supported on behalf of the Government of India the main points expressed by the authorities in Dacca – in particular the vital significance attached to the release of Sheikh Mujibur Rahman.

Mr. Winspeare then travelled to Rawalpindi and Islamabad where he remained from 5 to 10 January. He had meetngs there with President Bhutto and also the Foreign Secretary, Mr. Sultan Mohammed Khan, the Defence Secretary, Mr. Ghiasuddin Ahmed and, at their request, with the Government of Pakistan committee for repatriation of prisoners of war and civilians – a joint committee with a membership drawn from the armed forces an civilian administration chaired by Major-General Ehsan Malik. Mr. Winspeare also spoke with United Nations officials and delegates of the International Red Cross.

In response to inquiries, he reported at these meetings on the situation in Dacca in the humanitarian context of his mission. He was asked in particular about the circumstances of the non-Bengali minorities living in Mohammadpur and Mirpur. He described the situation as he had seen it. The Pakistan Government published subsequently, as a press communiqué, a resumé of his findings with a view to reassuring public opinion.

Mr. Winspeare raised with the Islamabad authorities at a meeting on 6 January the points which had been stressed in Dacca. He laid particular emphasis on the vital and urgent need for the return to Dacca of Sheikh Mujibur Rahman. He then conveyed the other concerns of the Dacca authorities and received certain assurances on these points from the Government of Pakistan. He was invited to speak freely to Bengalis and inspect their circumstances himself.

In addition to the problem of non-Bengali minorities in the East, the Government of Pakistan had two preoccupations. The first concerned the persons and condition of Dr. Malik and 33 senior officials of the former East Pakistan régime. The second concerned the state of prisoners of war. Finally, with regard to both prisoners of war and civilians, they wished to see established a tracing service. Since all of these areas fell within the traditional responsibilities of the Red Cross, a fact of which the Government of Pakistan was aware, Mr. Winspeare communicated them to the Red Cross delegates in both Islamabad and subsequently in Delhi. He was assured that arrangements to respond to these requests were in hand. On a personal basis Mr. Winspeare also spoke to a few wives of prisoners of war who had asked to see him.

In the early hours of 8 January, Sheikh Mujibur was released unconditionally and left Rawalpindi for London on his way to Dacca. Before leaving Rawalpindi Mr. Winspeare was given to understand that the

Pakistan Cabinet had approved in principle the free movement of Bengali officials and others should they wish to leave the West. He was asked by the Pakistan authorities to transmit to Delhi their continuing concern for the non-Bengali minorities in the East and their hope for a conciliatory approach to problems of common concern.

On 11 January Mr. Winspeare met the Foreign Secretary of India in Delhi and repeated to him the points which he had been requested to transmit. He also spoke at length with the ICRC Commissioner for Red Cross action in the sub-continent and other Red Cross representatives. He reiterated to them the areas of concern and the wishes of the Pakistan authorities.

Before travelling to New York to report to the Secretary-General on his mission, Mr. Winspeare was in contact in Geneva with the High Commissioner for Refugees and senior representatives of the ICRC and the Secretary-General of the League of Red Cross Societies. He communicated to them for their information, the relevant findings of his mission in their respective fields of involvement and action. On 14 January he received a further request from the Government of Pakistan, identical to that transmitted to the Secretary-General by the Permanent Representative of Pakistan in New York "for help in securing relief for two million Pakistani nationals rendered homeless" by recent military activity especially in the border areas of Sind and Punjab in West Pakistan. Details of estimated requirements were requested of the Permanent Representative of Pakistan in Geneva. The appeal was also conveyed to the Red Cross authorities directly concerned, with a view to their appraising the needs on the spot, and was transmitted to the relevant United Nations organizations.

The Secretary-General subsequently reported that in Delhi, Dacca and Islamabad, Mr. Winspeare received full assistance from government officials at all levels and the nature and scope of his mission within the terms of reference were generally well understood. Without the willingness of the relevant authorities to use the good offices of the Special Representative of the Secretary-General for the solution of humanitarian problems, the mission would have been ineffective. The Secretary-General recorded his satisfaction and appreciation for the objective, wise and efficient way in which Mr. Winspeare had carried out his important and delicate task and said that he would keep under review the various humanitarian problems of concern to his mission and take further action if deemed desirable in pursuance of the relevant provisions of Security Council resolution 307 (1971).

Subsequently, in the light of developments relating to humanitarian problems, the Secretary-General decided to ask Mr. Winspeare to go again to the subcontinent. Among his reasons for this decision was a message of 7 February 1972 from President Bhutto of Pakistan which referred in particular to the President's concern for the non-Bengali population, especially in the townships of Mirpur and Mohammedpur near Dacca. The Secretary-General asked Mr. Winspeare to visit New Delhi, Dacca and Islamabad.

In this connection, the Secretary-General despatched a message to the Prime Minister of Bangladesh, Sheikh Mujibur Rahman, in which he referred to increasingly disturbing news which had been reaching the outside world from various sources concerning both the condition of some of these minorities and the dangers and deteriorating position in which they found themselves. The Secretary-General appealed to him to do everything possible to allay the fears which were widely felt for the well-being, safety and future of certain non-Bengali minorities. He asked also that the International Red Cross should receive the fullest co-operation in performing its functions.

Before leaving Geneva, Mr. Winspeare consulted the Red Cross representatives concerned, principally the Red Cross Commissioner for the subcontinent, Mr. Bignami. Mr. Winspeare departed on 9 February accompanied by an aide, who travelled with him throughout as on the previous occasion. Mr. Winspeare arrived in Delhi the early morning of 10 February and continued to Calcutta the same evening. In Delhi he met Mr. D.P. Dhar, who briefed him on the Indian view of the background to the then obtaining situation and its implications. Mr. Winspeare flew to Dacca on 11 February and was received the same afternoon by the Prime Minister, Sheikh Mujibur Rahman. The Prime Minister welcomed Mr. Winspeare to Dacca and assured him of his full co-operation. He provided some explanations and invited Mr. Winspeare to visit personally the Bihari enclaves at Mirpur and Mohammedpur, adding that he and his Government had nothing to hide and that Mr. Winspeare was free to go wherever he wished and to meet whomever he chose.

On 12 February, Mr. Winspeare, accompanied only by an aide and a Foreign Office official, toured the Mirpur complex and Mohammedpur. Mr. Winspeare was given every opportunity to go wherever he wished and he made a point of responding to suggestions received from Biharis on the spot. Before departing from Dacca on 13 February, Mr. Winspeare was again received by the Prime Minister, having the previous evening spoken with the Foreign Minister, Mr. Abdus Samad. At both these meetings, Mr. Winspeare stressed that the Government of Bangladesh had the primary and principal responsibility for law and order and the welfare of all population groups in the country. The United Nations and the Red Cross stood ready to assist and were already actively involved in providing aid. However, neither the Red Cross nor the United Nations could ensure the conditions necessary to the well-being of the minorities.

The Prime Minister made it clear that he was aware of his responsibility and anxious to offer non-Bengalis as well as Bengalis the possibility of full citizenship in Bangladesh.

Mr. Winspeare arrived in Delhi on the night of 13 February and flew the following morning to Islamabad. On 15 February he was received in the morning by the Foreign Secretary, Mr. Sultan Khan, and in the evening by President Bhutto. He described to them the situation as he had seen it in Mohammedpur and Mirpur and conveyed the preoccupations of Dacca and the solution proposed.

President Bhutto expressed his interest in the report on conditions in and around Dacca and said he was grateful for the use of Mr. Winspeare's good offices in transmitting certain proposals of Sheikh Mujibur.

With regard to the situation of the displaced persons in Punjab, Sind and Azad-Kashmir, Mr. Winspeare consulted many of those responsible for relief action in Pakistan, including the United Nations system officials involved, and he subsequently met the Red Cross delegate. The representatives of the international organizations and voluntary agencies were in agreement that emergency assistance was required for a large number of people and that, while the Government infrastructure and local resources were fully engaged and contributing actively, neither local nor national means were adequate to the magnitude of the need. In consequence, there was general support for an appeal to the international community to supplement the efforts of the League of Red Cross Societies which had already received impressive support for its action in the border area from a number of national societies. The United Nations system could be expected to play a major role in contributing from its own resources to the extent possible and more particularly in channelling assistance from donor governments.

On his return to Geneva, Mr. Winspeare was advised by the International Committee of the Red Cross that the Government of India had agreed to repatriate a number of severely wounded and otherwise incapacitated Pakistan prisoners of war. A second plane could carry seriously sick and wounded Indian prisoners of war home from Pakistan. The initial flights had been for 24 February and subsequent flights from India to Pakistan were planned to take place in March.

Mr. Winspeare also spoke to the responsible officials of the International Red Cross regarding the movement of persons from east to west and vice versa; he asked that they should continue to pursue their examination of possible arrangements pending the time that the authorities concerned should reach agreement. Following the second visit of Mr. Winspeare, the Secretary-General in his report to the Security Council, said that in pursuance of the responsibilities given to him in Security Council resolution 307 (1972), he would keep the humanitarian problems involved under continuous review and would try to take whatever steps might seem feasible to assist in their solution.

The Secretary-General subsequently reported to the Security Council and to the General Assembly on other humanitarian relief activities carried out under his auspices until the crisis had improved.[11]

III. Concluding observations

The following features of the exercise of humanitarian good offices in this case may be particularly noted:

(1) The Secretary-General took the unprecedented step of initiating his activities in East Pakistan even without any supporting resolution from any United Nations organ because he felt that his obligations under the Charter must include any humanitarian action which he could take to save the lives of large numbers of human beings.

(2) The Secretary-General filled a vacuum created by the failure of United Nations organs to act in the face of a serious situation of gross violations of human rights.

(3) An agreement on conditions for the effective discharge of the functions of the United Nations East Pakistan Relief Operation was concluded by an exchange of letters between the Secretary-General and the Permanent Representative of Pakistan.

(4) The Secretary-General took the unusual step of reporting to the President of the Security Council on a question which had not been in-

scribed on the Council's agenda. The Secretary-General acted "under the broad terms of Article 99 of the United Nations Charter which provides that 'The Secretary-General may bring to the attention of the Security Council any matter which in his opinion may threaten the maintenance of international peace and security.' "[12]

(5) While acting discreetly for the most part, the Secretary-General did not hesitate to speak out when he felt that this was necessary. He did so in the case of Sheikh Mujibur Rahman, who had been taken into custody in Pakistan and he also expressed his views candidly to the Security Council and the General Assembly.

(6) The activities of his Special Representative pioneered efforts in the exercise of humanitarian good offices. The Special Representative made it known to the parties that it was for them to decide how best to avail themselves of his good offices. He was guided by their understandings of his terms of reference. He received the concerns of each party and transmitted them to the others concerned. He made visits on the spot unaccompanied by government representatives. He was forthright in stressing "that the Government of Bangladesh had the primary and principal responsibility for law and order and the welfare of all population groups in the country," a responsibility which the Prime Minister accepted; and he co-operated actively with the representatives of other humanitarian agencies such as the International Committee of the Red Cross.

(7) The initiatives and the activities of the Secretary-General were supported by the General Assembly and the Security Council.

(8) As former Under-Secretary-General Bradford Morse, at present Administrator of UNDP, has remarked: "significant legal issues" were raised by the programmes initiated by the Secretary-General: "The first issue is the question of the precedential value of the case. The Secretary-General initiated the beginning of a body of law by relying explicitly upon the statement of fundamental purposes in the Charter, and his responsibility as the executive of the Organization, to ensure that human well-being was protected and humanitarian principles upheld."[13]

NOTES

1. J. Salzberg, "UN Prevention of Human Rights Violations: The Bangladesh Case," 27 International Organization (1973), pp. 115-127, at p. 115.
2. A/PV.2003, p. 11, cited in Salzberg, *op. cit.*, p. 124.

3. UN press release SG/1763; IHA/93, 17 November 1971.
4. G. Gottlieb, "The United Nations and Emergency Humanitarian Assistance in India – Pakistan," 66 AJIL (1972), pp. 362-365 at p. 364.
5. S/10410, p. 2.
6. UN press release SG/1763; IHA/93, 17 November 1971.
7. S/10410, pp. 3-4.
8. A/8401/Add.1, para. 191.
9. Report of the Secretary-General concerning the implementation of Security Council resolution 307 (1971), S/10473, 25 December 1971.
10. The account which follows is based on the Report of the Secretary-General on the Good Offices Mission of his Special Representative for Humanitarian Problems under Security Council Resolution 307 (1971) – S/10512 and Add.1.
11. See the following reports of the Secretary-General: A/8662/Add. 1, 2 and 3 (1972); S/10539 (1972); S/10539, Add. 1 and 2 (1972); S/10539, Add. 3 (1972); A/8996/ Add. 1-4 (1973); S/10853 (and Corr.1), Add. 1 and 2 (1973), S/10853, Add. 3 and 4 (1973).
12. S/10410, para. 1.
13. B. Morse, "International Humanitarian Rescue Operation," 157 RCADI (1977, IV), pp. 150-194, at p. 150.

Chapter VII

CASE STUDY: CONFERENCE ON REFUGEES AND DISPLACED PERSONS IN SOUTH-EAST ASIA (1979)

The efforts made by Secretary-General Kurt Waldheim to deal with the humanitarian problems of refugees and displaced persons in South-East Asia, particularly the convening of an international meeting on these problems in 1979, offer examples of daring and imaginative exercise of humanitarian good offices from which much can be learned for the future. In the following case study the efforts of the Secretary-General will first be outlined, following which their significance will be analyzed.

I. The Conference

Between 1975 and 1979 there was a steady movement of people out of Indo-China. Nearly a million people left their countries, half of whom were received by the neighbouring countries of South-East Asia. The Secretary-General made frequent humanitarian appeals with regard to this situation. For example, on 2 December 1978, a United Nations spokesman made the following statement on behalf of the Secretary-General: "The Secretary-General is deeply concerned at the deteriorating situation of the refugees in South-East Asia. This humanitarian tragedy demands the compassion and the practical assistance of the world community. The United Nations High Commissioner for Refugees has been making all possible efforts to alleviate this appalling situation, and I appreciate the assistance already afforded by a number of Governments. However, in view of the continuing human tragedy which we are witnessing, I feel compelled to appeal to all Governments once again to consider urgently what measures they can take to assist these thousands of helpless people, who are now without hope for the future."[1]

By the end of 1978, the problem had begun to reach alarming proportions.[2] In the month of April 1979 alone, more than 25,000 "boat-people'' had arrived in the various countries of the region and tens of thousands had crossed the border into Thailand. During his visit to the area in April and May of 1979 the Secretary-General was able to obtain first-hand information concerning the situation and to discuss with the Heads of Governments directly involved measures that could be undertaken to alleviate a potentially explosive problem. In his discussions with the Heads of Government of Malaysia, Viet-Nam, China, Japan, the Philippines, Indonesia, Singapore and Thailand, the Secretary-General expressed the great concern of the United Nations about developments in the region and, in particular, his concern over the humanitarian problem of refuges in South-East Asia. He also expressed understanding of the problems faced by the countries of the region in trying to cope with the large increase in the number of refugees arriving as against the much lesser number who were departing for countries of resettlement.

On his return from the region, the Secretary-General decided to designate a senior official to follow developments closely from the region and to report to him on a regular basis on the humanitarian problems in all their aspects. On 11 June 1979, he appointed Ambassador I. Turkman of Turkey as his Special Representative for Humanitarian Affairs in South-East Asia to perform this function.

Considering the fact that the situation was rapidly assuming crisis proportions, and in support of the best efforts of the United Nations High Commissioner for Refugees, other agencies and governments to alleviate suffering and to find lasting solutions, the Secretary-General decided to send an appeal to the heads of a number of interested and concerned governments requesting their help and co-operation in urgently coping with this problem. In his communication of 24 May 1979, he emphasized the need for strict adherence to the internationally accepted humanitarian principle of asylum. Without a generous policy of at least temporary asylum, he pointed out, there could be no basis for humanitarian action. While appreciating the heavy burden of the countries of South-East Asia, he appealed to them to grant asylum while the United Nations High Commissioner for Refugees pursued his efforts to find places for their resettlement. He called on them to increase their financial contributions to the Office of the High Commissioner and to join in the search for lasting solutions by making an increased number of resettlement places available to enable those waiting in the camps to start a new and productive life.

Even as the governments were responding to the Secretary-General's appeal by increasing their contributions to the United Nations High Commissioner for Refugees and by offering limited possibilities of resettlement for the refugees, the situation continued to deteriorate. In a letter dated 31 May 1979, the Prime Minister of the United Kingdom of Great Britain and Northern Ieland proposed to the Secretary-General that an international conference be convened to deal with the problem. At the Tokyo Economic Summit Conference of industrialized countries, a special statement on Indo-Chinese refugees was issued on 28 June 1979, in which the heads of State and governments requested the Secretary-General to convene a conference as soon as possible with a view to attaining concrete and positive results. The twelfth Ministerial Meeting of the Association of South-East Asian Nations held in Bali, Indonesia, on 30 June 1979, supported the proposal for the convening of an international conference on Indo-Chinese refugees under the auspices of the United Nations Secretary-General, who also received suggestions from a number of the governments supporting the proposal of the Prime Minister of the United Kingdom of Great Britain and Northern Ireland and calling upon the Secretary-General to take up this matter and to hold a conference on Indo-Chinese refugees under the auspices of the United Nations.

Intensive consultations were conducted by the Secretary-General and, at his request, by UNHCR with a large number of interested governments to determine the most effective framework within which such a meeting could usefully be held with a view to achieving concrete results. Following these consultations, the Secretary-General informed governments of his intention to convene a meeting at Geneva on 20 July 1979, of governments in a position to make a contribution to a solution of the problem. He emphasized that the meeting should concentrate on the humanitarian aspects of the problem and should produce additional support to enable UNHCR to enlarge its efforts to meet the problem. The Secretary-General proposed that governments be represented at the ministerial level.

The meeting took place on 20 and 21 July 1979. Sixty-five governments attended, several other governments attended as observers and interested intergovernmental organizations and groupings of non-governmental organizations were also represented. In his opening statement, the Secretary-General emphasized that the purpose of the meeting should be to seek concrete ways of alleviating a crisis, the results of which would literally involve the life or death of many thousands of human beings. He said that the spectre of men, women and children cast on the waters to drift and drown and of others on land abandoned to famine and despair had been a deeply moving experience. Over 350,000 refugees remained in the ASEAN countries and Hong Kong, and there had been a steady increase in the number of new refugees arriving in those countries. It was, therefore, essential that the rest of the world should act in a decisive way to ease this tremendous burden imposed upon those countries. Such action, he said, would enable those States to adhere to the principle of first asylum and to contribute within the limit of their possibilities to an overall action that would lead to desirable solutions for the refugees.

The Secretary-General stressed that in dealing with this issue, everyone should be aware of the fact that the refugee problem had political roots. He felt, however, that finding adequate solutions to the humanitarian aspects of the question would surely also help contribute to the creation of an atmosphere in which other aspects of the problem were more likely to be resolved. In the meanwhile, the Secretary-General said that he hoped that, as a result of the meeting, there would not only be a significant increase in commitments for resettlement opportunities and in contributions of funds, but that specific suggestions would also be made as to how the programme of action could most quickly and successfully be translated into reality.

The Secretary-General emphasized the need for everyone concerned to realize the inter-relationship of obligations and responsibilities on the part of the countries of origin, those of first asylum and those of final settlement. The countries of origin had an obligation to respect the right of emigration and family reunification, while avoiding any action leading to the departure of their people under conditions which put their lives in jeopardy. These countries also had the responsibility of co-operating fully with the United Nations High Commissioner for Refugees and the other countries concerned to ensure an orderly outflow with the prospect of a safe journey. Since the countries of first asylum were developing countries confronted with serious economic and social constraints, it was essential that countries outside the area assume the principal responsibility for resettlement. The Secretary-General emphasized that, while the countries of initial arrival were expected to respect fully the principle of first asylum for refugees coming there by land and sea, they in turn expected an assurance that they would not be burdened with the residual problems and that no refugees would stay in their countries for more than a specified period. The countries of final settlement needed to set up local facilities in the region to expedite this process and were faced with significant financial problems.

The meeting had before it a paper prepared by the United Nations High Commissioner for Refugees which highlighted the various aspects of the problem.[3] The proceedings were marked by a spirit of co-operation, and a number of countries put forward concrete proposals. Offers of places of resettlement, of processing centres and of funds were made. The discussions at the meeting clarified a number of issues and a consensus also emerged on the framework of a plan of action: "In the first place, it was agreed that urgent efforts should be undertaken to reduce the backlog by resettlement on a larger and faster scale than hitherto. It was clearly understood that this movement should cover land cases as well as boat cases. Secondly, the Memorandum of Understanding concluded between the Socialist Republic of Viet-Nam and the United Nations High Commissioner for Refugees for the orderly departure from Viet-Nam of individuals to reunite with their families, as well as other cases involving humanitarian considerations, should be carried out, but not at the expense of those in the camps in South-East Asia. Thirdly, a major breakthrough was achieved on the establishment of processing centres. The availability of these facilities would make a direct and important contribution to reducing the hardships pertaining to the exodus of refugees and would provide a major reassurance to countries of first asylum. Work has already started on Galang Island, offered by Indonesia. The Government of the Philippines has also provided a new site for 50,000 refugees, the costs for which will be met by the United Nations High Commissioner for Refugees within the limits of available funds. Special attention was also paid to the question of rescue at sea for the so-called 'boat-people'. The High Commissioner for Refugees has already taken steps towards mobilizing international co-operative efforts to achieve this by ensuring that ships in the area are alerted to the vital need to rescue refugees in distress. Finally, the general principles of asylum and *non-refoulement* were endorsed."[4]

The Secretary-General had stressed that much of the success of any plan of action would depend on a substantial reduction of the disorderly exodus of thousands of persons from their homelands. During the meeting there was considerable discussion of the possibility of a moratorium on "illegal departures". Following extensive consultations, the Government of Viet-Nam gave assurances that, for a reasonable period of time, it would make every effort to stop illegal departures and to co-operate with UNHCR in expanding the seven-point programme designed to bring departures within orderly and safe channels.

The Secretary-General stated also that he would be following developments in the area personaly, and through his Special Representative for Humanitarian Affairs in South-East Asia. The role of the Special Representative would be, in particular, to maintain close contacts with the governments concerned.

In his closing remarks to the meeting, the Secretary-General observed: "When the idea of a conference was first launched, there were considerable doubts about its chances of achieving its purpose. There was even the fear that this gathering could stray into a sterile and acrimonious debate which would aggravate even further the political atmosphere surrounding the refugee crisis. I think we can say with gratification that this has not been the case. On the contrary, the very fact that the international community was about to focus its attention on the humanitarian issues in South-East Asia has created a momentum of its own. Before the Conference started, several countries increased substantially the number of resettlement places for refugees and their financial commitments. In addition, intensive contacts took place on a bilateral and multilateral basis to find ways and means of alleviating the suffering of the refugees in the area."[5]

The Secretary-General later assessed the results of the meeting in a report to the General Assembly as follows: "The Geneva Meeting has had a definite impact on the course of events in South-East Asia. Its conclusions reflected a consensus on the need to mobilize all efforts to alleviate human suffering. A combination of policy adjustments and intensified international action has created conditions under which a certain degree of optimism might be permissible. However, the new influx from Kampuchea has reminded all concerned of the fragility of the situation, so long as the root causes have not been resolved. The problem can be contained and gradually eased only if countries of origin, of first asylum and of final resettlement continue to adhere to the conclusions of the Geneva Meeting."[6]

The Secretary-General continued to act for humanitarian relief in this area. On 19 October 1979, for example, he appealed for emergency relief to the people of Kampuchea. On 26 October 1979, the Secretary-General sent the following message to the governments of all Member

States of the United Nations and the specialized agencies: "I have the honour to refer to the appeal I made on 19 October 1979 for emergency relief to the people of Kampuchea, who are facing suffering, misery and deprivation on a massive scale, including disastrous shortages of food, medical supplies, shelter and transport. There is appalling malnutrition, particularly among the children, 90 percent of whom are severely malnourished. The United Nations Childrens' Find and the International Committee of the Red Cross have been collaborating in mounting the first phase of the relief effort. The World Food Programme, the Food and Agriculture Organization and the United Nations High Commissioner for Refugees are already developing substantially increased programmes to meet this need. I have therefore decided to convene a pledging conference at United Nations Headquarters on Monday, 5 November 1979, at 10.30 a.m. for Governments interested in announcing contributions to the programme being carried out by the United Nations system of organizations for emergency humanitarian relief to the people of Kampuchea. The purpose of this undertaking is to obtain commitments for assistance on humanitarian grounds. I would be most grateful if your excellency could inform me whether your Government will participate in this pledging conference and at what level."[7]

II. General observations

The above-mentioned outline of the efforts made by Secretary-General Waldheim to deal with the humanitarian problems of refugees and displaced persons in South-East Asia provide various insights into the exercise of humanitarian good offices. In the first place, the Secretary-General quietly collected the facts and expressed concern in relation thereto. Second, the Secretary-General undertook visits on the spot with a view to familiarizing himself with the problems as well as to speaking with government leaders concerned. Third, appeals were made by the Secretary-General on behalf of the refugees and displaced persons; at the same time, appeals were made to the Secretary-General to act on their behalf. Fourth, the Secretary-General designated a special representative to assist him in dealing with the humanitarian problems in South-East Asia. Fifth, the meeting on refugees and displaced persons in South-East Asia was convened by the Secretary-General on his own authority, although there were some informal consultations on the matter. Sixth, the Secretary-General selected the countries to be invited; he drew up the agenda of the meeting and he chaired it personally. Seventh, the Secretary-General succeeded in stamping a humanitarian frame upon the deliberations, which otherwise could have taken political and controversial turns. Eighth, following the initiative of the Secretary-General in convening the meeting, further aid and assistance was generated in dealing with the humanitarian problems of refugees and displaced persons in South-East Asia. Ninth, the Secretary-General showed some nimbleness in dealing with a situation involving a potential conflict of humanitarian principles. As he was subsequently asked at a press conference: "You stated in your opening remarks that you were gratified that Viet-Nam had given assurances that it would curb what they call illegal departures. I believe the Charter of Human Rights of the United Nations, of which Viet-Nam is a member, states that the right to travel and the right of residence are fundamental human rights. Should the United Nations be gratified that Viet-Nam has undertaken to curb these basic human rights?"[8] To this, the Secretary-General replied: "You have quoted one part of my statement, not another in which I referred expressly to this point. I said we are in a dilemma. On the one hand we want to maintain the principles enshrined in the Charter and in the human rights convention, the right of asylum, the right of departure, etc. On the other hand, we ask that the exodus should be reduced or even stopped because the neighbouring countries cannot handle hundreds of thousands of refugees any more, and we do not have enough places in order to achieve the final resettlement. There is a dilemma and there is a certain contradiction. I fully understand this, but please be assured that we will do our best to handle the matter in such a way that we preserve the right of the refugees to leave if they so wish. On the other hand, we cannot accept, and this is the purpose of this measure, that these people should leave and drown in the sea. We must make sure that these people leave under conditions which, until now, have not been assured because, as we know, thousands of them have died on the seas. So this is the problem we are facing. We try to handle it in the best possible way, keeping in mind the principles enshrined in the Charter and in other international instruments."[9]

Tenth, the Secretary-General provided a way of dealing with a massive humanitarian problem and thereby offered a contribution by the Organization which might otherwise have been very difficult to bring about. Eleventh, the activities of the Secretary-General were expressly endorsed by the General Assembly at its thirty-fourth session held in 1979. The General Assembly commended the Secretary-General for his initiative in convening the meeting and for his Chairmanship of it, and requested the Secretary-General "to continue to follow the situation closely and to submit a report to the Member States if the situation so requires."[10]

NOTES

1. UN press release, SG/SM/2650, 2 December 1978.
2. The factual account which follows is based on the report of the meeting which the Secretary-General submitted to the thirty-fourth session of the General Assembly – A/34/627 and Corr.1.
3. A/34/627, Annex 1.
4. A/34/627, para. 15.
5. UN press release SG/SM/379, 21 July 1979, p. 1.
6. A/34/627, para. 51.
7. UN press release SG/SM/2816 – 26 October 1979.
8. UN press release SG/Ref/8, p. 4.
9. *Ibid.*
10. GA resolution 34/62.

Chapter VIII

CASE STUDY: HUMANITARIAN GOOD OFFICES IN CYPRUS

The United Nations Secretary-General's exercise of humanitarian good offices in relation to the situation in Cyprus provides various fascinating insights into the institution of good offices. In the first place, a combination of political and humanitarian questions were addressed at the same time. Second, there have been express and many-faceted mandates to the Secretary-General for the exercise of his good offices, addressed to him by the Security Council as well as the General Assembly and in relation, as we have just said, to political as well as humanitarian issues. Third, a combination of related efforts can be seen, on the part of the Secretary-General, his special representatives, peace-keeping forces, the United Nations High Commissioner for Refugees and an investigator designated by the Secretary-General to serve on a commission on the question of missing persons in Cyprus. Fourth, interesting legal questions have arisen regarding the competence of the Secretary-General in the face of reluctance by one of the parties concerned in the situation to accept an approach sought by the General Assembly.

I. The mandates

In examining the mandates entrusted to the Secretary-General we will be concerned primarily with questions in the humanitarian field, or which relate to the humanitarian aspects of the exercise of good offices by the Secretary-General. As far back as on 4 March 1964, the Security Council, by its resolution 186 (1964) recommended that the Secretary-General designate, in agreement with the Government of Cyprus and the Governments of Greece, Turkey and the United Kingdom, a mediator who shall use his best endeavours with the representatives of the communities and also with the aforesaid four Governments, for the purpose of promoting a peaceful solution and an agreed settlement of the problem confronting Cyprus, in accordance with the Charter of the United Nations, having in mind the well-being of the people as a whole and the preservation of international peace and security. It is interesting to note the formulation used in this resolution, namely, the reference to the "best endeavours of the Secretary-General" for in recent resolutions of the General Assembly we see these terms being used again, in relation to requests to the Secretary-General to use his efforts with regard to arbitrary and summary executions.[1]

Eleven years after the passage of Security Council resolution 186 (1964), in the light of the situation then existing in Cyprus, the Security Council, on 12 March 1975, adopted resolution 367 (1975) in which it requested the Secretary-General to undertake a new mission of good offices and, to that end, to convene the parties under new agreed procedures and place himself personally at their disposal, so that the resumption, the intensification and the progress of comprehensive negotiations, carried out in a reciprocal spirit of understanding and of moderation under his personal auspices and with his direction as appropriate, might thereby be facilitated. The Security Council called upon the representatives of the two communities in Cyprus to co-operate closely with the Secretary-General in the discharge of this new mission of good offices and asked them to accord high priority to their negotiations. Furthermore, the Security Council called upon all the parties concerned to refrain from any action which might jeopardize the negotiations between the representatives of the two communities and to take steps which will facilitate the creation of the climate necessary for the success of those negotiations.

The preceding year, the Security Council, by resolution 361 (1974) had already called upon all parties "to do everything in their power to alleviate human suffering, to ensure the fundamental respect of human rights for every person and to refrain from all action likely to aggravate the situation." It had also expressed its grave concern at the plight of the refugees and other persons displaced as a result of the situation in Cyprus and urged the parties concerned, in conjunction with the Secretary-General, to search for peaceful solutions to the problems of refugees, to take appropriate measures to provide for their relief and welfare and to permit persons who wish to do so to return to their homes in safety. The Security Council had further requested the Secretary-General to continue to provide emergency United Nations humanitarian assistance to all parts of the population of the island in need of such assistance.

The good-offices mandate extended to the Secretary-General by Security Council resolution 367 has been subsequently renewed by successive resolutions of the Council.

The good-offices mandates entrusted to the Secretary-General by the Security Council have also been expressly endorsed in a series of resolutions of the General Assembly, which has also added good-offices mandates of its own. For example, the General Assembly, by its resolution 32/128 of 16 December 1977 on the question of Missing Persons in Cyprus, requested the Secretary-General to provide his good offices, through his Special Representative in Cyprus, to support the establishment of an investigatory body, with the participation of the International Committee of the Red Cross, which would be in a position to function impartially, effectively and speedily so as to resolve the problem without undue delay. The General Assembly also invited the parties concerned to continue co-operating in the establishment of the investigatory body and to work out the modalities with a view to activating it expeditiously. The following year, on 20 December 1978, the General Assembly, regretting the delay in the implementation of its earlier resolutions on the question of the missing persons in Cyprus, adopted resolution 33/172, by which it urged the establishment of an investigatory body under the chairmanship of a representative of the Secretary-General with the co-operation of the International Committee of the Red Cross, which would be in a position to function impartially, effectively and speedily so as to resolve the problem without undue delay. The Assembly stated that the representative of the Secretary-General shall be empowered, in case of disagreement, to reach a binding independent opinion which shall be implemented. The General Assembly called upon the parties to co-operate fully with the investigatory body and, to this effect, to appoint their representatives thereto forthwith, and requested the Secretary-General to continue to provide his good offices through his Special Representative in Cyprus, to support the establishment of the investigatory body. The mission of good offices in relation to the problem of missing persons in Cyprus was recently renewed by the General Assembly, at its thirty-sixth session when, by resolution 36/164 it requested the Secretary-General to continue to provide his good offices for the unhindered functioning of the Committee.

II. Implementation

At the beginning of this chapter, we remarked upon some of the interesting characteristics of the exercise of humanitarian good offices in relation to the situation in Cyprus. We shall now examine some of these issues further. We may mention first of all, the personal involvement of the Secretary-General. In a report of 27 May 1981 submitted to the Security Council, Secretary-General Waldheim reported: ". . . I have continued, as part of the exercise of my good offices, to maintain direct personal contact with the parties at appropriate levels with a view to facilitating the conduct of the negotiations. In this connexion, I held talks in New York in December 1980 with Foreign Minister Rolandis; with Dr. Atakol, the spokesman for Foreign Affairs of the Turkish Cypriot community, and with the Permanent Representatives of Turkey and Greece to the United Nations. During my visit to the summit meeting of the Organization of the Islamic Conference at Taif, Saudi Arabia, I conferred on 25 January with His Excellency, Mr. Denktash, and on the next day with Mr. Ulusu, Prime Minister of Turkey, and Foreign Minister Turkmen. On my way back from Taif, I stopped over in Athens for a talk with Mr. Mitzotakis, Foreign Minister of Greece. When visiting New Delhi in February 1981 for the commemorative meeting of the Foreign Ministers of the Non-Aligned Countries, I had occasion to meet again with Mr. Rolandis. These talks enabled me and my Special Representative in Cyprus to explore the possible outlines of a partial interim agreement that might be negotiated by the interlocutors as a first step toward a comprehensive settlement."[2]

While maintaining his personal involvement, the Secretary-General has used various special representatives to assist him in the discharge of his good offices. An idea of the role of these special representatives can be obtained from the reports submitted regularly by the Secretary-General to the General Assembly and to the Security Council. For example, the Secretary-General reported to the General Assembly in 1980, that it was envisaged that Mr. Gobbi, his Special Representative at the intercommunal talks "would open the negotiations by delivering a statement designed to overcome the controversy between the parties concerning the implementation of the high-level agreements of 12 February 1977 and 19 May 1979 . . . At the meeting held on 9 August (1980), Mr. Gobbi delivered an opening statement on my behalf. The statement outlined my understanding of the common ground that had been worked out in the course of the consultations which had taken place over the preceding months, and listed the four items to be discussed in the inter-communal talks . . . Since then, there have been nine meetings of the resumed inter-communal talks and each of the four items has been discused . . . All meetings were held in private, in the presence of my Special Representative."[3]

The efforts of the Secretary-General and his Special Representatives to facilitate negotiations between the Cypriot communities may be particularly noted. In a report of 2 April 1980, submitted to the General Assembly, the Secretary-General stated "I and my Special Representative in Cyprus have . . . continued intensive consultations with all concerned within the framework of my good offices mission, and following the approach outlined in my reports (see A/34/620, paras. 12-14; S/13672, paras. 48-50), so as to circumvent the difficulties that were encountered in June 1979 and get down to concrete negotiations on the substantive aspects of the Cyprus problem. I suggested that the elements of that approach might be embodied in a statement to be delivered by my representative at the opening of the resumed round of talks, outlining my understanding of the common ground that had been worked out in the course of the consultations. The statement would simply be noted by the interlocutors, who might if desired put on record their views on the matters covered in it, and would then go on to the consideration of the substantive aspects of the Cyprus problem."[4]

The humanitarian objectives of the good offices of the Secretary-General and his Special Representatives emerge clearly from a statement in his report of 8 November 1979, submitted to the General Assembly: "In pursuance of the mission of good offices entrusted to me by the Security Council, and in the framework of the negotiating process called for by the General Assembly, I have endeavoured to promote a freely negotiated, just and lasting settlement of the Cyprus problem based on the legitimate interests of the two communities."[5]

Humanitarian functions are also performed by the United Nations Peacekeeping Force in Cyprus (UNFICYP). In his report of 27 May 1981, to the Security Council, on the United Nations operation in Cyprus, the Secretary-General reported that:

"22. UNFICYP continues to discharge humanitarian functions for the Greek Cypriots remaining in the north. Temporary visits to the south for family and other reasons continue on an *ad hoc* basis, both directly and through the good offices of UNFICYP . . . .

26. UNFICYP officers, in performing certain humanitarian tasks in the north, continue to have the opportunity of speaking in private with Greek Cypriots living there.

27. Periodic visits by UNFICYP officials to the Turkish Cypriots living in the south are continuing and contacts with their relatives in the north are maintained.

38. As part of its efforts to restore normal conditions, UNFICYP continues to facilitate economic activities in the area between the lines, especially by providing escorts for farmers in sensitive areas. During the period under review, economic activities in the buffer zone have increased."[6]

At the request of the Secretary-General, the United Nations High Commissioner for Refugees has provided assistance to displaced and needy persons in Cyprus in the capacity of co-ordinator of United Nations Humanitarian Assistance for Cyprus. UNFICYP has supported the High Commissioner's relief programme by, for example, delivering food supplies and other items. UNFICYP also provides emergency medical services, including medical evacuation by ambulance or helicopter. Delivery of medicines is made on a regular basis and emergency requests for medicines are met.[7]

Thus far, the inter-action of four entities has been seen, all of which render some form of humanitarian good offices in Cyprus: the Secretary-General; two emanations from the Secretary-General – his Special Representative and the Co-ordinator for United Nations Humanitarian Assistance for Cyprus; and UNFICYP.

There is still a fifth entity, partly representing a third emanation from the Secretary-General, which also renders humanitarian good offices in Cyprus. It was seen above that the Secretary-General had been requested by the General Assembly to use his good offices to support the establishment of an investigatory body on the question of the missing persons in Cyprus. In his report to the General Assembly of 20 November 1981, the Secretary-General reported that "as regards the question of setting up an investigatory body concerning the tracing of and accounting for missing persons, agreement was reached in April 1981 on the establishment of a Committee on Missing Persons in Cyprus. The Committee consists of three members, one 'humanitarian person' from each community and one official – Mr. Pilloud – selected for this purpose by the International Committee of the Red Cross, with the agreement of both sides, and appointed by me."[8] There are many interesting aspects of the Secretary-General's position vis-à-vis this Committee on Missing Persons which may merit further reflection. In the first place, as we have already seen, the General Assembly by its resolution 33/172 of 20 December 1978, had sought to empower the representative of the Secretary-General in cases of disagreement, "to reach a binding, independent opinion, which shall be implemented." When this resolution was being considered in the Third Committee of the General Assembly, on 12 December 1978, the Turkish Representative sought the opinion of the Legal Counsel on the following questions:

"First, does the Legal Counsel think that a General Assembly resolution can confer the role of compulsory arbitrator upon the Secretary-General or his representative in the absence of the explicit consent of both sides and even of the Secretary-General himself?

Secondly, has there been any precedent to this effect?

Thirdly, will such a provision be in conformity with established international practice?"[9] These questions were repeated in a letter dated 13 December 1978, which the Turkish Representative sent to the Secretary-General. On 15 December 1978, the Legal Counsel sent the following answers to the Turkish Ambassador in a letter:

". . . Before responding to the questions raised by the Permanent Representative of Turkey in his letter addressed to the Secretary-General dated 13 December 1978, it is useful first of all to characterise the particular procedure which is envisaged in the resolution adopted by the Third Committee. The 'investigatory body' to be established by this resolution is in the nature of an *ad hoc* body of inquiry or fact-finding rather than of arbitration or judicial settlement. The procedure, in other words, is diplomatic, not judicial, in nature. It follows from this that the assimilation of this body to a process of arbitration is not approprite. It is clear, however, that the procedure envisaged has the purpose of settling a dispute, a term which in its widest sense may be understood as a disagreement on a point of law or fact. All dispute settlement procedures, whether diplomatic or judicial, are based on the consent of the parties. In the light of the foregoing, it is possible to formulate the following answers to the questions raised:

1. In the absence of the explicit consent of both sides, the General Assembly cannot confer upon the Secretary-General the role of a compulsory arbitrator.

2. There is no precedent for conferring such a role upon the Secretary-General in the absence of the consent of the parties.

3. Established international practice in the matter of dispute settlement attaches primacy to the consent of the parties. Such consent must be express and not implied.''[10]

When the draft resolution was considered in the plenary of the General Assembly on 20 December 1978, the Turkish representative read the above answers to the meeting and appealed to those delegations that voted for the draft in the Third Committee to reconsider the matter. The representative of Cyprus replied that the Assembly was examining the recommendation of its humanitarian committee and was dealing with the human suffering of the relatives of missing persons in Cyprus. With a view to alleviating their plight, the establishment of an investigatory body to find out about them was sought. There was therefore no arbitration and no question of settlement of disputes.[11] In the end, the General Assembly proceeded to adopt the resolution as introduced, granting the powers indicated to the Secretary-General. Later, however, agreement was reached among the parties on the establishment of a Committee on Missing Persons in Cyprus and the Secretary-General was never called upon to act upon this aspect of the resolution. The Secretary-General reported to the Security Council on 27 May 1981 that he and his Representatives ''. . . continued their efforts aimed at bridging the gap between the two sides with regard to the establishment of an investigatory body for the tracing of and accounting for missing persons (S/14275, para. 31). As a result, Mr. Gobbi was able to announce on my behalf on 22 April 1981 that agreement had been reached by the two sides on the terms of reference for the establishment of a Committee on Missing Persons in Cyprus. The Committee wil consist of three members including one humanitarian person representing each of the two communities. The third member will be an official selected by the International Committee of the Red Cross for that purpose with the agreement of both sides, and appointed by the Secretary-General. The selection of Mr. Claude Pilloud having been agreed to by both sides, I intend to appoint him to that post at an early date.''[12] The Secretary-General reported further to the General Assembly on 20 November 1981 that ''procedural difficulties have made it impossible so far, for the Committee to embark upon its substantive work, despite intensive efforts by the members of the Committee and all possible assistance provided by my Representatives, including informal exchanges of views at United Nations Headquarters to facilitate the work of the Committee."[13] However, he did feel that "the intensive consultations and informal exchanges of views undertaken by my Representatives for the past few weeks appear to have improved the prospects of having the Committee resolve the outstanding procedural issues that have blocked its progress."[14]

III. General observations

The exercise of humanitarian good offices in Cyprus is generally considered by the parties concerned, to be the most successful part of the United Nations efforts with respect to the Cyprus situation. They have been accepted by the parties concerned and have brought relief, aid and assistance to thousands of persons. This case study shows once again that even in a situation with complex political dimensions, it is possible to provide humanitarian good offices successfully. This is a feature which was also seen in the East Pakistan (Bangladesh) situation and with regard to the refugees and displaced persons in South-East Asia.[15]

NOTES

1. See, e.g., GA resolutions 35/172 and 36/22.
2. S/14490, para. 44.
3. A/35/659, paras. 3-4.
4. A/35/161, para. 3.
5. A/34/620, para. 27.
6. S/14490, paras. 22, 26, 27 and 28.
7. S/14490, paras. 38, 40.
8. A/36/702, para. g.
9. Taken from text of original statement by Turkish representative.
10. A/33/PV.90, pp. 93-94.
11. A/33/PV.90, p. 106.
12. S/14490, para. 46.
13. A/36/702, para. 8.
14. *Ibid.*, para. 11.
15. See further on the Cyprus situation, R.St.J. Macdonald, "International Law and the Conflict in Cyprus," XIX CYIL (1981), pp. 3-49. J.A. Stegenga, The United Nations Force in Cyprus (1968). S.G. Xydis, Cyprus: Conflict and Conciliation (1967).

Chapter IX

CASE STUDY: THE AMERICAN HOSTAGES IN IRAN

I. Introduction

On 4 November 1979, 63 Americans as well as personnel of other nationalities were seized following the occupation of the United States Embassy in Teheran. Thirteen of those captured were released early; the remainder were released only in January, 1981.

On 25 November 1979, Secretary-General Waldheim invoked Article 99 of the United Nations Charter to request an urgent meeting of the Security Council, declaring that this crisis was a serious threat to international peace and security.[1]

On 4 December 1979, the Security Council adopted resolution 457 (1979) urgently calling upon the Government of Iran immediately to release the personnel of the American Embassy being held in Teheran, provide them protection and allow them to leave Iran. This resolution also called on the Secretary-General "to lend his good offices for the immediate implementation of this resolution and to take all appropriate measures to this end."

On 15 December 1979, the International Court of Justice issued an order calling for "the immediate release, without any exception," by Iran of all Americans held in Iran and for their safe departure from Iran.

On 22 December 1979, the Government of the United States of America requested the Security Council to consider measures to induce Iran to comply with its international obligations.[2] A draft resolution to this effect was subsequently vetoed in the Security Council.

II. The mandate of the Secretary-General

As was seen above, on 4 December 1979 the Security Council unanimously issued an urgent call to the Government of Iran to release immediately the personnel of the Embassy of the United States being held in Teheran, to provide them protection and to allow them to leave the country. Secretary-General Kurt Waldheim was asked to "lend his good offices for the immediate implementation of this resolution and to take all appropriate measures to this end." Following the vote, the Secretary-General told the Council he would devote all his efforts to carrying out his broad mandate as swiftly and effectively as possible. He remarked that there were few if any precedents for the situation in question and that innovation might be necessary.

III. The good offices of the Secretary-General

The first aspect which should be noted regarding the good-offices mandate entrusted to the Secretary-General in this case was the highly unusual situation and the need, as stated by the Secretary-General himself, for innovation. As was mentioned above, the Secretary-General remarked after his mandate had been assigned to him that "there were very few if any precedents for the present situation" and that "innovation might be necessary."[3] The circumstances were also quite unusual. As the Secretary-General was to say later, there was "a power struggle" going on in Iran, which meant that there was no single authority with whom he could deal in certainty.

An examination of the methods employed by the Secretary-General in this case shows that they included:

(a) *Definition of the issues.* The Secretary-General contributed in defining the issues to be addressed in order to resolve the situation. Thus, he defined the issues to include the release of the hostages as well as the grievances of the Government of Iran.

(b) *Consultations/contacts/representations.* The Secretary-General engaged in consultations and contacts with interested permanent missions in New York as well as with the parties concerned, and on occasions, he made representations to both parties: to the Government of Iran regarding the protection of hostages, and to the Government of the United States regarding the need for restraint.

(c) *Visits.* The Secretary-General undertook a visit to Teheran to discuss the situation with government authorities there with a view to working out possible formulas for resolving the situation. He also visited Washington for discussions with United States authorities.

(d) *Proposals.* The Secretary-General made concrete proposals aimed at resolving the situation. Thus, based on his contacts with the parties concerned he developed the idea of a commission of inquiry.

(e) *Negotiations.* Before, as well as after, the Secretary-General had launched his proposals, he entered into negotiations with the parties concerned on the terms of his proposals as well as on other matters.

(f) *Establishment of a commission of inquiry.* The Secretary-General decided to establish a commission of inquiry to hear Iran's grievances and to allow an early solution of the crisis between Iran and the United States and to report to him personally. According to one source, "the idea [of the commission of inquiry] – or at least its pursuit – was Waldheim's. Its very origin, less than 10 days after the occupation of the United States Embassy in Teheran was in the letter of the then foreign minister, Abolhassan Bani-Sadr, in which he asked that 'the United States Government should at least recognize an examination of the guilt of the former Shah'. The idea that the hostages could be freed in an exchange for a kind of international jury that would hear the case of Iran was thus born; Islamic diplomats argued in unison that that was the best avenue. Waldheim apparently needed little persuasion. By November 17 he officially, though only privately, broached the idea of an inquiry commission with both sides."[4] This was quite a remarkable development. It could have been asked before this instance whether the competence of the Secretary-General in the discharge of his good-offices functions could extend to the establishment of such a commission. After the present case, which received the endorsement of the membership of the United Nations, it may be taken as established that the Secretary-General can do so.

IV. The commission of inquiry

On 20 February 1980, the Secretary-General issued the following announcement:

"I wish to announce the establishment of a commission of inquiry to undertake a fact-finding mission to Iran to hear Iran's grievances and to allow an early solution of the crisis between Iran and the United States. Iran desires to have the commission speak to each of the hostages.

The commission will be composed of: Andres Aguilar (Venezuela); Mohamed Bedjaoui (Algeria); Adyb Daudy (Syrian Arab Republic); H.W. Jayawardene (Sri Lanka); and Louis-Edmond Petitti (France).

The members from Algeria and Venezuela will serve as its co-chairmen. The commission, which will leave for Tehran over the week-end, will complete its work as soon as possible and submit its report to the Secretary-General."[5]

It will be noted that the statement referred to "the members from Algeria and Venezuela" to "serve as its co-chairmen." This could have given the impression that the members were appointed as representatives of their Governments. However, since they were appointed by the Secretary-General it may be taken that he intended to designate them in their personal capacity.

Following the announcement of the appointment of the commission of inquiry, the White House issued an announcement in which it stated that: "in concurring, the United States has taken note of the Secretary-General's statement that the commission will undertake a fact-finding mission. It will not be a tribunal. The United States understands that the commission will hear the grievances of both sides and will report to the Secretary-General . . . The United States has also made clear its position that the meeting of the commission with our people must be consistent with international law and that the hostages must under no circumstances be subjected to interrogation. It is vital, however, for the commission to determine that they are all present, and to assess their condition."

The relationship between the establishment of the commission and the release of the hostages was not very clear. This led the International Herald Tribune to make the following comment on 21 February 1980:

"According to United Nations officials, as quoted by the New York Times, a specific time frame has been agreed upon for the release of the U.S. hostages in Tehran. According to Secretary-General Kurt Waldheim, as quoted by the Vienna newspaper Die Presse, the hostages will be released during the course of the work of the commission appointed to investigate the alleged crimes of Shah Mohammed Reza Pahlavi. Iranian President Abolhassan Bani-Sadr says no deal has been made linking the release of the hostages to the work of the commission. Iranian Foreign Minister Sadegh Ghotbzadeh holds that the hostages will not be released until the Shah is returned to Iran. According to the militants holding the hostages, as quoted by the Kuwaiti news agency, the commission 'is not authorized to deal with the hostage crisis, and we will oppose any attempt at such'. According to Mohammed Bedjaoui, a member of the commission, as reported by United Press International, a 'gentleman's agreement' exists to release the hostages. Ayatollah Khomeini has been silent on whether the convening of the commission and prospects for the release of the hostages are linked.

What are we to believe?"

The establishment of the commission, while the hostages continued to be held raised serious issues of principle. In the first place, there was an order of the International Court of Justice that "The Government of the Islamic Republic of Iran should ensure the immediate release, without any exception, of all persons of United States nationality who are or have been held in the Embassy of the United States of America or in the Ministry of Foreign Affairs in Tehran, or have been held as hostages elsewhere, and afford full protection to all such persons, in accordance with the treaties in force between the two States, and with general international law." The Court also stated in paragraph 42 of its decision that "continuance of the situation, the subject of the present request, exposes the human beings concerned to privation, hardship, anguish and even danger to life and health and thus to the serious possibility of irreparable harm."

The Times of London pointed out:

"In giving its imprimatur to the five-man commission investigating the alleged crimes of the former Shah of Iran, the United Nations is playing a dangerous game. It is saying, in effect, that it is prepared to accept, and submit to, one of the most serious and blatant acts of international illegality of the century in the hope of gaining the release of the American hostages . . .

The appointment of the commission . . . has conferred respectability on international terrorism by governments.

The commission has been set up as a direct response to blackmail. A government guilty of a gross violation of international law has been allowed to dictate the terms on which it may – and there is no certainty that it will – cease its illegal conduct. The very existence of the commission is a capitulation to terrorism. The composition of the commission is equally suspect. The Ayatollah Khomeini has, in fact, had the power of veto over the commission's membership . . . They are the chosen judges of a criminous party to the dispute they are considering.

That must destroy their claim to be regarded as impartial.''[6]

Following the announcement of its establishment the commission assembled in Geneva on Wednesday, 20 February and met on 21 February to exchange views on its procedures and collect documents necessary for its work. These included reports by various organizations on the situation in Iran and legal papers regarding the conduct of such missions. Commission members also had talks with Mr. Theo C. van Boven, the Director of the United Nations Division of Human Rights, with a delegation of the International Committee of the Red Cross and with the Secretary-General of the International Commission of Jurists.[7]

The commission arrived in Iran on 23 February 1980. After initial meetings with the Iranian President and the Iranian Foreign Minister a United Nations official said that ''the commission felt a sound basis had been established for its work from a substantive and practical standpoint.''[8]

In the ensuing days, it heard statements concerning grievances of the Iranian people, particularly about human rights violations, from the Association of Iranian Jurists and from people who said they were victims of the secret police of the former régime. The commission visited the Zehra cemetery, the Evin prison and one of the former Shah's palaces, Niavaran.

On Wednesday, 27 February, commission members met with the spokesman of the Islamic Revolutionary Council, Mr. Habibi, and later spent about 90 minutes with people voicing grievances against the previous régime. The commission spokesman said they went through a crowd of about 1200 victims examining particular cases of obvious physical mutilation and asking specific questions. One of the two cochairmen, Mohamed Bedjaoui of Algeria, assured the victims of the commission's compassion for their suffering.

During its stay the commission also met representatives of legal, banking, literary and academic groups. Members of the commission met several times with Foreign Minister Ghotbzadeh, who told them on Monday, 3 March that the Revolutionary Council had unanimously decided that the commission should see all the hostages in the United States Embassy. A United Nations official said the "modalities and timing" of the visit to the Embassy were discussed at a meeting with Mr. Ghotbzadeh on Wednesday, 5 March.[9]

However, the position of the Iranian Government was subsequently reversed and the commission left Iran without seeing the hostages. In a statement before leaving, a spokesman said that the panel was "not in a position to prepare its report." The statement added that the commission would confer with Secretary-General Waldheim "with a view to pursuing its task, which it regards as indivisible."[10] The commission thus suspended its activities in Iran on 11 March and returned to Headquarters for consultations.

Secretary-General Waldheim appealed for patience with the United Nations effort. He spoke of tremendous difficulties caused by a "power struggle" in Iran and recalled that the mandate of the United Nations commission was two-fold – to examine the grievances of the Iranian authorities, and to allow a solution of the crisis between Iran and the United States, which meant in the first instance, the question of the hostages and their release. What had to be clarified, he said, was when the Iranian Government would be in a position to implement the second part. The views of the Government, he noted, did not coincide with the views of the students holding the hostages. And that, he said, was one of the reasons why the commission had come back to Headquarters. Another aspect, he said, was the attitude of the Ayatollah Khomeini, who in a statement of Monday, 10 March had given the impression of support for the students in putting forward a number of conditions before the commission could see the hostages. These conditions, Mr. Waldheim said, were not foreseen in the arrangements for the commission, and it was felt better for it to return to Headquarters and give the Iranian Government time to clarify matters. Since the commission was unable to fulfill all aspects of its mandate and was not able to see the hostages, the Secretary-General said it could not issue a report for the time being.[11]

On 12 March 1980, United States Secretary of State Cyrus Vance visited the United Nations for exchanges of views with the Secretary-General and the members of the commission of inquiry. He told newsmen afterwards that "the door is still open" and that he had full confidence in the Secretary-General and in the commission. Mr. Vance said that the work of the commission had been useful, and he expressed appreciation to the Secretary-General for "his determination to continue to pursue this avenue."[12]

V. Conclusion

Subsequently, Secretary-General Waldheim continued to follow the situation, to call upon he parties to continue their efforts for a peaceful settlement of the dispute and to make himself available to the parties. He also hoped that the inquiry commission would be able to return to Iran in order to finish its work. As it turned out, this never materialized.

Some general assessments may now be offered of the approach of Secretary-General Waldheim in exercising his good offices in the present instance. The general approach of the Secretary-General was indicated in a statement which he made to the Security Council after receiving his mandate: "I shall," he said, "explore intensively the various modalities which might prove useful in resolving the present crisis. I am aware that there are few, if any, precedents for the present situation and that innovation may well be necessary . . . In carrying out my mandate, I shall be guided first and foremost by what is best for the achievement of the objectives we all have in mind."[13] In his first report on his efforts to the Security Council, he stated: "For my part I shall pursue my endeavours in exercise of the mandate entrusted to me . . . with the determination to find a means for achieving a mutually acceptable solution to this most serious situation."[14] His objective, he said later, "was to determine whether it was possible to agree upon the elements of a package which would be acceptable to the parties and would lead to a satisfactory resolution of the two main elements of the problem, namely the release of the hostages and a means of meeting the grievances of the Iranian Government."

The Secretary-General began by taking a principled approach. In his first report to the Security Council he stated that during his visit to Iran he had "explained to the Foreign Minister the position of the United Nations, referring to the relevant resolutions and decisions of the Security Council." He added: "I stressed the grave violation of international law constituted by the detention of the American diplomatic personnel in the United States Embassy. I stated that the international community did not accept such actions and requested repeatedly the immediate release of the hostages."[15] He stated that "the release of the hostages must take place either before or at least simultaneously with the establishment of an inquiry commission." The Foreign Minister, however, said that the release of the hostages would be one of the consequences of this procedure.

The efforts of the Secretary-General to resolve the crisis received high appreciation in the Security Council where high tributes were paid to him by all the members of the Council. Ambassador McHenry of the United States commented at one stage that "from the beginning of the crisis he has played an important and constructive role in the effort to help end this crisis and to have the hostages released . . . we are deeply appreciative of his enduring efforts and the work of his staff."[16]

What general conclusions may be drawn from the involvement of Secretary-General Waldheim in this affair? It should be recognized firstly that the issues were very complex, the situation was a post-revolutionary one, and there were no clear lines of authority in Iran. This made the efforts of the Secretary-General very difficult. Secondly, although he initially began with a principled position, faced with a protracted and deteriorating problem, the Secretary-General resorted to compromise formulas. His efforts amounted finally to a political response to an international crisis aimed at bringing about its resolution. Therefore, thirdly, pragmatism prevailed and human rights issues became secondary (except in so far as the commission of inquiry sought to investigate the grievances of the Iranian people as a means to bring about the release of the hostages). Fourthly, the commission of inquiry appointed by the Secretary-General was largely *sui generis*. It was established in a highly unusual situation, under the authority of the Secretary-General, and subject to no stated rules either of procedure or of substance. Fifthly, as an exercise in conflict resolution the efforts of the Secretary-General came very near to success in the short term and did assist eventually in the resolution of the crisis. In a message to the Secretary-General dated 19 January 1981, President Carter said that the United States had greatly appreciated Mr. Waldheim's tireless efforts to gain the release of the hostages.[17] United States Secretary of State, Alexander M. Haig Jr. on 28 January 1981, also commended the Secretary-General's role in the hostage crisis. Mr. Haig said that the United States was "deeply grateful" to the Secretary-General for his efforts on behalf of the hostages.[18]

NOTES

1. S/13646.
2. S/13705.
3. UN press release WS/948, 7 December 1979.
4. L. Halasz, "Iran Panel puts Secretary-General in picture," UN Observer, Vol. III, No. 1.
5. United States Permanent Mission, Geneva, Daily Bulletin, No. 34, 21 February 1980.
6. Reproduced in the International Herald Tribune of 22 February 1980.
7. UN press release, WS/959, 22 February 1980.
8. UN press release, WS/960, 29 February 1980.
9. UN press release, WS/961, 7 March 1980.
10. International Herald Tribune, 12 March 1980.
11. UN press release, WS/962, 14 March 1980.
12. UN press release, WS/962, 14 March 1980.
13. S/PV.2178.
14. S/13704.
15. S/13704.
16. Ambassador McHenry's remarks came in response to a Washington Post article suggesting that the Secretary-General had "bungled" the negotiations: "The article written by reporter J.C. Randal after a visit to Teheran, maintained that Waldheim had botched 'a carefully negotiated – and purposefully vague – tacit Iranian-American understanding' on the commission's assignment. U.N. officials denied it. But well-informed sources in Teheran said that Waldheim acting under U.S. pressure, had pushed the commission forward too quickly, claiming too much credit for the U.N. and leaving too little time and manoeuvering room for Bani Sadr. As a result, Khomeini had deferred a decision on releasing the prisoners, and Bani Sadr had been forced to assume a more militant posture." Newsweek, 10 March 1980, p. 19. In reply to his critics the Secretary-General said in Newsweek of 24 March 1980, "Have any critics presented a better alternative? Patience and perseverance are the only approach we have." The Secretary-General himself said of his efforts "this is an honest effort. I have never in my whole career tried so hard to solve a problem."
17. UN press release WS/1007, p. 2.
18. UN press release WS/1008, p. 4.

Chapter X

HUMANITARIAN GOOD OFFICES IN SITUATIONS OF MASS EXODUSES

In recent years, there has been much international concern about problems stemming from massive exoduses of peoples on account of various types of man-made disasters, such as internal or international conflicts or gross violations of human rights. In discussions of these problems within the United Nations, much faith has been placed in the possibilities offered by humanitarian good offices.

I. The practice

In a resolution[1] adopted on 11 March 1980, the Commission on Human Rights requested the Secretary-General of the United Nations, in cases where large-scale exoduses become a matter of international concern and solidarity, to consider establishing direct contacts with the appropriate governments, to assess the relationship between the situation and full enjoyment of human rights, and to make concrete recommendations for ameliorating such situations.[2] In paragraph 5 of the same resolution, the Secretary-General was requested, where warranted, to submit to the next session of the Commission, or General Assembly, as appropriate, a summary of his findings and recommendations to assist governments in restoring full enjoyment of human rights. Following the adoption of this resolution, the General Assembly adopted a resolution without a vote on 15 December 1980, which expressed deep concern at the continued incidences of large-scale exoduses and displacements of populations and at the resulting hardships and problems of the persons and States concerned. The Assembly endorsed the requests to the Secretary-General contained in the resolution of the Commission on Human Rights, and requested the Commission to "examine the report of the Secretary-General to be submitted to it . . . and on the basis of that report to make recommendations for further action."[3]

In compliance with the request of the Commission, Secretary-General Waldheim submitted a report to the Commission on Human Rights at its thirty-seventh session in which he recalled that "in all situations of international concern, the Secretary-General, in accordance with his responsibilities under the Charter and with any specific mandate given to him by a relevant United Nations organ, seeks to facilitate solutions as well as to alleviate human suffering. The Secretary-General does this in a variety of ways, for example, through contacts and consultations with the parties concerned, through exercise of his good offices and through appeals for international assistance."[4] He added, however, that the root causes of situations involving mass exoduses were often very complex and could relate to political or military conflicts, internal or external, to civil strife, persecution or other forms of violations of human rights, be they civil and political, or economic, social and cultural rights. Hence, in seeking to be of assistance in such situations the Secretary-General reported, he used the methods which he considered were the most appropriate for each situation; insofar as the root causes of mass exoduses were concerned, the Secretary-General said he often discussed them in his contacts and consultations with the parties concerned and, through the use of his good offices, he sought to alleviate the circumstances leading to such exoduses. He also sought to support the humanitarian assistance activities of the United Nations High Commissioner for Refugees.[5] The Secretary-General added that there were doubtless many situations in which mass exoduses were caused by denials of human rights, and that he did not fail to point this out in his contacts and consultations with the parties concerned. However, he said that he often found that considerable caution needed to be exercised in the public disclosure of the precise substance of his contacts with governments concerned, including those on the nexus between mass exoduses and the full enjoyment of human rights, so as to avoid prejudicing future contacts and closing the possibility of his being of assistance in the future to the victims of such situations. Without entering into details of the situations involved, the Secretary-General said that in respect of situations of mass exoduses which had recently occurred, he had, while supporting and assisting the activities of the United Nations High Commissioner for Refugees, also adopted various approaches of his own, including: "consultations and direct contacts with the parties concerned; the use of his good offices, including appeals to the parties concerned; the designation of special representatives to follow situations; the dispatch of inter-agency missions; personal visits to the areas or regions concerned; and, the mobilization of humanitarian assistance, including the convening of international conferences for this purpose."[6]

The Secretary-General referred to the introduction to his Annual Report of 1980, in which he had expressed the following view:

"Political and humanitarian factors are sometimes difficult to separate . . . Unfortunately, most of the great human tragedies of our time are deeply rooted in political and military developments. This is particularly true of the various humanitarian demands of Indo-China. In the face of human misery on the scale which exists in that part of the world, it is essential to provide humanitarian assistance even though a political solution has yet to be found. I appeal to all Governments to understand this dilemma and to support the humanitarian efforts of the United Nations system and associated international and voluntary organizations to provide assistance on a non-discriminatory basis to the afflicted civilian population. Above all, there is a need to make renewed efforts to move in the direction of political settlements which will allow the agonized populations of that tortured region to look at last to a future of peace."

The Secretary-General concluded that he was of the view that through approaches such as those described above, he had been able to use his influence to the maximum extent possible. He was of the view that further investigation or articulation of the nexus between violations of human rights and mass exoduses were subjects which were deserving of consideration by United Nations organs such as the Commission on Human Rights with a view to devising appropriate, complementary approaches or procedures for dealing with such situations.

II. Recent proposals

(a) *Report on human rights and mass exoduses*

After considering the above-mentioned report of the Secretary-General, the Commission on Human Rights adopted a resolution[7] in accordance with which Prince Sadruddin Aga Khan was appointed as "a special rapporteur to study the question of human rights and mass exoduses" and to submit his study to the Commission, together with his conclusions and recommendations.

In the report which he submitted to the Commission at its thirty-eighth session, Prince Sadruddin Aga Khan recommended that consideration be given, *inter alia*, to "the introduction of an early-warning system based on impartial information-gathering and data-collection concerning potential mass exodus situations, leading to expeditious reporting to the Secretary-General of the United Nations and competent intergovernmental organs for the purpose of timely action, if required."[8] He was of the view that the basic concept of an appropriate United Nations "presence" could be extended to humanitarian emergencies, as had been done in peace-keeping operations in the accepted sense. He explained that in order to give birth to an "early-warning system" it would be necessary to gather, on an ongoing basis, impartial information from proven sources such as governments, the United Nations representatives in the countries concerned (whether the UNDP resident representative, specialized agencies, United Nations information centres or other) and other informed parties in order to gain an understanding of the background and all the facets of a situation, including the ethnic, economic, political and social aspects. There could also be visits to the field. After assessing all available data, an appreciation to include a number of possible scenarios for the future development of the situation could be given to the Secretary-General of the United Nations and to the competent intergovernmental organs.

A "trigger mechanism", he said, could be provided by the Secretary-General deciding, after due study of the above-mentioned materials and using his executive authority, what action would be required on the part of the United Nations. The Secretary-General might, for example, call for further study of the situation, including discussion with the government or governments most closely concerned and/or with the appropriate regional body (Arab League, Council of Europe, Organization of African Unity, Organization of American States) to try to determine how regional containment of the problem could be achieved, to save it becoming internationalized (that is to say, requiring involvement of large-scale United Nations operations).

In the next stage, Prince Sadruddin continued, the executive entrusted with the task would bring the situation to the attention of those who deal with causes (as distinct from effects) to try to encourage, as appropriate, preventive action before the start of a mass movement. In the case of a political question, the executive could propose to the Secretary-General that the latter take the initiative appearing most indicated, whether it be consulting interested States or drawing the attention of the Security Council, in a suitable manner, to the problem. In the case of human rights issues, the responsible officer could relay the situation to the Commission on Human Rights which could make an investigation and take follow-up action. After this, there could be liaison on an informal basis with the humanitarian agencies for purposes of consultation. They would thus be alerted and enabled to act swiftly if an exodus did indeed occur. Furthermore, the executive entrusted with responsibility in the situation should keep abreast of the relevant work of the General Assembly, the Security Council, the Commission on Human Rights or other competent body tackling "causes", as the case might be, while at the same time ensuring that humanitarian needs were being covered. He would be responsible for seeing that the question is kept under review by the relevant bodies. Simultaneously, he would be in a position to advise on the best way to apportion aid as between areas affected by the crisis in order to reduce to the maximum extent possible the stress/distress involved. Where necessary, an agency or agencies not so far working on the problem whose expertise were seen to be needed would be invited to participate. Follow-up work, Prince Sadruddin thought, could include monitoring of developments in order to report them to the Secretary-General and informal reporting to governments on the progress of international efforts. In the longer term, work could be carried out on seeking to promote regional reflexes to crisis situations, for example, through encouraging the creation and/or development of regional human rights mechanisms, in co-operation with the Commission on Human Rights.

The measures to be undertaken, he emphasized, should be speedy. Their success would be largely dependent on an informed appreciation of each complex situation and its respective origins, based on ongoing research and analysis. Only an impartial monitoring of situations could, he felt, lead to a more balanced assessment of circumstances lying at the root of potential exodus and contribute thereby to a more adapted response from humanitarian agencies.

Another suggestion made by Prince Sadruddin was for the appointment of a "Special Representative of the Secretary-General for Humanitarian Questions" whose task would basically be (a) to forewarn; (b) to monitor; (c) to de-politicize humanitarian situations; (d) to carry out those functions which humanitarian agencies cannot assume because of institutional/mandatory constraints; (e) to serve as an intermediary of goodwill between the concerned parties.

The special rapporteur also suggested the identification from among groups experienced in humanitarian questions of men and women willing and able to be called upon to form a corps of "humanitarian observers" which, in case of need, could monitor situations and contribute through their presence to a de-escalation of tensions. A pre-requisite for this role, he said, would be the concurrence of the governments concerned. The corps, he felt, would facilitate the work of the Special Representative for Humanitarian Questions. He stressed that the role of such a corps of humanitarian observers should be entirely non-political and purely humanitarian. Consequently, any decision in this regard by the United Nations should be taken in a humanitarian context and care should be taken that it is not viewed as an effort parallel to, or in conflict with, the work of the Security Council. The benefit would be similar to that of delegates of bodies such as the International Committee of the Red Cross in situations of armed conflict. In addition to having a calming effect in the areas where they will be stationed, these observers might carry out general monitoring functions both in regard to the rhythm and nature of the exodus and the international aid provided. The corps would consist of volunteers whose lists may be established in advance on the basis of availability of human resources essentially within the United Nations system, for short rounds of duty in the field. A pre-requisite for this role would be the concurrence of the governments concerned. The corps would then spring into action in the context of the trigger mechanism suggested above.

With respect to this suggestion of Prince Sadruddin, it may be recalled that in his Annual Report of 1980, Secretary-General Waldheim had made a similar proposal: "It has until now been generally accepted that security and peace-keeping are political matters and separate from emergency humanitarian efforts, although past experience has shown that when the two have happened to co-incide the humanitarian task has been greatly facilitated by the presence of peace-keeping operations. A relatively small United Nations presence can have a calming effect on a violent situation out of all proportion to its numbers, armaments or military capacity. I fully recognize the political and other complexities involved. Clearly, the authority of the Security Council must be respected, and the principle of national sovereignty strictly observed. On this basis, I believe however, that Member States might consider the possibilities of extending in some form the Organization's very considerable experience of peace-keeping into humanitarian emergencies where conditions call urgently for an element of security."[9]

(b) *International co-operation to deal with problems of mass exoduses*

When the problems of mass exoduses were discussed in the Special Political Committees at the thirty-fifth session of the United Nations General Assembly in 1980, the main idea proposed was to utilize some form of good-offices approach by the United Nations in dealing with such massive exoduses. Thus, the Federal Republic of Germany, which had raised the problem before the United Nations, suggested that in cases in which neither the "classical" methods for a bilateral settlement of differences nor regional organizations were able to prevent a flow of refugees, suitable instruments for consultation within the United Nations were necessary. It suggested that consideration be given to what extent those talks could be performed within existing United Nations institutions and whether it might be advantageous for the General Assembly to create a body which, in such situations, could take quick action to determine the facts of the matter and offer its good offices in preparation for the work of existing institutions. That body might be designated the United Nations Good Offices Committee for the Promotion of International Co-operation to Avert New Flows of Refugees. Its services would be available at all times and it would be kept informed of developments in its area of concern. Its members would be elected at regular intervals and, with due regard for the areas of competence of existing United Nations organs and special organizations. It could initiate fact-finding missions; call upon the States involved to discuss jointly ways of averting the danger of a new flow of refugees; direct the attention of the regional organizations to critical developments within their respective areas; call the attention of other United Nations organs and specialized agencies to such developments, and lastly, offer its own good offices to the States involved.[10]

This approach was supported by various countries including New Zealand, Singapore, Pakistan, Austria, Somalia, Tunisia and Morocco. On the other hand, reservations were expressed by the representatives of the USSR, the German Democratic Republic, China, Laos, Czechoslovakia, Democratic Yemen and Cuba. It may be useful to examine the arguments which were advanced on both sides.[11] The representative of New Zealand "like the Federal Republic of Germany, thought that the best way to tackle the problem was at its source. It too felt that there was a need for more effective machinery to deal with refugees situations as they developed, and it found the proposals for the use of good offices attractive."[12] The representative of Singapore felt that "The international community needed an institutionalized body of that kind, a group of experts, drawn from Member States, who would be available at all times to deal with refugees problems."[13] The representative of Pakistan was of the view that "the proposal put forward by the Federal Republic of Germany for the creation of a 'United Nations good offices committee for the promotion of international co-operation to avert new flows of refugees' seemed to offer good prospects of supplementing the efforts of the United Nations and deserved full support."[14] The Austrian representative "supported the initiative of the Federal Republic of Germany and was prepared to study with interest any institutional proposal in that regard, such as that for the creation of the appropriate body to study the ideas and suggestions of Member States on the question. Such a body could present in a comprehensive manner the relevant and accepted principles of international law and international relations, including the right to seek asylum, and elaborate guidelines of a preventive nature, as well as for coping with the problems raised by mass flows of refugees, with a view to avoiding the economic disruption and internal destabilization of the recipient countries."[15] The Somali representative "hoped that serious consideration would be given to the proposals made by the Federal Republic of Germany and that Member States would make an active contribution to the development and implementation of those proposals."[16] The Tunisian representative submitted that "The proposal submitted by the Federal Republic of Germany, whose purpose was to avert new flows of refugees, would have his country's support. Any organ entrusted with studying the refugee problem should do everything possible to avert new flows of refugees, concentrating its efforts on the problems still pending."[17]

On the other hand, the representative of the USSR argued that "the establishment of a good offices committee would amount to creating an organ that was unprecedented in the United Nations, in that it would be able to interfere in the internal affairs of States. The establishment of such an organ, as a supranational institution, was an attempt to judge, outside the State concerned, complex and delicate problems pertaining to its internal life and ethnic relations. It was clear that this was completely unacceptable and that no sovereign State, Member of the United Nations, could accept such a situation."[18] The representative of Czechoslovakia also felt that "the result of establishing a supranational body of that kind, whose functions would include making proposals concerning the conduct of Governments, might involve the United Nations in policing activities and in interference in the internal affairs of Member States." Also, "the establishment of a United Nations good offices committee to avert new flows of refugees could have unforeseen adverse effects and be harmful to the vital interests of the majority of the States Members of the Organization."[19] The representative of Democratic Yemen was of the view that "the proposal before the Committee was aimed at the establishment of a supranational body, or good offices committee, to strengthen international co-operation so as to avert new flows of refugees. The objective was in fact to establish a body empowered to intervene in the internal affairs of States, in violation of the principles of the United Nations Charter."[20] The Cuban delegation "could see no point whatsover in establishing a good offices committee. It could not accept the idea that the refugee problem was a threat to international peace and security, and even if that was the case, the question would be the exclusive responsibility of the Security Council. It also rejected the formulation of guidelines for the conduct of States, which it considered to be flagrant interference in the internal affairs of States."[21] The representative of Laos was "apprehensive that such an initiative, particularly the proposal to establish a United Nations good offices committee, might only lead to involvement by the Organization in the internal affairs of States by virtue of the committee's supranational powers."[22] The Chinese representative felt that "the United Nations should investigate and examine the causes of flows of refugees . . . and that all Member States should adopt the necessary measures to prevent flows of refugees and to strengthen international co-operation."[23]

The representative of Morocco, however, "believed that the proposed body represented no threat to the national sovereignty of countries. A sincere effort to analyze in an innovative way the real causes of the evil, together with a will to seek solutions in which all would cooperate, could not constitute interference in the domestic affairs of a State or be an attempt to dictate the policy it should adopt. The States

Members of the United Nations must help to find a solution for a problem which was as old as the world but was currently acquiring dimensions that could exceed the means available for dealing with it."[24]

In the end, the General Assembly, on the recommendation of its Special Political Committee, adopted resolution 35/124 by which it invited all Member States to convey to the Secretary-General their comments and suggestions on international co-operation to avert new flows of refugees and to facilitate the return of those refugees who wished to do so. The Assembly requested the Secretary-General to report to it, at its thirty-sixth session, for its further examination and thorough study, the views, comments and suggestions expressed by Member States, together with those expressed on this item at its thirty-fifth session, including all additional contributions pertaining to the matter which he may receive from other United Nations organs.

At its thirty-sixth session, the General Assembly after considering the above-mentioned report submitted by the Secretary-General containing observations received from governments, adopted resolution 36/148 establishing a Group of Governmental Experts on International Co-operation to Avert New Flows of Refugees, to undertake as soon as possible, in order to improve international co-operation to avert new massive flows of refugees, a comprehensive review of the problem in all its aspects, with a view to developing recommendations on appropriate means of international co-operation in this field, having due regard to the principle of non-intervention in the internal affairs of sovereign States. The Assembly requested the Group of Governmental Experts to be mindful of the importance of reaching general agreement whenever it has significance for the outcome of its work and called on the Group to take into account the comments and suggestions communicated to the Secretary-General in accordance with resolution 35/124 and any further comments and suggestions from Member States and United Nations organs, organizations and specialized agencies as well as the views expressed during the debate on this item at the thirty-sixth session of the General Assembly and also the study submitted to the Commission on Human Rights at its thirty-eighth session by its special rapporteur, and furthermore the deliberations on this study by the Commission. The Group was requested to submit a report to the General Assembly at its thirty-seventh session in 1982.

III. Conclusion

In this chapter we have seen the Secretary-General acknowledging that he used his good offices in situations of mass exoduses. However, in his report to the Commission on Human Rights he was cautious. He gave a broad outline of the nature of his activities but he was reluctant to go into details. Also, he discreetly urged the Commission to undertake action of its own. A preference was thus indicated for a parallel approach on the part of the Secretary-General and United Nations organs. The suggestions made by Prince Sadruddin Aga Khan could ensure optimum use of the potential of the United Nations system and seek, essentially, to reinforce the leadership of the Secretary-General. These suggestions are currently under consideration and their outcome must be awaited. In the debates in the Special Political Committee consideration was given to the notion of collective good offices by a committee or group of experts. It will be interesting to see whether, and how, this notion is applied in this field in the future.

NOTES

1. Resolution 30 (XXXVI).
2. This account is based on a report which the Secretary-General submitted to the thirty-seventh session of the Commission on Human Rights, E/CN.4/1440.
3. GA resolution 35/196.
4. E/CN.4/1440, para. 4.
5. *Ibid.*, para. 5.
6. *Ibid.*, para. 7.
7. Resolution 29 (XXXVII).
8. E/CN.4/1503, Recommendation No. 7. See also paras. 110-140.
9. A/35/1.
10. A/SPC/35/SR.43, para. 9.
11. For the records of discussion see A/SPC/35/SR.43-46.
12. A/SPC/35/SR.44, para. 22.
13. A/SPC/35/SR.44, para. 29.
14. A/SPC/35/SR.44, para. 33.
15. A/SPC/35/SR.45, para. 7.
16. A/SPC/35/SR.46, para. 14.
17. A/SPC/35/SR.46, para. 5.
18. A/SPC/35/SR.44, para. 35.
19. A/SPC/35/SR.46, paras. 29-30.
20. A/SPC/35/SR.46, para. 43.
21. A/SPC/35/SR.46, para. 56.

22. A/SPC/35/SR.46, para. 18.
23. A/SPC/35/SR.45, para. 31.
24. A/SPC/35/SR.46, para. 5.

Chapter XI

GOOD OFFICES OF THE PROPOSED UNITED NATIONS COMMISSIONER FOR HUMAN RIGHTS

Since the early years of the United Nations, proposals for the establishment of a post of, or akin to, United Nations High Commissioner for Human Rights, have been considered by various United Nations organs.[1] Some merits in the proposals are recognized by nearly all sides involved in the debate. Nevertheless, it has not yet obtained political agreement, remains controversial, and continues to attract strong resistance, particularly on the part of governments which feel that the High Commissioner's office could be abused so as to become a vehicle for interference into the internal affairs of States. Despite this, the faith of supporters of the proposal continues to increase.

The notion of good offices has been, especially in the more recent phases of the debate, a central issue of discussion, and our purpose, in the present chapter, is to examine this aspect of the question. This examination appears timely and pertinent in view of the request made in 1982 by the Commission on Human Rights, to its Sub-Commission, to examine possible terms of reference for the proposed High Commissioner.

I. The proposals

For present purposes, we shall limit ourselves to an examination of the resolution proposed to the General Assembly by the Economic and Social Council in 1967, upon the recommendation of the Commission on Human Rights[2] and to the last proposal which was extensively discussed by the General Assembly, namely a seventeen-power proposal submitted to the General Assembly's Third Committee in 1977.[3]

By its resolution 1237 (XLII) of 6 June 1967, the Economic and Social Council recommended that the General Assembly should adopt a resolution deciding to establish a United Nations High Commissioner's Office for Human Rights. According to the draft resolution, the General

Assembly would have instructed the High Commissioner to assist in promoting and encouraging universal and effective respect for human rights and for fundamental freedoms for all persons. The High Commissioner would be mandated to maintain close relations with organs of the United Nations system concerned with human rights and "upon their request, give advice and assistance," as well as to "render assistance and services to any State . . . at the request of that State" and "submit a report on such assistance and services with the consent of the State concerned."[4]

Engaging in humanitarian good offices was inherent in the abovementioned functions. Indeed, as a protagonist of the idea was to say in the Dag Hammarskjöld Memorial Lecture at Columbia University in 1963, "Such a High Commissioner would, amongst other things, lend his good offices to Governments and be available at their request to investigate situations where there have been alleged violations of human rights; he could assist underdeveloped countries in the organization of various institutions for the promotion of human rights; he could advise the Economic and Social Council on the human rights aspects of the Development Decade; and he could assist the Commission on Human Rights in its review of the periodic reports from Governments on human rights . . ."[5]

The controversy surrounding the proposal has turned particularly around the mandate to be entrusted to the High Commissioner. This led the sponsors of the seventeen-power proposal submitted to the General Assembly in 1977, 10 years after the proposal of the Economic and Social Council referred to above, to modify the proposed terms of reference in the hope of making it more acceptable. Paragraph 2 of the 1977 draft resolution would have had the General Assembly decide that

"the High Commissoner shall act within the framework of the Charter of the United Nations in order to:

(a) Promote and strengthen universal and effective understanding and respect for human rights and fundamental freedoms for all without distinction as to race, religion, sex or language, as set forth in the Charter of the United Nations, the Universal Declaration of Human Rights and other instruments of the United Nations and in particular:

(i) Consider as areas of special concern and attention such massive violations of human rights as *apartheid*, racism and racial discrimination, colonial domination, foreign occupation and alien subjugation;

(ii) Give special attention to the critical importance of ensuring the effective enjoyment by all of their civil and political rights and their economic, social and cultural rights and such other rights as are recognized by the Charter of the United Nations and by the General Assembly, bearing in mind that all human rights and fundamental freedoms are indivisible and interdependent;

(iii) Actively promote the understanding of the basic human rights inherent in the establishment of a new international economic order and of the necessity to link the traditional concept of human rights with the rights of all to have their economic, social and cultural needs met;

(b) Render, at the specific request of any State, assistance and services, including good offices, to that State; the High Commissioner may submit a report on such assistance and services and on its results with the consent of the State concerned;

(c) Maintain close relations with the Secretary-General and all other organs of the United Nations, specialized agencies and other intergovernmental organizations concerned with human rights, and give advice and assistance in order to ensure co-ordination of their activities in the human rights field;

(d) Report annually to the General Assembly on his activities and on developments in the field of human rights;''

The reference to ''good offices'' in sub-paragraph (b) appeared to have been intended to give an indication of the kind of assistance and services which the High Commissioner was to offer and, hopefully, to make the proposal more acceptable. In introducing the draft resolution before the Third Committee of the General Assembly on 17 November 1977, the representative of Italy explained on behalf of the sponsors that the High Commissioner would be under the authority of the Secretary-General, and that his position would be practically analogous to that of an Under-Secretary-General, although he would be assured of the prestige deriving from his title and from the process of confirmation by the General Assembly. The intent of the sponsors was that the High Commissioner would act under powers delegated by the Secretary-General. It therefore followed that the Secretary-General must retain the right to be consulted in delicate situations and to take the initiative himself whenever he deemed it necessary. That position would be consistent with the principle that the direction of and responsibility for action in all areas must, in conformity with the letter and spirit of the Charter, remain in the hands of the Secretary-General as chief administrative officer of the Organization.[6] Later, in response to questions which had been raised by the representative of Oman,[7] the Italian representative added that "the good offices of the High Commissioner could be extremely helpful."[8] Other representatives, such as those of Denmark spoke approvingly of the role of the Secretary-General in providing good offices[9] in the field of human rights, while the representative of Yugoslavia thought that the good-offices function of the Secretary-General had not been sufficiently used.[10]

The representative of the USSR however, referring to the "good offices" mentioned in the draft resolution as being one of the High Commissioner's main functions, asked what those "good offices" were. They were one way of settling international disputes, in other words, disputes between States. What that meant was that, at the request of one State, the High Commissioner would interfere in the affairs of another State without the latter's consent. In other words, any State could draw the High Commissioner's attention to reports concerning violations of human rights in another State of its own choosing, and the High Commissioner would have to act by rendering his "good offices". Furthermore, as some of the sponsors had admitted, the High Commissioner could act "on his own initiative" and "at his own discretion", even on the basis of reports from individuals and non-governmental organizations. The potential consequences were clear to everyone.[11]

A representative who participated in the debate subsequently wrote: "*'Good Offices' – For which purpose?* An old stipulation that was included in all versions of the High Commissioner proposal said that the High Commissioner should render assistance and services to every United Nations' Member State or specialized agency if they so request . . . To the term 'assistance and services' have been added the words 'including good offices'. At the request of any State the High Commissioner shall render his good offices. The importance of 'good offices' has been described in detail and repeatedly emphasized by the authors. It was described as the main task of the High Commissioner apart from the so-called co-ordinating function . . . However, it was never said just exactly what the issue was. It was the Soviet delegate and the representative from Oman who pointed this out. The term 'good offices' is used to describe a procedure to settle a dispute between two States with the help of a mediator. If in the field of human rights – as the draft stipulates – any State has the right to request good offices from the High Commissioner, this no longer means that the State which has asked for assistance to implement human rights on its territory receives such help. Such a possibility has existed for a long time and to this end neither a new decision or the new post is needed. It does mean, however, that a State can request the 'good offices' of the High Commissioner as assistance in a dispute with another State which it accuses of violating human rights . . .

When the representative of Oman asked just exactly what would it mean that *any* State could request the 'good offices' of the High Commissioner and obviously wanted to know whether it would be necessary to have the consent of that State in which the alleged violation of human rights had taken place, the authors replied that relating to the rendering of assistance and services at the specific request of any State, the paragraph referred to all States, whether or not they were members of the United Nations. But they quietly ignored the question of just what 'good offices' would mean in such a case in practice when at least two States were involved. They obviously meant that any State can apply for the 'good offices' of the High Commissioner to make his charges against any other State."[12]

From the above account, it can be seen that while the performance of "good offices" was visualized by the sponsors as being of the essence of the functions of the High Commissioner, difficulties were experienced in explaining what such "good offices" would mean. This dilemma is far from having passed away.

II. General observations

The debate on possible good offices to be entrusted to, or exercised by, a future High Commissioner for Human Rights, does not add much by way of international practice which can help to elucidate the nature, content or meaning of humanitarian good offices. It does bear out, however, the need for a better understanding of the concept which is the purpose addressed in the present volume. The conclusion may be drawn that, insofar as the proposed High Commissioner is concerned, it would be necessary to rely on international practice and on international customary law in order to arrive at an understanding of what would be encompassed within the range of his or her humanitarian good offices.

Inasmuch as nearly all of the proposals for the establishment of the Office of High Commissioner for Human Rights envisage that he or she would act under the auspices of the Secretary-General of the United Nations and in accordance with the Charter of the United Nations, it may be concluded that the humanitarian good offices of the High Commissioner would be within the same range as those exercised by the Secretary-General of the United Nations. Those of the High Commissioner could conceivably be even slightly narrower, for there may be some actions which the Secretary-General of the United Nations can take, but which would be beyond the province of a High Commissioner. The functions of the Secretary-General under, or related to, Article 99 of the Charter come to mind in this regard. At the same time, some specialized good-offices practices could develop within the office of a High Commissioner for Human Rights, as have developed within the office of the United Nations High Commissioner for Refugees.

The conclusion that the good offices of the proposed High Commissioner for Human Rights would be within the range of those of the Secretary-General of the United Nations is an important one. For if the good offices of the High Commissioner must stay within the range of those of the Secretary-General of the United Nations, then the argument that the High Commissioner might intervene in the internal affairs of States would lose some of its force. It would also appear that many of the activities of the proposed High Commissioner could already be carried out under the existing areas of competence of the Secretary-General. This appears to have been the rationale behind the Canadian proposal for a UN Under-Secretary-General for Human Rights which was submitted to the General Assembly in 1979. The establishment of the office of High Commissioner for Human Rights could, however, be seen as a means of assisting the Secretary-General as well as a means of spreading the political responsibilities. The Secretary-General presently carries direct political responsibility for any humanitarian intercession which he makes and he always has to weigh this against his other responsibilities and duties under the Charter. A High Commissioner appointed by the General Assembly could provide a first line in facing the political responsibilities while leaving the Secretary-General freer to act as a detached arbiter later, if necessary.

In chapter III above, we enumerated a list of activities which have, in international practice, been undertaken as part of the exercise of humanitarian good offices. It would seem that practically all of these activities could also be engaged in by a future High Commissioner for Human Rights, while being mindful of existing competences, such as those of the United Nations High Commissioner for Refugees. For purposes of convenience, the list is reproduced here. They are:

(1) To promote human rights generally, including the ratification of human rights treaties.

(2) To facilitate the establishment or restoration of an attitude of respect for human rights.

(3) To alleviate situations of gross violations of human rights.

(4) To ease tensions and facilitate the movement of refugees.

(5) To initiate consultations to help reach solutions to human rights problems.

(6) To assist individuals or groups.

(7) To assist in the drafting of legislation or the establishment of national or local institutions for the promotion and protection of human rights.

(8) To resolve practical or legal difficulties encountered in the application of a human rights convention.

(9) To provide for contingencies, cases, or situations outside regular mandates or to provide *ad hoc* protection where there is a lack of specific authorization.

(10) To support the activities of human rights organs through discreet facilitative action behind the scenes.

(11) To fill gaps left by human rights organs, particularly in responding to urgent situations.

(12) To bring about friendly settlements of complaints.

(13) To provide equitable relief in cases where the strict application of rules might result in lack of justice.

(14) To engage in fact-finding, diplomatic, mediatory, or conciliatory activities.

(15) To respond to human needs generally, particularly in situations of emergency or those entailing human suffering.

NOTES

1. See R.S. Clark, A United Nations High Commissioner for Human Rights (1972), chapter 2, "The Development of the High Commissioner Proposal."
2. ECOSOC resolution 1237 (XLII) reproduced by Clark, *op. cit.* in annex I.

3. A/C.3/32/25/Rev. 1.
4. Para. 2, sub-paras. (a) and (b).
5. J. Blaustein, "Human Rights – A Challenge to the United Nations and to our Generation," (1963), p. 23, cited in R. Clark, *op. cit.*, p. 46.
6. A/C.3/32/SR.50, para. 49.
7. A/C.3/32/SR.67, para. 9.
8. A/C.3/32/SR.67, para. 55.
9. A/C.3/32/SR.51, para. 11; A/C.3/32/SR.67, para. 9.
10. A/C.3/32/SR.52, para. 31.
11. A/C.3/32/SR.55, para. 35.
12. B. Graefrath, "On the 6th Version of the Proposal for a High Commissioner for Human Rights," Bulletin of the GDR Committee for Human Rights, No. 4/78, pp. 36-37.

CONCLUSION

In this review of the humanitarian good offices of the United Nations Secretary-General we have seen how, though convinced of the importance of the human rights activities of the UN, Secretaries-General Lie and Hammarskjöld were faced with the tasks of pioneering the operational responsibilities of the Organization and of the Office of the Secretary-General in the area of the maintenance of international peace and security. The most pressing human rights issue of the early days of the United Nations was the realization of the right to self-determination, and the organization certainly launched itself into a historic mission against colonialism. Some humanitarian good offices were exercised and humanitarian relief efforts undertaken, but, for the most part, the development of operational United Nations action in the field of human rights did not feature among the core strategies of Secretaries-General Lie or Hammarskjöld.

However, the pressure on the United Nations to act against gross violations of human rights increased throughout this period and, as we have seen, the matter was raised in the General Assembly in 1957, as it was again raised later, in the 1960s, the 1970s and the 1980s. The question became a matter of credibility for the world organization during the tenure of Secretary-General U Thant who, being the ascetic figure he was, often spoke out publicly against such violations. He did this methodically, acting with discretion and lack of publicity at first, and publicly later as necessary. In the Bangladesh case we saw the lengths to which he went, as he broke new ground in trying to give justice a world-wide dimension. The Bangladesh case underscored the need for action by the Secretary-General when the United Nations organs concerned failed to act.

During the tenure of Secretary-General Kurt Waldheim the need for action by the Secretary-General continued to build up. This was seen dramatically in relation to the situation of refugees and displaced persons in South-East Asia. Secretary-General Waldheim developed the line taken by U Thant. He acted occasionally without any enabling resolution of a policy-making organ and was successful in containing the consideration of some complex situations within a humanitarian context.

During the tenureship of these four Secretaries-General we see: first, a continually growing recognition of the need for the United Nations to act against gross violations of human rights; second, the need for the Secretary-General to act when United Nations organs fail to do so; third, that in situations which are very grave and in which there is a great deal of human suffering, an initiative by the Secretary-General, though it may not necessarily succeed entirely, may run fewer risks of political controversy and could have the moral backing of world public opinion.

From the case studies undertaken we have seen that in relation to the situation in Bangladesh, the Secretary-General's special representative pioneered methods in the exercise of humanitarian good offices. The Secretary-General "initiated the beginning of a body of law by relying explicitly upon the statement of fundamental purposes in the Charter, and his responsibility as the executive of the Organization, to ensure that human well-being was protected and humanitarian principles upheld."[1]

In relation to the situation in Cyprus, where humanitarian good offices were exercised at the request of the Security Council and the General Assembly, the issues involved were political as well as humanitarian. However, even in such a complex situation, the Secretary-General and his representatives were able to make a contribution to the humanitarian aspects of the problems while, at the same time, seeking to assist with the political issues. The Secretary-General operated under many hats and contributed to the development of negotiating and other humanitarian processes – e.g. the establishment of the Committee on Missing Persons in Cyprus.

With respect to Iran, the situation was unusually complex, particularly having regard to the lack of a clear governmental authority at the time, and Secretary-General Waldheim was imaginative and innovative in his search for solutions. He came very near to success in obtaining the release of the hostages, but in the end it eluded him. Nevertheless, it should not be discounted that the efforts of the Secretary-General may have acted as a calming and mitigating influence in a volatile situation. That alone would have justified his efforts. The establishment of the commission of inquiry into alleged human rights violations under the régime of the Shah was decidedly a new and bold type of action for the Secretary-General of the United Nations.

In the case studies on mass exoduses and on the proposal to appoint a UN High Commissioner for Human Rights, we saw how much reliance continues to be placed on the possibilities of utilizing good offices in order to deal with situations of gross violations of human rights.

The following general concluding observations may now be offered:

(1) Humanitarian intercessions by the Secretary-General of the United Nations (or by the heads of organizations such as ILO and UNESCO) are an invaluable and indispensable part of the response of the international community to cases or situations of violations of human rights. Sometimes such intercessions may be the only channel of action available or acceptable.

(2) The label "good offices" has frequently been used to indicate this form of intercession. Good offices have acquired wide usage as a term of art indicating the rendering of some service, attention or kindness, either at the request of a government, an international organ or on a voluntary basis, which is usually carried out in co-operation with the government concerned.

(3) The content and meaning of humanitarian good offices must be derived from international practice. The forms, methods and modalities of humanitarian good offices vary considerably and flexibility of action must be allowed.

(4) The good offices of the United Nations Secretary-General in the field of human rights have become a fully established part of, to use the words of Hammarskjöld, the "common law of organized international co-operation", and therefore of international customary law.

(5) Good offices in the field of human rights have certain characteristics that distinguish them from traditional good offices or that may not even exist in contemporary good offices in the settlement of international disputes generally. Among these the following may be mentioned:

(a) There may be only one government involved.
(b) The matter may be internal to a State (though not within its exclusive domain).
(c) The consent of the State concerned is not necessarily a pre-requisite to the good-offices initiative, though its co-operation will be essential to success.

(d) Good offices may be exercised with respect to situations involving gross violations as well as with respect to individual cases.

(6) Good-offices initiatives must be in accordance with the general principles of the Charter of the United Nations. However, the requirements of the Universal Declaration of Human Rights and the International Covenants on Human Rights must also be taken into account. Good offices should be carried out in a spirit of mutual respect and with discretion.

(7) The exercise of good offices by the United Nations Secretary-General is always discretionary. No element of compulsion or automaticity can or should be injected into this function.

(8) In practice, Secretaries-General in dealing with individual cases, act on the following principles, *inter alia*:

(a) They use their personal judgement as to whether an intercession on their part would be appropriate or helpful.
(b) They are guided mainly by the welfare of the persons concerned.
(c) They act mainly on humanitarian grounds, mindful as a general rule of the injunction against intervention in internal affairs.
(d) They take into account the circumstances and responsibilities of the government(s) concerned.
(e) They normally act confidentially and discreetly, but on occasion they may speak out publicly when necessary.
(f) They may on occasion send a representative to consult with the government concerned.

(9) In dealing with situations of gross violations of human rights, Secretaries-General have adopted the following approaches, *inter alia*:

(a) They may establish contacts with the governments concerned.
(b) They may send a representative for discussion with the government concerned.
(c) They may personally make a visit on the spot.
(d) They may designate a special representative to deal with the situation.
(e) They may seek to provide international humanitarian assistance, particularly through the Office of the United Nations High Commissioner for Refugees.

(f) They may offer United Nations technical assistance.
(g) They may convene an international conference to consider the situation.
(h) They may establish an inquiry into the situation.
(i) They may, if they consider it necessary, comment on the situation publicly or express their concern about it.

Perhaps we should end this work on a cautionary note: while the humanitarian good offices of the Secretary-General are an indispensable part of any system for the promotion and protection of human rights and the need for good offices is felt particularly when United Nations organs fail to act in situations of gross violations of human rights, the humanitarian good offices of the Secretary-General are not a substitute for appropriate action by United Nations organs, and it may not be possible to exercise them in all cases in which they are needed. The need to develop adequate ways and means within the United Nations for dealing with gross violations of human rights must therefore continue to be pressed with full vigour. As the United Nations General Assembly reaffirmed on 17 December 1979, "mass and flagrant violations of human rights are of special concern to the United Nations" and "the appropriate United Nations bodies [must] . . . take timely and effective action in existing and future cases of mass and flagrant violations of human rights."[2]

NOTES

1. B. Morse, "International Humanitarian Rescue Operations," 157 RCADI (1977, IV), pp. 150-194 at p. 150.
2. GA resolution 34/175, reproduced in annex II below.

Annex I

RESOLUTION 27 (XXXVI) OF THE UN COMMISSION ON HUMAN RIGHTS

Good offices role of the Secretary-General in the field of human rights[1]

The Commission on Human Rights,

Bearing in mind General Assembly resolution 34/175 of 17 December 1979 on the need for effective action by the United Nations against mass and flagrant violations of human rights, which, *inter alia*, stressed the important role that the Secretary-General can play in such situations,

Recalling that the Economic and Social Council in its resolution 1979/36 of 10 May 1979 expressed its appreciation to the Secretary-General for his efforts to continue rendering the good offices envisaged in the Charter of the United Nations in the field of human rights,

Welcoming the statement of the Secretary-General in his Report on the Work of the Organization submitted to the General Assembly at its thirty-fourth session that he has continued to exert his best endeavours on behalf of human rights whenever he considers that his actions may be of assistance to the persons or groups concerned,

1. *Requests* the Secretary-General to continue and intensify the good offices envisaged in the Charter of the United Nations in the field of human rights;

. . .

NOTE

1. Adopted at the 1577th meeting, on 11 March 1980, without a vote.

Annex II

RESOLUTION 34/175 OF THE UN GENERAL ASSEMBLY

Effective action against mass and flagrant violations of human rights

The General Assembly,

Mindful of the importance given in the Charter of the United Nations to promoting and encouraging respect for human rights and fundamental freedoms for all without distinction as to race, sex, language or religion,

Recognizing that, in accordance with the Universal Declaration of Human Rights, the ideal of free human beings enjoying civil and political freedom and freedom from fear and want can be achieved only if conditions are created whereby everybody may enjoy his civil and political rights as well as his economic, social and cultural rights,

Conscious of the responsibility of the United Nations, expressed *inter alia* in General Assembly resolution 32/130 of 16 December 1977, in dealing with situations of mass and flagrant violations of human rights,

Believing that disregard and contempt for human rights have resulted in barbarous acts which have outraged the conscience of mankind,

Recalling the statements made at the current session of the General Assembly by representatives of countries which have recently experienced mass and flagrant violaations of human rights,

1. *Expresses satisfaction* that during the current year several situations of mass and flagrant violations of human rights have ceased, though many serious situations remain to be resolved;

2. *Notes with appreciation* the assistance being offered by the Secretary-General and by various United Nations bodies to countries which have recently experienced situations of mass and flagrant violations of human rights;

3. *Reaffirms* that mass and flagrant violations of human rights are of special concern to the United Nations;

4. *Urges* the appropriate United Nations bodies, within their man-

dates, particularly the Commission on Human Rights, to take timely and effective action in existing and future cases of mass and flagrant violations of human rights;

5. *Stresses* the important role that the Secretary-General can play in situations of mass and flagrant violations of human rights.

Annex III

RESOLUTION 25 (XXXIII) OF THE SUB-COMMISSION ON PREVENTION OF DISCRIMINATION AND PROTECTION OF MINORITIES

Question of the violation of human rights and fundamental freedoms, including policies of racial discrimination and segregation and of apartheid, in all countries, with particular reference to colonial and other dependent countries and territories

The Sub-Commission on Prevention of Discrimination and Protection of Minorities,

Recalling resolution 8 (XXIII) of the Commission on Human Rights,

Mindful of its experience in considering situations of violations of human rights, including those referred to it by the Commission on Human Rights,

Noting that as regards forms of urgent action, the Sub-Commission has been used in the past as a forum to discuss situations, to adopt resolutions expressing concern thereon, or to draw situations to the attention of organs such as the General Assembly and the Commission on Human Rights,

Recalling the provisions of paragraphs 4 and 5 of resolution 28 (XXXVI) of the Commission on Human Rights on the possibility of the creation of an international role for the Commission's Bureau and on the possible need for convening emergency sessions of the Commission in order to consider responding to reports of mass and flagrant violations of human rights of an urgent nature,

Conscious of the needs to develop further the possibilities open to the United Nations for dealing with situations of gross violations of human rights of an urgent nature which may arise, particularly in periods when neither the Commission nor the Sub-Commission is in session,

1. *Decides* to inform the Commission of its readiness to assist the Commission in responding to reports of mass and flagrant violations of human rights of an urgent nature and, to this end, recommends that the Commission, in considering this matter, should give attention also to

ways and means by which the Sub-Commission, particularly having regard to the expert character of its composition, can contribute to the response of the United Nations to reports of mass and flagrant violations of human rights of an urgent nature;

2. *Decides,* in this regard, to draw the attention of the Commission to the ideas contained in the annex to the present resolution in connexion with possible future roles of the Sub-Commission as part of United Nations responses to emergency situations of violations of human rights;

3. *Urges* the Commission to consider approaches to the handling of emergency situations by the United Nations which seek to complement the activities of the Commission by utilizing the possibilities of the various Charter-based human rights organs which meet outside of the annual session of the Commission, such as the General Assembly, the Security Council and the Economic and Social Council, and by drawing upon the possible assistance of subsidiary organs such as the Sub-Commission on Prevention of Discrimination and Protection of Minorities;

4. *Recommends* to the Commission on Human Rights that it recommend the Economic and Social Council to consider including as a regular item on its agenda the question of emergency situations of violations of human rights;

5. *Suggests also* that due consideration be given to the various useful avenues open to the Secretary-General in responding to reports of mass and flagrant violations of human rights of an urgent nature by, for example, bringing a United Nations presence to bear on situations through the exercise of his good offices, through personal contacts, the use of special representatives, members of the United Nations Secretariat, United Nations field officers, other emissaries, or through other appropriate discreet methods;

6. *Requests* the Secretary-General to inform the Sub-Commission at its thirty-fourth session of the deliberations of the Commission on this matter, as well as of any consideration which may be given to it by the General Assembly, the Economic and Social Council or the Security Council.

Annex

Ideas which may be considered in connexion with possible future roles of the Sub-Commission as part of United Nations responses to urgent situations of violations of human rights

(1) The Sub-Commission may be used as a forum for discussing emergency situations or for expressing international concern thereon.
(2) The Sub-Commission may seek appropriate channels within the United Nations to bring a United Nations presence to bear upon situations as a matter of urgency. This could be done, for example, by the Sub-Commission drawing a situation to the attention of the President of the General Assembly, the President of the Security Council, the President of the Economic and Social Council, the Chairman of the Commission on Human Rights, or the Secretary-General, as appropriate, with a view to their interceding with the Government concerned or taking other appropriate action.
(3) In particularly serious instances the Sub-Commission could draw a situation directly to the attention of the General Assembly, which meets shortly after the sessions of the Sub-Commission.
(4) The Sub-Commission could suggest the inclusion in the agenda of the next session of the Commission of an iem or a subitem on a specific situation or on emergency situations.
(5) The Sub-Commission could, in situations which it considers especially serious, designate one of its members to make an analysis of the information available on that situation and present that analysis to the Commission on Human Rights at its next session.
(6) In situations considered by the Sub-Commission, the Sub-Commission could be granted the competence to intercede, through the Secretary-General, directly with Governments concerned if this appears necessary in order to save lives or to prevent imminent danger to life or physical integrity or security.
(7) Consideration could be given to the possibility of utilizing the Bureau of the Sub-Commission to respond to emergency situations of violations of human rights, particularly having regard to the expert character of the membership of the Sub-Commission and of its Bureau.

Annex IV

FUNCTIONS OF THE OFFICE OF THE UNDER-SECRETARIES-GENERAL FOR SPECIAL POLITICAL AFFAIRS

Functions

Undertakes special political, economic and social assignments, including supervision of peace-keeping operations under the Secretary-General's direction.

Organization

Under-Secretaries-General for Special Political Affairs

Office of the Under-Secretaries-General

Provides a special staff to assist the Secretary-General in overseeing United Nations peace-keeping operations and certain *ad hoc* or special political missions;

Provides advice to certain humanitarian missions and relief operations on the political aspects of their work;

Assists the Secretary-General in the exercise of his good offices for the settlement of certain political or humanitarian issues.[1]

NOTE

1. Emphasis added. Text taken from UN doc. ST/SGB/Organization, Section D/Rev. 1, September, 1976.

Annex V

EXTRACT FROM THE VERBATIM RECORDS OF THE 2301ST PLENARY MEETING OF THE UN GENERAL ASSEMBLY[1]

The PRESIDENT (Mr. Bouteflika (Algeria)) (interpretation from French): I should like to summarize the situation to make sure that I have correctly understood what action is being called for from the Secretary-General of the United Nations and the President of the twenty-ninth session of the General Assembly.

The representative of the United Republic of Tanzania, speaking on behalf of the African Group, has informed the General Assembly, after consultation with various heads of regional groups, of the concern of the members of the General Assembly over recent events in Ethiopia.

The representative of Saudi Arabia, on the one hand, and that of Canada, on the other, have spoken in support of the request made by the representative of Tanzania on behalf of the African Group as a whole. The Foreign Minister of Ethiopia has given the General Assembly the clarifications available to him, given the means of communication that are at his disposal at the moment. He has given an undertaking to the General Assembly that he will inform his Government of the legitimate concern of Members of our Organization.

I infer from this short debate – in view of the differences in time zones, and also in view of the increasingly alarming nature of the press releases reaching us, to the effect that another group of people might be executed tomorrow, Thursday, and a third group on Saturday – that the General Assembly would wish both the Secretary-General of the United Nations and the President of the twenty-ninth session of the General Assembly acting in accordance with the United Nations Charter, and with the principles set forth in the Universal Declaration of Human Rights, to do all they can to save the human lives now in danger and provide them with a minimum of protection through what the Minister of Foreign Affairs of Ethiopia has referred to as "a fair trial under normal judicial processes."

It is quite clear, therefore, that in the minds of members of the General Assembly, collectively and individually, the action does not in any way represent interference in the domestic affairs of a Member State.

Is there any objection to my interpretation? Since there is none, I take it that I have correctly understood the significance of the action.

NOTE

1. A/PV.2301, pp. 16-17.

Annex VI

AGREEMENT BETWEEN UN SECRETARY-GENERAL AND GOVERNMENT OF PAKISTAN ON CONDITIONS FOR DISCHARGE OF FUNCTIONS OF UNITED NATIONS RELIEF OPERATIONS IN EAST PAKISTAN (1971)[1]

In a letter dated 20 September 1971 to the President of Pakistan, General Agha Muhammad Yahya Khan, the Secretary-General put on record his understanding of the principles upon which the United Nations East Pakistan Relief Operation (UNEPRO) is based, as follows:

"Now that the United Nations relief operation is established and functioning in East Pakistan, I should like to put on record my understanding of the principles on which this United Nations effort is based.

As Your Excellency knows, this operation was initiated because it seemed imperative to act with speed in order to forestall by a strictly humanitarian action the possibility of famine and related disasters which might cost the lives of vast numbers of human beings in East Pakistan. This meant that the operation had to be launched solely on the basis of Your Excellency's acceptance of my offer of humanitarian assistance by and through the United Nations for the relief of the distressed people of East Pakistan, and of the assurances given by Your Excellency to my Personal Representative, Mr. Ismat Kittani, during his visit to Islamabad in June of this year. On that occasion, as Your Excellency will recall, you welcomed and gave your full support to the United Nations operation being set up in such a way as to enable me to give contributors and donors the requisite assurances that the relief provided by and through the United Nations was reaching those for whom it was destined, the people of East Pakistan.

The United Nations effort in East Pakistan is an unusual – even an unprecedented – form of activity for the Organization. I initiated this operation, even without any supporting resolution from any United Nations organ, because I felt that my obligations under the Charter must include any humanitarian action which I could take to save the lives of large numbers of human beings. The operation is, as Your Excellency knows, entirely dependent on the response by governments and other donors to my various appeals for help and is based exclusively on voluntary contributions. I need not emphasize here that this is a purely humanitarian operation unrelated to economic assistance of a more long-term nature.

Especially in view of the unusual nature of this operation, it is now necessary for its smooth functioning that we fill in the legal and other details which are normally required in an undertaking of this kind and which were omitted during the initial phase because of the speed with which the emergency had to be met. The arrangements outlined below are designed to put the operation on a more customary and regular basis without of course affecting any standing agreements or arrangements the various organizations or agencies engaged in the operation may have with Your Excellency's Government.

In sending this message to Your Excellency I have in mind, first, the necessity of a good working relationship on the ground between United Nations personnel and all those with whom they will have to deal in East Pakistan. Second, I am very conscious of my obligations to those governments and agencies who have made voluntary contributions to this relief operation and their desire to be assured as to the use of the relief provided. Thirdly, I am anxious to clarify the record so as to avoid any possible misunderstandings between the Government of Pakistan and the United Nations concerning the way in which this operation is to be run."

On the basis of this letter, discussions were held at Headquarters with the Permanent Representative of Pakistan, resulting in an agreed statement of "Conditions for the effective discharge of the functions of the United Nations East Pakistan Relief Operation". The agreement was finalized by an exchange of letters between the Secretary-General and the Permanent Representative of Pakistan dated 15 and 16 November 1971. The agreed text of the "Conditions for the effective discharge of the functions of UNEPRO" is reproduced below:

Conditions for the effective discharge of the functions of the United Nations East Pakistan Relief Operation (UNEPRO)

1. A Chief of Mission shall be appointed by the Secretary-General, who shall exercise full authority, on behalf of the Secretary-General,

over the conduct of UNEPRO. In selecting the Chief of Mission, the Secretary-General shall take into consideration the views of the Government of Pakistan.

2. UNEPRO shall consist of such officials as the Secretary-General may assign or appoint for the purpose of discharging the Operation's functions, namely, international officials of the United Nations, its programmes and Specialized Agencies, and officials locally recruited for the purposes of UNEPRO. Such officials, with the exception of those locally recruited and employed at hourly rates, shall be accorded the privileges and immunities specified in Article V of the Convention on the Privileges and Immunities of the United Nations and Article VI of the Convention on the Privileges and Immunities of the Specialized Agencies, to both of which instruments Pakistan is a Party. UNEPRO personnel shall respect the laws and regulations of Pakistan and shall refrain from any action incompatible with their status as officials of the United Nations or of the Specialized Agencies.

3. UNEPRO associated personnel shall consist of persons, other than those referred to in paragraph 2 above, who are not of Pakistan nationality and who are engaged in relief activities forming part of UNEPRO. UNEPRO associated personnel shall, in particular, include international members of the crews of vessels engaged in activities forming part of UNEPRO and such additional categories of personnel (other than those covered under paragraph 2 above) as may be agreed between the Government of Pakistan and the United Nations. The Secretary-General shall provide to the Government of Pakistan at its request lists of UNEPRO associated personnel, and shall from time to time inform it of any changes in those lists. The Government of Pakistan shall grant UNEPRO associated personnel immunity from legal process in respect of words spoken or written and all acts performed by them in the course of such activities. UNEPRO associated personnel shall respect the laws and regulations of Pakistan and shall refrain from any action incompatible with their functions.

4. UNEPRO personnel and associated personnel shall enjoy freedom of access to, and freedom of movement within East Pakistan. In particular they shall have free access to the places and facilities where relief supplies brought in by, or under the auspices of, the United Nations, are discharged, stored, transported or distributed. Such freedom of access and movement shall include the use of motor vehicles, vessels used for sea and river navigation, and equipment, required in connexion with

UNEPRO activities. The freedom of access and movement envisaged in this paragraph may be subject to temporary restriction for security reasons. The Chief of Mission shall be informed when such restrictions are imposed and shall be consulted with a view to ensuring that activities forming part of UNEPRO can continue to be conducted so far as possible without interruption.

5 (a). All property, equipment and forms of transport used as part of UNEPRO, as well as all relief supplies brought in by, or under the auspices of, the United Nations, shall be afforded free entry into Pakistan and expeditious handling. They shall not be diverted to any purpose incompatible with the functions of UNEPRO.

(b). The Government of Pakistan shall provide free storage facilities for relief supplies brought in by, or under the auspices of, the United Nations. Arrangements shall be made for regular on-the-spot consultations between officials of the Government of Pakistan and UNEPRO personnel and associated personnel regarding customs formalities and similar matters.

6. UNEPRO personnel and associated personnel shall enjoy an unrestricted right of communication, by radio, telephone, telegraph or other means when performing duties forming part of UNEPRO. The United Nations may for this purpose, establish a system of radio communication in East Pakistan connected with the UN radio network, which shall be operated in accordance with such international agreements, conventions and regulations as may be in force.

7. The United Nations flag, markings and emblem may be used in connexion with UNEPRO as the Chief of Mission shall determine.

8. The Government of Pakistan shall take all necessary measures to ensure the security and safety of all UNEPRO personnel and associated personnel, and of all premises, facilities, means of transport and equipment used in connexion with UNEPRO activities.

9. The United Nations and the Government of Pakistan shall extend to each other the fullest possible co-operation in order that activities forming part of UNEPRO may fulfil the strictly humanitarian purposes of the Operation."

NOTE

1. Text taken from UN press release SG/1763; IHA/93, 17 November 1971.

Annex VII

GENERAL ASSEMBLY RESOLUTION 2816 (XXVI)

Assistance in cases of natural disaster and other disaster situations

The General Assembly,

Bearing in mind that throughout history natural disasters and emergency situations have inflicted heavy loss of life and property, affecting every people and every country,

Aware of and concerned about the suffering caused by natural disasters and the serious economic and social consequences for all, especially the developing countries,

Also aware of the varying needs of nations experiencing such disorders, which present new challenges for international co-operation,

Concerned about the ability of the international community to come to the aid of countries in a disaster situation,

Recalling its resolutions 2034 (XX) of 7 December 1965, 2435 (XXIII) of 19 December 1968, 2608 (XXIV) of 16 December 1969 and 2717 (XXV) of 15 December 1970, and Economic and Social Council resolutions 1533 (XLIX) of 23 July 1970 and 1546 (XLIX) of 30 July 1970 on assistance in cases of natural disaster,

Expressing appreciation of the Secretary-General's comprehensive report[1] and of its perceptive examination of all aspects of the question, and taking note of the relevant passage in his statement to the Economic and Social Council on 5 July 1971,[2]

Taking note of Economic and Social Council resolution 1612 (LI) of 23 July 1971 on assistance in cases of natural disaster and other emergency situations,

Noting the study, annexed to the Secretary-General's report, on the legal status of disaster relief units made available through the United Nations,[3]

Mindful of the need to strengthen and make more effective the collective efforts of the international community, and particularly the United Nations system, in the field of international disaster assistance,

Bearing in mind that assistance provided at the request of the stricken countries, without prejudice to their individual country programmes under the United Nations Development Programme, can be an effective contribution to the rehabilitation and development of the stricken areas,

Bearing in mind also that the possible response of the International Bank for Reconstruction and Development and other credit organizations and development agencies to a request from the Governments concerned for complementary assistance to the stricken areas, without prejudice to the assistance provided by those organizations for the normal development programmes of the stricken countries, can be an important element in the reconstruction and development of those areas,

Noting the competence of the United Nations and its related agencies, the United Nations Children's Fund, the United Nations High Commissioner for Refugees and the World Food Programme to render assistance in cases of natural disaster and other disaster situations,

Noting further the key role which the resident representatives of the United Nations Development Programme could play at the country level,

Recognizing the vital role in international relief played by the International Red Cross and other voluntary societies,

Recognizing further the necessity to ensure prompt, effective and efficient response to a Government's need for assistance, at the time of a natural disaster or other disaster situation, that will bring to bear the resources of the United Nations system, prospective donor countries and voluntary agencies,

1. *Calls upon* the Secretary-General to appoint a Disaster Relief Co-ordinator, who will report directly to him and who will be authorized, on his behalf:

(a) To establish and maintain the closest co-operation with all organizations concerned and to make all feasible advance arrangements with them for the purpose of ensuring the most effective assistance;

(b) To mobilize, direct and co-ordinate the relief activities of the various organizations of the United Nations system in response to a request for disaster assistance from a stricken State;

(c) To co-ordinate United Nations assistance with assistance given by intergovernmental and non-governmental organizations, in particular by the International Red Cross;

(d) To receive, on behalf of the Secretary-General, contributions offered to him for disaster relief assistance to be carried out by the United Nations, its agencies and programmes for particular emergency situations;

(e) To assist the Government of the stricken country to assess its relief and other needs and to evaluate the priority of those needs, to disseminate that information to prospective donors and others concerned, and to serve as a clearing-house for assistance extended or planned by all sources of external aid;

(f) To promote the study, prevention, control and prediction of natural disasters, including the collection and dissemination of information concerning technological developments;

(g) To assist in providing advice to Governments on pre-disaster planning in association with relevant voluntary organizations, particularly with the League of Red Cross Societies, and to draw upon United Nations resources available for such purposes;

(h) To acquire and disseminate information relevant to planning and co-ordinating disaster relief, including the improvement and establishment of stockpiles in disaster-prone areas, and to prepare suggestions to ensure the most effective use of available resources;

(i) To phase out relief operations under his aegis as the stricken country moves into the stage of rehabilitation and reconstruction, but to continue to interest himself, within the framework of his responsibilities for relief, in the activities of the United Nations agencies concerned with rehabilitation and reconstruction;

(j) To prepare an annual report for the Secretary-General, to be submitted to the Economic and Social Council and to the General Assembly;

2. *Recommends* that the Disaster Relief Co-ordinator should be appointed by the Secretary-General normally for a term of five years and at a level comparable to that of an Under-Secretary-General of the United Nations;

3. *Endorses* the Secretary-General's proposals for an adequate permanent office in the United Nations which shall be the focal point in the United Nations system for disaster relief matters;

4. *Recommends* that that office should be headed by the Disaster Relief Co-ordinator and located in Geneva, be a distinct element within the United Nations Secretariat and be augmented as necessary by short-term secondment of personnel for individual emergencies;

5. *Requests* the Secretary-General to prepare for the Economic and

Social Council at its fifty-third session, taking into account any relevant suggestions and the experience gained by the Disaster Relief Co-ordinator, a report on any further steps which may be required to enable the Disaster Relief Co-ordintor adequately to perform the functions entrusted to him under the present resolution;

6. *Further endorses* the plan for a roster of volunteers, to be drawn from experienced staff members of the United Nations system and interested non-governmental organizations, who could be made available at very short notice;

7. *Recommends* that the Disaster Relief Co-ordinator should maintain contact with the Governments of States Members of the United Nations or members of specialized agencies or of the International Atomic Energy Agency concerning available aid in emergency situations, such as food supplies, medicines, personnel, transportation and communications, as well as advice to countries in pre-disaster planning and preparedness;

8. *Invites* potential recipient Governments:

(a) To establish disaster contingency plans with appropriate assistance from the Disaster Relief Co-ordinator;

(b) To appoint a single national disaster relief co-ordinator to facilitate the receipt of international aid in times of emergency;

(c) To establish stockpiles of emergency supplies, such as tents, blankets, medicines and non-perishable food-stuffs;

(d) To make necessary arrangements for the training of administrative and relief personnel;

(e) To consider appropriate legislative or other measures to facilitate the receipt of aid, including overflight and landing rights and necessary privileges and immunities for relief units;

(f) To improve national disaster warning systems;

9. *Invites* potential donor Governments:

(a) To respond promptly to any call by the Secretary-General or, on his behalf, by the Disaster Relief Co-ordinator;

(b) To consider and to continue offering on a wider basis emergency assistance in disaster situations;

(c) To inform the Disaster Relief Co-ordinator in advance about the facilities and services they might be in a position to provide immediately, including where possible relief units, logistical support and means of effective communication;

10. *Decides* to authorize the Secretary-General to draw on the Work-

ing Capital Fund in the amount of $200,000 for emergency assistance in any one year, with a normal ceiling of $20,000 per country in the case of any one disaster;

11. *Further invites* all organizations of the United Nations system and all other organizations involved to co-operate with the Disaster Relief Co-ordinator.

NOTES

1. E/4994.
2. See Official Records of the Economic and Social Council, fifty-first session, 1773rd meeting.
3. E/4994, annex III.

Annex VIII

GENERAL ASSEMBLY RESOLUTION 36/225

Strengthening the capacity of the United Nations system to respond to natural disasters and other disaster situations

The General Assembly,

Recalling its resolutions 2816 (XXVI) of 14 December 1971, by which it established the Office of the United Nations Disaster Relief Co-ordinator, 3243 (XXIX) of 29 November 1974 on the strengthening of that Office, 3440 (XXX) of 9 December 1975, in which it provided, *inter alia*, for measures to be taken in support of the activities of the Office, and 3532 (XXX) of 17 December 1975 on the financing of emergency relief assistance and technical co-operation activities of the Office,

Recalling also its resolution 31/173 of 21 December 1976 on financial arrangements for the Office of the United Nations Disaster Relief Co-ordinator,

Recalling further the International Development Strategy for the Third United Nations Development Decade,[1]

Recalling the report of the United Nations Conference on the Least Developed Countries containing the Substantial New Programme of Action for the 1980s for the Least Developed Countries, in particular the section concerning disaster assistance for least developed countries,[2]

Deeply concerned about the increasing number of natural disasters and other disaster situations, the economic burden borne by disaster-stricken and affected countries, particularly the developing countries, and the disruption thereby caused to their development process,

Also recalling its resolution 35/107 of 5 December 1980,

Further recalling Economic and Social Council resolution 1980/43 of 23 July 1980 regarding international efforts to meet humanitarian needs in natural disaster and other disaster situations,

Fully cognizant of the sovereign interests and rights of affected countries and of the primacy of their role in caring for the victims of natural disasters and other disaster situations,

Anxious that the international community should respond speedily and effectively to calls for emergency humanitarian assistance,

Recognizing that the quality and appropriateness of material and other assistance provided by the international community should meet the particular needs of the populations of disaster-affected areas,

Recognizing the contribution made by the United Nations system to the relief of suffering and provision of humanitarian relief in natural disasters and other disaster situations,

Recognizing that the primary responsibility of administration, relief operations and disaster preparedness lies with the affected countries and that the major part of the material assistance and human effort in disaster relief comes from the Governments of those countries,

Recognizing also the importance in international relief of the contribution of the International Committee of the Red Cross, the League of Red Cross and Red Crescent Societies and appropriate voluntary organizations,

Recognizing further that, in order to attain an effective co-ordination system of humanitarian and disaster relief assistance, it is essential to strengthen and improve the capacity and effectiveness of the Office of the United Nations Disaster Relief Co-ordinator and the United Nations system as a whole in order to enable the Office to respond to natural disasters and other disaster situations speedily, efficiently and effectively, and thereby ensure prompt delivery of concerted relief,

Recognizing that a major constraint for the United Nations system to respond effectively to natural disasters and other disaster situations has been the shortage of resources,

1. *Takes note* of the reports of the Secretary-General and other reports on international efforts to meet humanitarian needs in emergency situations, as well as on measures for strengthening the capacity of the United Nations system to respond to natural disasters and other disaster situations[3] and of the statement made by the United Nations Disaster Relief Co-ordinator before the Second Committee on 5 November 1981;[4]

2. *Reaffirms* the sovereignty of individual Member States, recognizes the primary role of each State in caring for the victims of disasters occurring in its territory and stresses that all relief operations should be carried out and co-ordinated in a manner consistent with the priorities and needs of the countries concerned;

3. *Reaffirms* the mandate of the Office of the United Nations Disaster Relief Co-ordinator, established by the General Assembly in resolution 2816 (XXVI) as the focal point of the United Nations system for disaster relief co-ordination and calls for strengthening and improvement of the capacity and effectiveness of the Office;

4. *Endorses* the approaches outlined by the Secretary-General in his comments on the report of the Joint Inspection Unit concerning the role of the Office of the United Nations Disaster Relief Co-ordinator in the various phases of disaster assistance;[5]

5. *Requests* the Secretary-General to continue to take the necessary steps to strengthen the management operations of the Office of the United Nations Disaster Relief Co-ordinator;

6. *Stresses* the need to take full advantage of information provided by existing early-warning monitoring systems that have been developed to strengthen the capacity of the United Nations system in responding to natural disasters and other disaster situations and to co-ordinate, as far as feasible and useful, all the relevant early-warning systems, and stresses, to this effect, the capability of the Office of the United Nations Disaster Relief Co-ordinator in information collection and dissemination should be further strengthened and improved;

7. *Urges* the appropriate organs, organizations and bodies of the United Nations system, including the United Nations Children's Fund, the Food and Agricultural Organization of the United Nations, the World Health Organization, the Office of the United Nations High Commissioner for Refugees, the World Food Programme and other appropriate bodies, to co-operate closely, in their respective areas of competence, with the Office of the United Nations Disaster Relief Co-ordinator in disaster relief activities and other disaster situations, to respond effectively to the needs of the situation and to comply promptly with the requests of disaster-affected countries;

8. *Decides* that, in response to a request for disaster relief from a disaster-stricken State and, as necessary, in particular in disaster-prone countries, the United Nations resident co-ordinator shall, with the full concurrence, consent and participation of the Government, convene meetings of the concerned organs, organizations and bodies of the United Nations system to plan, monitor and take immediate action to provide assistance; the International Committee of the Red Cross, the League of Red Cross and Red Crescent Societies and appropriate voluntary organizations may be invited to participate in such meetings with the approval of the host country;

9. *Decides* that, following a request for disaster relief from a disaster-stricken State and whenever required to deal effectively with complex disasters and emergencies of exceptional magnitude, the Secretary-General or his representative, who would normally be the United Nations Disaster Relief Co-ordinator, shall convene meetings of the concerned organizations of the United Nations system in order to develop a concerted relief programme and conduct *ad hoc* consultations with the heads or representatives of the agencies concerned with disaster-relief questions, with a view to ensuring speedy and efficient delivery of goods and services to the disaster-stricken areas, and decides that these *ad hoc* consultations should draw on information provided by the Government concerned, as well as on the assessments of the United Nations Disaster Relief Co-ordinator, the resident co-ordinator and representatives of other United Nations organizations in the countries concerned, and take into account advice offered by the International Committee of the Red Cross, the League of Red Cross and Red Crescent Societies and appropriate voluntary organizations in the field; all agencies with responsibilities for natural disasters and other disaster situations should be involved at the appropriate level in such consultations;

10. *Decides* that, once it has been determined – on the basis of the above-mentioned information and consultations – that an exceptional or complex natural disaster or other disaster situation requiring system-wide action exists, the Secretary-General shall designate, at the international level, a lead entity from among the United Nations organizations, agencies and bodies, including the Office of the United Nations Disaster Relief Co-ordinator, and, at the country level, the appropriate entity of the United Nations system to carry out relief operations, taking into account the specific requirements of the situation and in consultation with the host Government, and calls on all organs, organizations and bodies of the United Nations system to co-operate closely with one another in their relief operations;

11. *Invites* the Administrative Committee on Co-ordination to examine urgently the role of the lead entity and participating organs, organizations and bodies of the United Nations system in complex disaster situations, taking into account decision 1981/2 of the Administrative Committee on Co-ordination, and requests the Secretary-General to submit a report, through the Economic and Social Council at its second regular session of 1982, to the General Assembly at its thirty-seventh session, on the deliberations of the Committee;

12. *Strongly calls upon* all States to respond positively and expeditiously to the Secretary-General's appeals for contributions to meet natural disasters and other disaster situations;

13. *Reiterates*, in particular, its appeal in resolution 35/107 for increased contributions to the trust fund of the Office of the United Nations Disaster Relief Co-ordinator, in particular to the sub-account for humanitarian emergency relief;

14. *Stresses* in this regard the need to strengthen the operational capacity and the human, material and financial resources available to individual agencies and organizations, in order to enable them to play their respective roles more promptly, efficiently and effectively in natural disasters and other disaster situations;

15. *Requests* all States to ensure a full flow of information to the Office of the United Nations Disaster Relief Co-ordinator, especially regarding relief actions, and also to provide the United Nations system with the necessary personnel and logistical support;

16. *Urges* Governments in disaster-prone countries to explore further, with the assistance of the donors, appropriate organs, organizations and bodies of the United Nations system, the possibility of improving storage, communication and transportation facilities, as well as measures to ensure disaster prepardness and prevention;

17. *Also urges* the international community to assist disaster-prone countries, upon their request, with the establishment of effective national and early-warning systems, the development of contingency plans for disasters and the strengthening of assessment capacity for relief requirements and for distribution and monitoring of relief supplies;

18. *Calls upon* organs, organizations and bodies of the United Nations system involved in the provision of humanitarian assistance and disaster relief to establish emergency units or focal points if they are not already in existence;

19. *Reaffirms* the need for the international community to respond fully to requests for emergency and humanitarian assistance, in particular through increased financial contributions for affected developing countries, bearing in mind the relevant provisions of the International Development Strategy for the Third United Nations Development Decade, the Substantial New Programme of Action for the 1980s for the Least Developed Countries,[6] as well as those of the trust fund of the Office of the United Nations Disaster Relief Co-ordinator;

20. *Requests* the Secretary-General to submit a preliminary progress

report on the implementation of the present resolution to the General Assembly at its thirty-seventh session through the Economic and Social Council at its second regular session of 1982, and a comprehensive report to the Assembly at its thirty-eighth session through the Council at its second regular session of 1983.

NOTES

1. General Assembly resolution 35/56, annex.
2. A/CONF.104/22 and Add.1, part one, para. 59.
3. See A/36/73 and Add.1; A/36/259; E/1981/16 and Corr.1, annex; and decision 1981/2 of the Administrative Committee on Co-ordination.
4. A/C.2/36/SR.29, paras. 33-40.
5. A/36/73/Add.1.
6. A/CONF.104/22 and Add.1, part one, para. 59.

Annex IX

UNITAR'S PROPOSED MODEL RULES FOR DISASTER RELIEF OPERATIONS[1]

A. Model rules for bilateral agreement between an assisting state and a receiving state

Rule 1
The receiving State shall designate a national relief authority to co-ordinate the relief activities.

Rule 2
The assisting State shall, *inter alia*,
(1) Give to the designated national authority information about the assistance it can immediately provide.
(2) Ensure that the relief assistance it provides is restricted to appropriate relief needs. In particular, it shall consult the designated national authority with respect to the needs of the receiving State.
(3) Ensure that the relief assistance it provides is correctly timed. In particular, it shall promptly notify the designated national authority of impending relief shipments.

Rule 3
The receiving State shall employ disaster assistance exclusively for the purpose for which it has been supplied. Relief supplies shall be distributed without discrimination.

Rule 4
The assisting State shall, in accordance with agreed standards, appropriately pack, classify and mark relief supplies, and shall include detailed manifests with each shipment.

Rule 5
The receiving State and the assisting State shall waive normal commer-

cial documentation requirements or use simplified documentation and procedures in regard to designated relief supplies. The receiving State shall duly notify the assisting State of the precise documentation and procedures required. In any event absolute priority shall be granted to relief supplies.

Rule 6

The receiving State and the assisting State shall exempt the designated relief supplies from customs duties, taxes, fees, or tolls chargeable by reason of exportation or importation.

Rule 7

The receiving State and the assisting State shall relax to the extent compatible with standards of hygiene and animal protection normal requirements regarding fumigation and prohibitions and restrictions on food imports and exports in regard to the designated relief supplies.

Rule 8

(1) The receiving State and the assisting State shall take all possible measures for their airlines to provide transport on a priority basis for designated relief personnel and relief supplies.

(2) The receiving State and the assisting State shall take all possible measures so that their airlines accord free transportation or transportation at minimal fares or rates for the designated relief personnel and relief supplies.

Rule 9

The receiving State and the assisting State shall waive limitations imposed on aircraft not possessing traffic rights when such waiver is necessary for taking on or discharging the designated relief personnel and relief supplies.

Rule 10

The receiving State shall grant permission for overflight and landing of aircraft transporting designated relief personnel and relief supplies.

Rule 11

(1) The receiving State and the assisting State shall provide, subject to availability, adequate means of transport and handling equipment on a priority basis for the movement of designated relief supplies.

(2) The receiving State and the assisting State shall provide, to designated relief supplies using facilities operated or administered by the State, free transportation or tariffs or charges that are reasonable as regards both their rates and the method of their application. These charges shall not be higher than the charges applied by the State for the transport of its own supplies.

Rule 12

The receiving State shall authorize the designated relief personnel in the performance of their duties to use on a priority basis, free or at rates not higher than the rates applied by the receiving State, telex, cable, wire, telephone, and other means of communication. The receiving State may also authorize the designated relief personnel to establish a system of radio communication.

Rule 13

The receiving State shall allow the assisting State to maintain bank accounts and to convert currency held by it into local currency as necessitated by the relief function and at the most favourable rate of exchange.

Rule 14

The receiving State shall extend to the designated relief personnel the necessary facilities with a view to securing the expeditious performance of relief functions. Relief personnel shall co-operate at all times with the appropriate authorities of the receiving State to facilitate the proper administration of justice, secure the observance of police regulations and prevent the occurrence of any abuse in connection with the facilities granted.

Rule 15

The receiving State shall waive requirements for entry and exit visas, provide with minimum delay visas at points of entry and exit, or issue multiple entry and exit visas, for the designated relief personnel. The assisting State shall waive requirements for, or provide with the minimum delay, exit visas for its designated relief personnel.

Rule 16

The receiving State shall permit the designated relief personnel freedom of access to, and freedom of movement within, disaster-stricken areas that are necessary for the performance of their specifically agreed functions.

Rule 17
The receiving State shall take all necessary measures to ensure the security and safety of the designated relief personnel and of all premises, facilities, means of transport and equipment used in connection with relief activities.

B. Model rules for bilateral agreement between an assisting organization and a receiving State

Rule 1
The receiving State shall designate a national relief authority to coordinate the relief activities.

Rule 2
The assisting organization shall, *inter alia*,
(1) Give to the designated authority information about the assistance it can immediately provide.
(2) Ensure that the relief assistance it provides is restricted to appropriate relief needs. In particular, it shall consult the designated national authority with respect to the needs of the receiving State.
(3) Ensure that the relief assistance it provides is correctly timed. In particular, it shall promptly notify the designated national authority of impending relief shipments.

Rule 3
The receiving State shall employ disaster assistance exclusively for the purpose for which it has been supplied. Relief supplies shall be distributed without discrimination.

Rule 4
The assisting organization shall, in accordance with agreed standards, appropriately pack, classify and mark relief supplies, and shall include detailed manifests with each shipment.

Rule 5

The receiving State shall waive normal commercial documentation requirements or use simplified documentation and procedures in regard to designated relief supplies. The receiving State shall duly notify the assisting organization of the precise documentation and procedures required. In any event absolute priority shall be granted to relief supplies.

Rule 6

The receiving State shall exempt the designated relief supplies from customs duties, fees or tolls chargeable by reason of importation.

Rule 7

The receiving State shall relax to the extent compatible with standards of hygiene and animal protection normal requirements regarding fumigation and prohibitions and restrictions on food imports and exports in regard to the designated relief supplies.

Rule 8

(1) The receiving State shall take all possible measures for its airlines to provide transport on a priority basis for designated relief personnel and relief supplies.

(2) The receiving State shall take all possible measures so that its airlines accord free transportation or transportation at minimal fares or rates for designated relief personnel and relief supplies.

Rule 9

The receiving State shall waive limitations imposed on aircraft not possessing traffic rights when such waiver is necessary for taking on or discharging the designated relief personnel and relief supplies.

Rule 10

The receiving State shall grant permission for overflight and landing of aircraft transporting designated relief personnel and relief supplies.

Rule 11

(1) The receiving State shall provide, subject to availability adequate means of transport and handling equipment on a priority basis for the movement of designated relief supplies.

(2) The receiving State shall provide to designated relief supplies using

facilities operated or administered by the State free transportation or tariffs or charges that are reasonable as regards both their rates and the method of their application. These charges shall not be higher than the charges applied by the State for the transport of its own supplies.

Rule 12

The receiving State shall authorize the designated relief personnel in the performance of their duties to use on a priority basis, free or at rates not higher than the rates applied by the receiving State, telex, cable, wire, telephone, and other means of communication. The receiving State may also authorize the designated relief personnel to establish a system of radio communication.

Rule 13

The receiving State shall allow the assisting organization to maintain bank accounts and to convert currency held by it into local currency as necessitated by the relief function and at the most favourable rate of exchange.

Rule 14

(1) (i) The receiving State shall extend to disaster relief units that are subsidiary organs of the United Nations or are made available through the United Nations the privileges and immunities contained in Article I, II and III of the Convention on the Privileges and Immunities of the United Nations. It shall also extend to relief personnel who are:

(a) officials of United Nations, the privileges and immunities contained in Article V and sections 24 and 25 of Article VII of the Convention; (b) experts on missions for the United Nations, the privileges and immunities contained in Article VI of the Convention; (c) holders of certificates that they are travelling on the business of the United Nations, the privileges contained in section 26 of Article VII of the Convention.

(ii) The receiving State shall extend to disaster relief units that are subsidiary organs of the United Nations Specialized Agencies the privileges and immunities contained in Article II, III and IV of the Convention on the Privileges and Immunities of the Specialized Agencies. It shall also extend to relief personnel who are:

(a) officials of the Specialized Agencies the privileges contained in

Article VI and section 27 and 28 of Article VII of the Convention; (b) experts and other persons, holders of certificates that they are travelling on the business of the Specialized Agencies, the privileges contained in section 29 of Article VIII of the Convention.

(iii) The receiving State shall extend to disaster relief units that are subsidiary organs of the International Atomic Energy Agency the privileges and immunities contained in Articles II, III and IV of the agreement on the Privileges and Immunities of the International Atomic Energy Agency. It shall also extend to relief personnel who are:
(a) officials of the Agency, the privileges and immunities contained in Article VI and sections 29 and 30 of Article IX of the agreement; (b) experts on missions for the Agency, the privileges and immunities contained in Article VII of the Agreement; (c) holders of certificates that they are travelling on the business of the Agency the privileges contained in section 31 of Article IX of the Agreement.

(iv) Relief personnel shall co-operate at all times with the appropriate authorities of the receiving State to facilitate the proper administration of justice, secure the observance of police regulations and prevent the occurrence of any abuse in connection with privileges, immunities and facilities granted.

(2) The receiving State shall extend to designated relief personnel the necessary facilities with a view to securing the expeditious performance of relief functions. Relief personnel shall co-operate at all times with the appropriate authorities of the receiving State to facilitate the proper administration of justice, secure the observance of police regulations and prevent the occurrence of any abuse in connection with the facilities granted.

Rule 15

The receiving State shall waive requirements for entry and exit visas, provide with minimum delay visas at points of entry and exit or issue multiple entry and exit visas for designated relief personnel.

Rule 16

The receiving State shall permit the designated relief personnel freedom of access to, and freedom of movement within, disaster-stricken areas that are necessary for the performance of their specifically agreed functions.

Rule 17
The receiving State shall take all necessary measures to ensure the security and safety of the designated relief personnel and of all premises, facilities, means of transport used in connection with relief activities.

C. Model rules for bilateral agreement between an assisting State or organization or a receiving State and a transit State

Rule 1
The transit State shall waive normal commercial documentation requirements or use simplified documentation and procedures in regard to designated relief supplies. The transit State shall duly notify the requesting party of the precise documentation and procedures required. In any event absolute priority shall be granted to relief supplies.

Rule 2
The transit State shall exempt the designated relief supplies from customs duties, taxes, fees or tolls chargeable by reason of importation or exportation or any special dues in respect to transit.

Rule 3
The transit State shall relax to the extent compatible with standards of hygiene and animal protection normal requirements regarding fumigation and prohibitions and restrictions on food imports and exports in regard to the designated relief supplies.

Rule 4
(1) The transit State shall take all possible measures for its airlines to provide transport on a priority basis for designated relief personnel and relief supplies.

(2) The transit State shall take all possible measures so that its airlines accord free transportation or transportation at minimal fares or rates for designated relief personnel and relief supplies.

Rule 5
The transit State shall waive or relax to the minimum limitations imposed on aircraft not possessing traffic rights when such action is necessary for taking on or discharging the designated relief personnel and relief supplies.

Rule 6
The transit State shall grant permission for overflight and landing of aircraft transporting designated relief personnel and relief supplies.

Rule 7
(1) The transit State shall grant freedom of transit for the designated relief supplies.

(2) The transit State shall provide, subject to availability at the points of entry and exit, and as required at points of transshipments, adequate means of transport and handling equipment on a priority basis for the movement of designated relief supplies.

(3) The transit State shall provide to designated relief supplies in transit using facilities operated or administered by the State tariffs or charges that are reasonable as regards both their rates and the method of their application. These charges shall not be higher than the charges applied by the transit State for the transport of its own supplies.

Rule 8
The transit State shall waive requirements for entry and exit visas, provide with minimum delay visas at points of entry and exit, or issue multiple entry and exit visas, for designated relief personnel.

NOTE

1. Contained in UNITAR Policy and Efficacy Studies No. 8: Model Rules for Disaster Relief Operations, UN Sales No. E.82.XV.PE/8.

Annex X

CANADIAN DRAFT RESOLUTION ON GOOD OFFICES OF THE UN SECRETARY-GENERAL IN CASES OF HUMAN RIGHTS VIOLATIONS, CONSIDERED BY UN GENERAL ASSEMBLY AT ITS THIRTY-FIFTH SESSION (UN doc. A/C.3/35/L.78)

The General Assembly,

Conscious of the responsibility of the United Nations expressed, *inter alia*, in resolution 32/130 of 16 December 1977, in dealing with situations of mass and flagrant violations of human rights;

Recalling its resolution 34/175 on Effective Action against Mass and Flagrant Violations of Human Rights;

Taking note of the pertinent provisions of resolutions 1979/36 of the Economic and Social Council and 27 (XXXVI) of the Commission on Human Rights, which requested the Secretary-General to continue and intensify the good offices envisaged in the Charter of the United Nations in the field of human rights;

Further recalling resolution 1980/43 of the Economic and Social Council on international efforts to meet humanitarian needs in emergency situations, as well as resolution 30 (XXXVI) of the Commission on Human Rights on human rights and massive exoduses;

Believing that in cases of mass and flagrant violations of human rights the United Nations should be informed of the facts of a situation as urgently as possible, and should seek to take timely action in dealing with and responding to the humanitarian requirements of such situations;

Recognizing the valuable role performed by the Secretary-General in exercising good offices in respect of situations of mass and flagrant violations of human rights, and in co-operating with Governments in dealing with these situations, by means of personal endeavours, or the use of special representatives, emissaries or experts or by other means;

1. *Reiterates* that mass and flagrant violations of human rights are of special concern to the United Nations;

2. *Urges once again* the appropriate United Nations bodies, within their mandates, particularly the Commission on Human Rights, to take timely and effective action in existing and future cases of mass and flagrant violations of human rights;

3. *Requests* the Secretary-General, when urgent situations of mass and flagrant violations of human rights arise, to consider establishing direct contact with the Government concerned, with a view to assisting the Government concerned in the full restoration of respect for human rights and fundamental freedoms as quickly as possible, and also with a view to considering what forms of assistance the United Nations can provide to the Government concerned;

4. *Further requests* the Secretary-General to keep the President of the Economic and Social Council or Chairman of the Commission on Human Rights informed of developments regarding such situations as well as regarding any action which is to be undertaken in relation thereto.

Annex XI

CANADIAN STATEMENT DELIVERED 19 NOVEMBER 1980 BY MRS. SYLVIA SUTHERLAND TO THE THIRD COMMITTEE OF UNGA 35

Good offices role of the Secretary-General in Situations Involving Human Rights

Mr. Chairman,

In the course of consideration of the previous item on our agenda, a number of proposals, old and new, have been discussed to improve the effective enjoyment of human rights and fundamental freedoms. Many of these are, in the view of my Delegation, potentially very useful and deserve further examination. It is, however, obvious that there does not exist, at this time, the necessary consensus within this Committee to realistically envisage their rapid implementation. We must, therefore, while the search continues for mutually agreed solutions to some of the questions remaining before us, concentrte our efforts on ensuring that machinery and procedures already at our disposal within the UN system are put to the best and most effective use possible.

One such means which has gradually evolved over the years to the point where it has now become universally accepted is the resort to the good offices of the Secretary-General envisaged in the UN Charter in the field of human rights. In the course of the debate just concluded under alternative approaches, a great number of speakers have referred to the good offices role of the Secretary-General and have stressed the constructive contribution that role has made in the past to the effective enjoyment of human rights in the situations when it has been resorted to judiciously. The good offices role of the Secretary-General in the human rights field has gradually been developed over the years by successive Secretaries-General in response to changing circumstances in the world. It has become universally accepted by all members of the United Nations as an integral and essential part of his functions, and it has been employed on many occasions with welcome results.

I believe, Mr. Chairman, that it would be useful to recall the manner in which successive Secretaries-General have perceived their role in the human rights field. Secretary-General Trygvie Lie disclosed in his memoires that he had frequently undertaken efforts on behalf of individuals and groups whose basic freedoms and human rights appeared imperilled. Secretary-General Dag Hammarskjöld relentlessly pursued the search for arrangements to safeguard human rights in South Africa in accordance with United Nations principles. The late U Thant stated "there are great humanitarian emergencies which the United Nations is still not equipped to meet. I am glad that steps are now being taken to fit the organization to deal with natural disasters. The next step is to expand its capability to cover unnatural disasters." In connection with emergencies U Thant wrote "I have felt that an initiative on my part was essential to fill the gap until more regular arrangements can be made and that the Secretary-General's obligations under the Charter include any humanitarian action that he can take to save the lives of large numbers of human beings. The political aspects of such situaions on the other hand must obviously fall as far as the United Nations is concerned primarily within the competence of the Security Council."

In 1978, our current Secretary-General, Dr. Waldheim, said of his activities in the field of human rights "My own efforts in the field – in the exercise of my good offices in specific humanitarian cases – have met with some success. To secure the maximum benefit for the individuals involved, past experiences demonstrated that it is best to proceed on purely humanitarian grounds and usually with the utmost confidentiality. Not only does this approach work to the advantage of the system, but it also avoids the political sensitivity often associated with such cases. I shall continue these efforts whenever and wherever they best serve the welfare of the individuals concerned." Similar statements have been made by Dr. Waldheim in 1979 and again this year.

From these observations I believe, Mr. Chairman, that a number of conclusions come to mind. The first is that all Secretaries-General have effectively resorted to their good offices in the human rights field. The second is that they have all viewed this aspect of their function as constituting an integral part of their mandate. Third, they have all approached their role in this respect from a strictly humanitarian point of view and the role has therefore consistently been regarded as non-political. Finally, it has always been performed with the expressed consent of the countries concerned and as such, has never been regarded as interference in internal affairs.

In this connection, a number of interesting parallels can be drawn between the Secretary-General's role in the human rights field and his activities in the area of humanitarian assistance and relief. Both have been developed progressively in response to changing circumstances in the world, rather than being specifically destined as such in an article of the Charter. Both have become universally accepted as one of those functions which the United Nations in general, and the Secretary-General in particular, could most appropriately and effectively perform. Both spring from a strictly humanitarian concern for alleviating the fate of human beings in dire need of assistance from the international community which often constitutes their only resort. Both have been performed in such a manner that they have never been regarded as constituting unjustified interference in the internal affairs of the countries concerned. Finally, Mr. Chairman, neither has ever been regarded as entrusting the Secretary-General with a political function not provided for in the Charter.

I suggest, Mr. Chairman, that the protection of innocent individuals from the flagrant abuses of their human rights is as important a function of this organization as the assistance it may provide to distressed persons who are the victims of man-made or natural catastrophes. The four Secretaries-General to date have obviously come to the same conclusion, and it is the view of my Delegation that it is entirely proper that they should have done so.

It is interesting to note, Mr. Chairman, that a similar good offices role in humanitarian matters or the human rights field has also developed over the years in other international organizations such as the UNHCR, the ILO, UNESCO and the ICRC, confirming, if such a confirmation is indeed necessary, that it corresponds to a need of our times.

With your permission, I would like, Mr. Chairman, to dwell for a moment on the ILO practice which is highly illustrative of the effective use to which resorts to the good offices can be put in practice. There are elements of good offices in the procedure of direct contacts for example, introduced by the ILO in 1968 to permit the representative of the Director-General to examine directly with competent government authorities practical or legal difficulties encountered in the application of a ratified convention. Resort to such procedure is subject to the consent of the government concerned, and has been used on occasion to examine questions relating to human rights conventions. Direct contacts have also been used under the ILO Governing Body freedom of association procedure to examine in co-operation with the country concerned, problems raised by complaints including infringements on the principle of freedom of association.

Results achieved so far in the ILO through this process have amply demonstrated that "quiet diplomacy" in the human rights field can be made to work in practice. In resolving a number of situations, which would otherwise, through misunderstandings or other reasons, have developed into unproductive confrontations, the good offices role of the Director-General of the ILO has proved an invaluable instrument.

Experience has demonstrated that it is appropriate to leave to the discretion of the Secretary-General the precise manner in which he will elect to intervene in any given circumstances. His decision will always be predicated on the assumptions which have prompted the action of Secretaries-General in the past, namely: a determination that a resort to his good offices is likely to have any beneficial results in improving a given situation; a willingness to provide any assistance which might appear useful from a strictly humanitarian point of view; the consent of the country concerned; and finally, a clear understanding that the Secretary-General's concern relates to humanitarian and non-political considerations.

Mr. Chairman, we firmly believe that the informality of this procedure is conducive to the rapid improvement of situations of gross violations of human rights, while contributing to the alleviation of the fate of victims of such situations. The high regard which we have for the function of the Secretary-General and for the present incumbent is our best guarantee that his expression of concern and offers of assistance will receive the most serious consideration on the part of all parties concerned.

With these considerations in mind, Mr. Chairman, my Delegation is tabling a resolution designed to reaffirm our support for his important role in this area. It requires the Secretary-General, when urgent situations of flagrant violations of human rights arise, to consider establishing direct contacts with the government concerned for the dual purpose of assisting governments concerned in the full restoration of the respect for human rights and fundamental freedoms as quickly as possible, and also of considering what forms of assistance the United Nations can provide to governments involved.

What is involved in this resolution, Mr. Chairman, is the full development of the well-established and universally-accepted instrument at our disposal to enable the United Nations system to cope more adequately with the all-too-frequent situations of mass and flagrant violations of human rights which persist throughout the world today. We therefore hope that it will command itself to all members of this Committee. The adoption of this resolution would not distract us from our concerted search for alternative approaches and ways and means within the United Nations system for improving the effective enjoyment of human rights and fundamental freedoms. It will, however, signal our renewed commitment and determination to put to the best use possible existing procedures and bodies such as this Committee, the ECOSOC, the Human Rights Commission, the Division of Human Rights and the United Nations Secretariat, in our quest for a more productive approach to the improvement of the human rights situation throughout the world.

Annex XII

EXTRACTS FROM STATEMENT BY JEROME J. SHESTACK, UNITED STATES REPRESENTATIVE TO THE UN COMMISSION ON HUMAN RIGHTS IN THE THIRD COMMITTEE OF THE UN GENERAL ASSEMBLY ON 13 NOVEMBER 1980

(Press release USUN 143 (80) – 13 November 1980)

1. The good offices role

. . .

The concept of good offices, of course, is well known in diplomacy and has often been employed in the settlement of disputes.[1] In the field of human rights, the good offices approach is more vague but still has considerable precedent to support it, having been employed for human rights purposes within the ILO, the UNHCR, UNESCO, the ICRC, the Council of Europe, and other international bodies.[2]

In the ILO, the Director General frequently exercises good offices as does the International Labour Office under his direction. Thus, the ILO has employed the "good offices" practice of making direct contacts with a government experiencing difficulties in the application of a ratified convention, or with respect to complaints alleging infringement of the freedom of association.[3]

In UNESCO, the Executive Board has expressly recognized the good offices of the Director General to initiate consultations with governments to help reach solutions to particular problems.[4] In the case of the High Commissioner for Refugees, as early as 1959, the General Assembly in resolution 1388 (XIV) authorized the High Commissioner to use his good offices with respect to refugee matters encouraging him to expand considerably his most useful role.[5]

The European Convention on Human Rights authorizes the European Commission to place itself at the disposal of parties concerned with a view to securing a friendly settlement of complaints on the basis of respect for human rights (Article 28). The American Convention on Human Rights has a comparable provision (Article 4F(1)(b)). Similarly, Article 41(1)(e) of the International Covenant on Civil and Political Rights requires the Human Rights Committee to make available its good offices to state parties concerned in inter-state complaints in order to obtain friendly solutions on the basis of respect for human rights.

The General Assembly and the Commission on Human Rights has also requested the Secretary-General to exercise his good offices or to undertake direct contacts, and various resolutions to this effect have been adopted.[6] The Secretariat serves as a principal organ of the United Nations to carry out Charter imposed obligations which include promoting and encouraging respect for human rights.[7] There can be little doubt, therefore, that there is a firm legal basis for the Secretary-General to use his good offices in the human rights area.

In practice, various Secretaries-General of the United Nations have used their good offices in the field of human rights in varying degrees. Secretary-General Trygvie Lie used his good offices on behalf of Greek children. Secretary-General Dag Hammarskjöld used his good offices in trying to safeguard human rights in South Africa. Secretary-General U Thant has described his good offices role on behalf of Soviet citizens of the Jewish faith who wanted to leave the Soviet Union.[8] The current Secretary-General in various reports has indicated that he, too, has used his good offices on behalf of human rights concerns, preferring to do so, according to his reports, on a confidential basis.

We believe that the use of the good offices of the Secretariat is most useful and could be employed more frequently and consistently. We have examined a resolution before this Committee which procedurally broadens the "good offices" compass moderately; it should be non-controversial. We suggest, however, that in the future this body or the Commission on Human Rights should evolve detailed and objective criteria for employing the good offices role of the Secretary-General. That role could, for example, encompass the following ways and means:

(a) ascertain the facts in a case of gross violation of human rights;

(b) maintain communications and contacts with the governments concerned;

(c) send routinely a special representative or working group to the government concerned;

(d) bring to the attention of the government the report of the special representative;

(e) attempt to influence the government to restore respect for human rights;

(f) make available technical assistance or advisory services to help accomplish the task;

(g) raise and report on the issue before the Commission on Human Rights or its Sub-commission;

(h) convene international conferences to consider the situation, if necessary;

(i) make public comment on the situation; and

(j) refer the matter to appropriate UN bodies for public consideration.

These are illustrative. Hopefully, this Committee or the Commission will elaborate on these functions. Of course, we are sensitive to the danger that a particular use of good offices will be viewed politically. However, this should not be a deterrent to the use of good offices on behalf of human rights concerns. In this connection, we note that the Hague Conventions of 1899 and 1907 specifically provided that the exercise of a good offices role by a friendly power should not be regarded by any of the parties in a dispute as an unfriendly act.

We believe that the good offices role has enormous potential and hope that this Committee and the Commission will continue to play a significant role in evolving and institutionalizing that process.

NOTES

1. For example, the Hague Conventions of 1899 and 1907 on the Pacific Settlement of Disputes has a procedure whereby in cases of serious disputes, recourse may be had in the good offices by one or more friendly powers.
2. Even in the League of Nations system, it was a regular practice for the Minorities Committee, acting through the Secretariat, to use its good offices in trying to settle questions raised in communications by negotiating with the Government concerned in an informal and friendly manner (see, *e.g.*, UN doc. E/CN.4 Sub. 2/6 of Nov. 7, 1946: The International Protection of Minorities under the League of Nations, pp. 27-32).
3. A recent example of use of offices by the ILO occurred in August, 1980, with respect to a dispute in a particular state regarding the formation of free trade unions. The Director General placed "his good offices and those of the International Labour Office" at the disposal of the authorities concerning the framework of legislation assuring the free exercise of trade union rights.
4. In a report which the Director General of UNESCO submitted to the 20th session of UNESCO in 1978, he noted that his role with respect to "intercessions on humanitarian grounds and representations of a conciliatory nature" was no longer confined to individual cases but had been extended to cover questions.
5. The International Committee of the Red Cross likewise has made considerable use

of its good offices role under the Geneva Conventions of 1949 and under the ICRC statutes. It engages in "ad hoc protection" which is another way of saying that it exercises its good office in many areas where there is not specific authorization for ICRC involvement but where there is serious domestic trouble and prima facie evidence of inhumane treatment.

6. See, *e.g.*, GA res. 33/173; CHR res. 30 (XXVI); 32 (XXVI).
7. This is apart from the specific authority under Article 99.
8. U Thant, *View from the UN.*

Annex XIII

THE EFFECTS OF GROSS VIOLATIONS OF HUMAN RIGHTS ON INTERNATIONAL PEACE AND SECURITY (UN doc. E/CN.4/Sub.2/1982/18)

Note by the Secretary-General

1. At its 931st meeting on 10 September 1981, the Sub-Commission decided to include in the provisional agenda of its thirty-fifth session an item entitled "The effects of gross violations of human rights on international peace and security." In accordance with a wish expressed by members of the Sub-Commission at that time, the Secretary-General submits below, for the consideration of members of the Sub-Commission, the following basic information which appears relevant to the discussion of this item:

(a)In his Annual Report on the work of the Organization, which was submitted to the General Assembly at its thirty-sixth session, the Secretary-General of the United Nations stated: "In the contemporary world, the relationship between human rights and questions of peace and security is emerging into sharper focus. The purposes and principles of the Charter are mutually supporting and interdependent. Thus, it is increasingly clear that peace and development are necessary for the full realization of human rights. At the same time, in the absence of respect for human rights, peace and development lose much of their meaning."[1]

(b) In the United Nations medium-term plan for the period 1980-83, it is stated that "in the conception of the Charter, the promotion and encouragement of respect for human rights and fundamental freedoms for all was placed in direct relationship with the maintenance of international peace and security and the creation of conditions for economic and social progress and development. The interdependence between human rights, peace and development means that freedom from fear and freedom from want belong as much to the heart of the concept of human rights as political freedoms. This same interdependence assumes and requires that the wider recognition and acceptance of the human factor be made the central theme in all human endeavours."[2]

(c) In the Preamble of the Universal Declaration of Human Rights the General Assembly proclaimed that "recognition of the inherent dignity and of the equal and inalienable rights of all members of the human family is the foundation of freedom, justice and peace in the world" and that "it is essential, if man is not to be compelled to have recourse, as a last resort, to rebellion against tyranny and oppression that human rights should be protected by the rule of law." In the Declaration on Principles of International Law concerning Friendly Relations and Co-operation among States in accordance with the Charter of the United Nations, which it approved by its resolution 2625 (XXV) of 24 October 1970, the General Assembly stated that international peace must be "founded upon freedom, equality, justice and respect for fundamental human rights."[3] In its resolution 5 (XXXII) adopted on 27 February 1976, the Commission on Human Rights recalled that "everyone has the right to live in conditions of international peace and security and fully to enjoy his economic, social and cultural rights and civil and political rights." The General Assembly, in its resolution 33/73 proclaiming the Declaration on the Preparation of Societies for Life in Peace, stated that "Every nation and every human being, regardless of race, conscience, language or sex, has the inherent right to life in peace. Respect for that right, as well as for the other human rights, is in the common interest of all mankind and an indispensable condition of advancement of all nations, large and small, in all fields."

(d) The International Conference on Human Rights recognized, in the preamble to the Proclamation of Teheran, that "peace is the universal aspiration of mankind and that peace and justice are indispensible to the full realization of human rights and fundamental freedoms."[4] In the preamble to the International Convention on the Elimination of All Forms of Racial Discrimination the States Parties reaffirmed that "discrimination between human beings on the grounds of race, colour or ethnic origin is an obstacle to friendly and peaceful relations among nations and is capable of disturbing peace and security among peoples and the harmony of persons living side by side even within one and the same State."[5]

(e) In a report on the right to development[6] which the Secretary-General submitted to the Commission on Human Rights in 1979, it was stated that: "Violations of human rights frequently pose a threat to the enjoyment of world peace. This may often be the case, for example, with respect to denials of the right to self-determination, the widespread occurrence of discriminatory practices, and the practice of racial discrimination and racism.[7] In paragraph 1 of the Declaration on the granting of independence to colonial countries and peoples the General Assembly declared that: "The subjection of peoples to alien subjugation, domination and exploitation constitutes a denial of fundamental human rights, is contrary to the Charter of the United Nations and is an impediment to the promotion of world peace and co-operation."[8]

(f) In principle VI of the "Principles of International Law recognized in the Charter of the Nuremberg Tribunal and in the Judgement of the Tribunal" which were submitted by the International Law Comission to the General Assembly in 1950, crimes against humanity are defined as follows: "Murder, extermination, enslavement, deportation, and other inhuman acts done against any civilian population, or persecutions on political, racial or religious grounds, when such acts are done or such persecutions are carried on in execution of or in connection with any crime against peace or any war crime."[9] Article 2, paragraph 11, of the Draft Code of Offences against the Peace and Security of Mankind drawn up by the International Law Commission in 1954 and submitted to the General Assembly, includes among the acts considered as offences against the peace and security of mankind: "inhuman acts such as murder, extermination, enslavement, deportation or persecutions, committed against any civilian population on social, political, racial, religious or cultural grounds by the authorities of a State or by private individuals acting at the instigation or with the toleration of such authorities."[10]

(g) Article 19 of the draft articles on State Responsibility submitted by the International Law Commission to the General Assembly in 1976, states that:

"1. . . .

2. An internationally wrongful act which results from the breach by a State of an international obligation so essential for the protection of fundamental interests of the international community that its breach is recognized as a crime by that community as a whole, constitutes an international crime.

3. Subject to paragraph 2, and on the basis of the rule of international law in force, an international crime may result, *inter alia*, from:

(a) A serious breach of an international obligation of essential importance for the maintenance of international peace and security, such as that prohibiting aggression;

(b) A serious breach of an international obligation of essential importance for safeguarding the right of self-determination of peoples, such as that prohibiting the establishment or maintenance by force of colonial domination;

(c) A serious breach on a widespread scale of an international obligation of essential importance for safeguarding the human being, such as those prohibiting slavery, genocide and *apartheid*;

(d) A serious breach of an international obligation of essential importance for the safeguarding and preservation of the human environment, such as those prohibiting massive pollution of the atmosphere or of the seas."[11]

(h) Article 34 of the Charter of the United Nations provides that the Security Council may investigate any dispute or any situation which might lead to international friction or give rise to dispute, in order to determine whether the continuance of the dispute or situation is likely to endanger the maintenance of international peace and security. Articles 33 to 38 of the Charter contain further provisions on the pacific settlement of disputes. Chapter VII of the Charter, dealing with action with respect to threats to the peace, breaches of the peace and acts of aggression, provides that the Security Council shall determine the existence of any threat to the peace, breach of the peace or act of aggression, and shall make recommendations, or decide what measures shall be taken in accordance with Articles 41 and 42 to maintain or restore international peace and security. Article 40 provides that in order to prevent an aggravation of the situation, the Security Council may call upon the parties concerned to comply with such provisional measures as it deems necessary. Article 99 of the Charter provides that the Secretary-General may bring to the attention of the Security Council any matter which, in his opinion, may threaten the maintenance of international peace and security. From the formulations used in the above-mentioned articles of the Charter, it may be seen that reference is made to "disputes", "situations" or "matters" which might lead to international friction or give rise to a threat or breach of the peace. Conceivably, all three concepts could encompass gross violations of human rights.

(i) In paragraph 8 of the Declaration on the occasion of the Twenty-Fifth Anniversary of the United Nations, which it adopted on 4 November 1970, the General Assembly stated: "Although some progress has been achieved, serious violations of human rights are still being committed against individuals and groups in several regions of the world. We pledge ourselves to a continued and determined struggle against all violations of the rights and fundamental freedoms of human beings, by eliminating the basic causes of such violations, by promoting universal respect for the dignity of all people without regard to race, colour, sex, language or religion, and in particular through greater use of the facilities provided by the United Nations in accordance with the Charter."[12]

2. In its resolution 32/130 adopted on 16 December 1977, the General Assembly decided that the approach to future work within the United Nations system with respect to human rights questions should take account of certain concepts, including the following:

"In approaching human rights questions within the United Nations system, the international community should accord, or continue to accord, priority to the search for solutions to the mass and flagrant violations of human rights of peoples and persons affected by situations, such as those resulting from *apartheid*, from all forms of racial discrimination, from colonialism, from foreign domination and occupation, from aggression and threats against national sovereignty, national unity and territorial integrity, as well as from the refusal to recognize the fundamental rights of peoples to self-determination and of every nation to the exercise of full sovereignty over its wealth and natural resources."

3. In its resolution 34/175 adopted on 17 December 1979, the General Assembly, conscious of the responsibility of the United Nations in dealing with situations of mass and flagrant violations of human rights and believing that disregard and contempt for human rights have resulted in barbarous acts which have outraged the conscience of mankind, reaffirmed that "mass and flagrant violations of human rights are of special concern to the United Nations" and urged the appropriate United Nations bodies, within their mandaes, particularly the Commission on Human Rights, to take timely and effective action in existing and future cases of mass and flagrant violations of human rights.

4. Account may be taken of the mandates relating to, and the practice of the Commission on Human Rights and the Sub-Commission regarding the items on their respective agendas on the question of violations

of human rights and fundamental freedoms in all countries. It may be recalled that by its resolution 2144 A (XXI) of 26 October 1966, the General Assembly invited the Economic and Social Council and the Commission on Human Rights to give urgent consideration to ways and means of improving the capacity of the United Nations to put a stop to violations of human rights wherever they may occur. Pursuant to that resolution, the Commission on Human Rights, on 16 March 1967, adopted resolution 8 (XXIII) entitled "Study and investigation of situations which reveal a consistent pattern of violations of human rights," in which it decided to give annual consideration to an item on the question of violations of human rights and fundamental freedoms in all countries. The Commission also requested the Sub-Commission to prepare, for the use of the Commission in its examination of this question, a report containing information on violations of human rights and fundamental freedoms from all available sources. The Commission further invited the Sub-Commission to bring to the attention of the Commission any situation which it has reasonable cause to believe reveals a consistent pattern of violations of human rights and fundamental freedoms, in any country, including policies of racial discrimination, segregation and *apartheid*, with particular reference to colonial and other dependent territories. The provisions of resolutions 1235 (XLII) and 1503 (XLVIII) of the Economic and Social Council may also be kept in mind.

5. The deliberations of the United Nations seminar on the relations that exist between human rights, peace and development, may be of relevance in the consideration of this item. The report of the seminar (ST/HR/SER.A.10) will be made available to the Sub-Commission. The seminar concluded by consensus that "human rights, peace and development are interrelated and interdependent and that the fostering of one promotes the enhancement of the others. The absence of peace, or the achievement of development by a people, can never exempt a State from its obligation to ensure respect for the human rights of its nationals and of the persons residing in its territory."[13] Among the conclusions which were widely supported at the seminar was one to the effect that "peace is not merely the absence of war. It is also the promotion of a state of harmonious relations within a State, or between States. The promotion of peace at the international level is linked to the achievement of peace within each State. Mass and flagrant violations of human rights, including those stemming from *apartheid*, racism and racial dis-

crimination, foreign domination and occupation, aggression and threats against national sovereignty and territorial integrity, and the denial of the right to self-determination of a people are flagrant breaches of international peace and security."[14]

6. The report of the Secretary-General on "Present international conditions and human rights" (A/36/440) which was submitted to the General Assembly at its thirty-sixth session may be of interest to the Sub-Commission in the consideration of this item; it will be made available to members of the Sub-Commission.

7. The item on the agenda of the General Assembly concerning the draft Code of Offences against the Peace and Security of Mankind, may also be of relevance in the consideration of this item. By its resolution 36/106 adopted on 10 December 1981, the General Assembly, having considered the draft Code of Offences against the Peace and Security of Mankind prepared by the International Law Commission and submitted to the General Assembly in 1954[15] and having considered a related report of the Secretary-General,[16] invited the International Law Commission to resume its work with a view to elaborating the draft Code of Offences against the Peace and Security of Mankind, taking duly into account the results achieved by the process of the progressive development of international law. The General Assembly further decided to include in the provisional agenda of its thirty-seventh session an item entitled "Draft Code of Offences against the Peace and Security of Mankind". Information will be provided to the Sub-Commission on the consideration of this question by the International Law Commission, which is in session at the time of the preparation of the present Note. It may be observed that in a report which the Secretary-General presented to the General Assembly at its thirty-sixth session, containing the views of Governments and international organizations, the view was expressed that "The international protection of human rights is closely linked to the maintenance of international peace, and repeated and systematic violations at least should be considered an offence against mankind."[17]

8. The consideration currently being given in the General Assembly and related organs to the question of the peaceful settlement of disputes may also be relevant to the consideration of this item. In this regard, it

may be noted that by its resolution 36/110 adopted on 10 December 1981, the General Assembly requested the Special Committee on the Charter of the United Nations and on the Strengthening of the Role of the Organization to finalize the draft Manila declaration on the peaceful settlement of disputes with a view to its consideration and adoption by the General Assembly and to submit it to the Assembly at its thirty-seventh session. The Special Committee has since finalized the draft declaration and submitted it to the General Assembly for consideration and adoption. The text of the draft declaration will be made available to members of the Sub-Commission.

NOTES

1. Official Records of the General Assembly, thirty-sixth session, Supplement No. 1 (A/36/1), section VIII.
2. Official Records of the General Assembly, thirty-third session, Supplement No. 6 (A/33/6/Rev.1), vol. I, chapter 9.
3. Third preambular paragraph.
4. See Human Rights – A Compilation of International Instruments (United Nations publication, Sales No. E.78.XIV.2), pp. 18-19.
5. General Assembly resolution 2106 A (XX).
6. E/CN.4/1334, para. 133.
7. See, generally, the Proclamation of Teheran, paras. 7 and 11; International Convention on the Suppression and Punishment of the Crime of *apartheid* (General Assembly resolution 3068 (XXVIII), Article I, para. 1); United Nations Declaration on the Elimination of All Forms of Racial Discrimination (General Assembly resolution 1904 (XVIII), Article 1); Declaration adopted by the World Conference to Combat Racism and Racial Discrimination held in Geneva 14-25 August 1978 (A/CONF.92/L.2; and A/33/262), paras. 3 and 4.
8. General Assembly resolution 1514 (XV).
9. Yearbook of the International Law Commission, 1950, vol. II.
10. Yearbook of the International Law Commission, 1954, vol. II.
11. Report of the International Law Commission on the work of its twenty-eighth session, Official Records of the General Assembly, thirty-first session, Supplement No. 10 (A/31/10), p. 226.
12. General Assembly resolution 2627 (XXV).
13. ST/HR/SER.A.10, p. 53.
14. *Ibid*., p. 55.
15. Official Records of the General Assembly, ninth session, Supplement No. 9 (A/2693), para. 54.
16. A/36/535.
17. A/36/416, part III, para. 7 (d).

BIBLIOGRAPHY

S.D. Bailey, The Secretariat of the United Nations. London, Pall Mall Press (1964).

M. El Baradei and others, Model Rules for Disaster Relief Operations. UNITAR Policy and Efficacy Studies, No. 8 (1982).

J. Barros, Betrayal from Within. Joseph Avenol, Secretary-General of the League of Nations, 1933-1940. New Haven, Yale University Press (1969).

J. Barros, Office Without Power. Secretary-General Sir Eric Drummond, 1919-1933. Oxford, Clarendon (1979).

A.W. Cordier *et al.* Public Papers of the Secretaries-General of the United Nations, vols. I-VIII (1969-1977).

R. Fisher *et al.*, International Mediation: A working guide; Ideas for the Practitioner (1978).

D.P. Forsythe, Humanitarian Politics. The International Committee of the Red Cross. Baltimore and London, The Johns Hopkins University Press (1977), chapters 3 and 4, "Ad Hoc Diplomacy."

L. Gordenker, The United Nations Secretary-General and the Maintenance of Peace. New York, Columbia University Press (1967).

D. Hammarskjöld, Servant of Peace. A selection of the speeches and statements of Dag Hammarskjöld, Secretary-General of the United Nations, 1953-1961. Edited and introduced by Wilder Foote. New York, Harper and Row (1962).

Interpretation of Peace Treaties (Second Phase), Advisory Opinion: ICJ Reports (1950), p. 221.

T. Lie, In the Cause of Peace. Seven Years with the United Nations. New York, Macmillan (1954).

B. Morse, "Practice, Norms and Reform of International Humanitarian Rescue Operations," 157 RCADI (1977, IV), pp. 150-194.

C.Y. Pak, The Political Role of the Secretary-General of the United Nations in Theory and Practice. Ann Arbor, Michigan University Press (1963).

B.G. Ramcharan, "The Good Offices of the United Nations Secretary-General in the Field of Human Rights," 76 AJIL (1982), pp. 130-141.

Reparation for Injuries Suffered in the Service of the United Nations. Advisory Opinion: ICJ Reports (1949), p. 174.

A.W. Rovine, The First Fifty Years: The Secretary-General in World Politics 1920-1970. Leiden, A.W. Sijthoff (1970).

S.M. Schwebel, The Secretary-General of the United Nations. His political powers and practice. Cambridge, Harvard University Press (1952).

K.R. Simmonds, " 'Good Offices' and the Secretary-General," 29 Nordisk Tidsskrift for International Ret og Jus Gentium (1959), pp. 330-345.

J. Siotis, Essai sur le sécretariat international. Genève (1963).

U Thant, "A Quiet United Nations Road to Accord," VII UN Monthly Chronicle, No. 7 (July 1970), pp. 122-131.

U Thant, "The United Nations and Some Problems of Public Understanding," VIII UN Monthly Chronicle, No. 1 (January 1971), pp. 98-105.

U Thant, "The Role of the Secretary-General," VIII UN Monthly Chronicle, No. 9 (October 1971), pp. 178-187.

U Thant, View from the United Nations. New York, Doubleday (1978).

B. Urquhart, Hammarskjöld. New York, Alfred A. Knopf (1972).

M. Virally, "Le rôle politique du Secrétaire général des Nations Unies," IV Annuaire français de droit international (1958), pp. 380-399.

D.W. Wainhouse *et al.*, International Peace Observations: a History and Forecast. Baltimore, Johns Hopkins Press (1966).

O.R. Young, The Intermediaries: Third Parties in International Crises. Princeton, NJ. Published for the Center for International Studies, Princeton University, by Princeton University Press (1967).

K. Waldheim, Un métier unique au monde. Paris, Editions Stock (1977).

K. Waldheim, Building the Future Order. New York, The Free Press (1980).

M. Zacher, Dag Hammarskjöld's United Nations. New York, Columbia University Press (1970).

INDEX